COMPLETE
Folding Kayaker

Second Edition

Ralph Díaz

Ragged Mountain Press / McGraw-Hill

Camden, Maine | New York | Chicago | San Francisco | Lisbon
London | Madrid | Mexico City | Milan | New Delhi
San Juan | Seoul | Singapore | Sydney | Toronto

Para mis padres, Aurelio Díaz y Teresa O'Halloran Díaz, e hijo Jason

The McGraw·Hill Companies

1 2 3 4 5 6 7 8 9 0 DOC DOC 0 9 8 7 6 5 4 3

Copyright © 2003 Ragged Mountain Press

All rights reserved. The publisher takes no responsibility for the use of any of the materials or methods described in this book, nor for the products thereof. The name "Ragged Mountain Press" and the Ragged Mountain Press logo are trademarks of The McGraw-Hill Companies. Printed in the United States of America.

Library of Congress Cataloging-in-Publication Data
Díaz, Ralph.
  Complete folding kayaker / Ralph Díaz.—2nd ed.
      p.   cm.
Includes bibliographical references and index.
   ISBN 0-07-140809-6 (pbk.)
  1. Sea kayaking. 2. Kayaks. I. Title.
   GV788.5 .D53 2003
   796.1′224—dc21   2002152835

Questions regarding the content of this book should be addressed to
Ragged Mountain Press
P.O. Box 220
Camden, ME 04843
www.raggedmountainpress.com

Questions regarding the ordering of this book should be addressed to
The McGraw-Hill Companies
Customer Service Department
P.O. Box 547
Blacklick, OH 43004
Retail customers: 1-800-262-4729
Bookstores: 1-800-722-4726

All photos by the author unless otherwise noted.
Illustrations on pages 177, 195 (2), 196 (bottom), 199, and 205 by Christopher Hoyt.

Contents

Acknowledgments

This second edition of the *Complete Folding Kayaker* continues the voyage of discovery of folding kayaks that began in the late 1980s when I first purchased a foldable. At the time, my teachers were Dieter and Eric Stiller at the old Klepper shop on Union Square in the heart of New York City. Their generous hand-holding broadened my understanding of folding kayaks, and their tales of epic deeds of folding-kayak adventurers—including Eric's—made clear to me that folding kayaks are a very special breed of vessel indeed.

Others have helped along the way. Doug Simpson and the crew at Feathercraft in Vancouver let me poke around the factory on Granville Island and suffered my many questions with good cheer. Over the years, Doug has shared his insights on how folding kayaks interact with their watery element and made me aware of just how much folding kayaking is a lifestyle, not merely a sport.

I'm thankful to other makers of folding kayaks who also see it as more than a business. Phil Cotton of Folbot in Charleston, South Carolina, and Philippe Guyot of Nautiraid in Vaiges, France, have consistently been helpful and shared their visions of the future. Dr. Henning Isbruch, who became owner of Klepper in Rosenheim, Germany, several years ago, was kind enough to arrange a visit to the new factory (a fire destroyed the old one in 1995) as well as to an exciting new museum devoted to folding kayaks inaugurated in 2001. Days spent in the museum gave me new insights into and appreciation of the simplicity and complexity of folding kayaks. Others in the business have been most supportive: Peter Schwierzke, owner of the Western Folding Kayak Center, which sells most makes of folding kayaks; Mark Balogh and Ms. Sam Carroll of Balogh Sail Designs, makers of premier kayak sails; Mark Eckhart, owner of Long Haul Folding Kayaks, which produces accessories and repairs boats, and now has introduced its own line of folding kayaks; Randy Henriksen, owner of New York Kayak Company, who has always been generous with his time and energies; Janice and Bill Lozano of Atlantic Kayak Tours, who did some early work with foldables before being bitten by the hardshell kayak bug; and Ken Fink, an early importer and promoter of hardshell kayaks, who acted as a friendly foil to keep me on my toes and who now champions at least some folding kayaks.

Most of all, I give a special thanks to the readers of *Folding Kayaker*, the newsletter I started in 1991. I cannot say enough about them. Their unflagging support has encouraged me to pursue the potential of folding kayaks in the pages of that publication. They have fed me hundreds of ideas for modifications and ways to use these vessels. And their many questions—in letters, on the phone, in person, and in cyberspace—are what I'm attempting to answer with the writing of this book.

Finally, I thank Donna Deeprose, my wife. She read first drafts of the book and prodded me toward better writing and clarity of thought. Readers will no doubt appreciate her persistence as much as I do.

Foreword
by Paul Theroux

Just the other workday morning I looked out the window and saw a clear sunny day, with only a slight wind, pleasant sea conditions; and without hesitating I turned my back on my work and put my kayak on the roof rack. At Ala Wai Harbor—this was in Honolulu—another kayaker was setting up his boat. He said to me, "I look out the window this morning, see the sun, see the ocean, and I say to myself, *ono* [perfect], no work for me, I'm paddling today." So I felt vindicated, even happier, knowing that someone else was of exactly the same mind.

All over the world there are people who know the pleasures of paddling, who would rather be kayaking than doing practically anything else. And a kayaker does not need perfect weather—doesn't even need good weather. I bought my first boat ten years ago because I was sick of drydocking my boats in the winter and exercising from October until May indoors on a rowing machine. A kayak is the answer. Of course, a headwind more than 15 or 20 knots can be tiresome, and heavy surf can be dangerous; but those are the only limits. A kayak, the most adaptable (and I think among the safest) craft, can be paddled in almost any weather. Kayaks evolved in regions noted for heavy weather; they were designed for extreme conditions. Severe cold is not much of a problem.

My first kayak was a hardshell, and I remember how that first winter, paddling home through a marsh in the late afternoon, I turned back to look at the setting sun and saw that the water I had splashed had frozen in great pale casts to the stern deck. But I was warm enough (overheating is a greater danger than frostbite in winter paddling), and I was convinced that I had found the right recreation. Paddling to me is the healthiest, most liberating, and adaptable outdoor activity on earth.

It took me a while to find the right boat. But of course there is no all-purpose kayak; each style has its specific use. I have owned five different kayaks. I own three at the moment, and two of them are foldables—a Klepper Expedition single and a Feathercraft K1. Hardshells bristle with adaptations, but the foldable is pretty close in basic shape to the old hull shape that was paddled in the Northern Hemisphere 10,000 years ago. An Inuit paddler might be bemused by my Kevlar Nordkapp (a light, fast, low-volume boat) but would easily recognize any one of my foldables.

As a restless soul, not a practitioner of horizontal or sedentary vacations, I realized that one of the annoyances of traveling in remote places was the absence of reliable transportation. Many times, on the Scottish coast, in the Mediterranean, in Southeast Asia, or in the Pacific, I found myself standing on a beach and looking at an offshore island I wished to visit. There used to be a boat that took people out, I would be told. Nowadays no one goes there. But I wanted to go there. And maybe I wanted to stay there; carry enough food and equipment to last me a week or more. Perhaps I did not want to be pinned down by a hired boatman who would have said, "Mister, what time do you want to go back?" I might never want to go back.

I began to travel with a folding kayak (I always think of them as collapsibles) and my life changed. I learned what all kayakers eventually find out: You head for the offshore island, and when you get there you see another, more distant island—invisible from the mainland shore; and so you are led onward, self-contained and self-reliant, island-hopping and utterly uplifted. That is the greatest experience in travel, the discovery of something new and unexpected. It can happen anywhere. Paddling off Cape Cod in the winter I often see seals. Many people on Cape Cod are fair-weather beachgoers, unaware that these seals exist. Paddling in Hawaii in the winter, it is not unusual to see whales. But only the paddler is able to leap into the water and hear the whales singing; everyone else is subjected to the chugging of an outboard motor.

It is almost impossible to exaggerate the usefulness of a folding kayak. Even the hackneyed phrase "flying carpet" is appropriate to this ingeniously conceived craft. When I traveled around China by train in aid of getting material for a book, I kept wishing I had my boat with me, to go from city to city the most revealing way, by river. It was not accidental that my next travel book was the series of paddling journeys I recounted in *The Happy Isles of Oceania*, and the book would have been impossible without a folding kayak. Many Pacific islanders are still people of the sea. They watched me set up my kayak on the beach; they always recognized the uniqueness of the craft and never failed to ask where they could get one.

There is an immense amount to be known about this deceptively simple boat. I suspect the reason for the folding kayak's complexity is inherent in the boat's design. All other sailing craft have conventional similarities—a little plastic motorboat has many features in common with the *QE II*, but these have nothing in common with a folding kayak. Consider the shape and construction of the folding kayak, or any skin boat, and you have to reach the conclusion that its nearest equivalent is an animal's body, not a fish but a mammal, a vertebrate. It has an interior skeleton, ribs, joints, a spine; it has a head and a tail, it has a hide, it flexes. To this animal shape the paddler brings a brain, and energy, and guts.

Ralph Díaz is a solitary but resourceful evangelist. I was impressed when he started the first folding kayak newsletter, and I am delighted that he has written the first complete guide to these boats. It is valuable, plain-spoken and, best of all, exhaustive. I am happy to help launch this book.

God bless it and all who paddle the seas.

Preface
to the Second Edition

When the first edition of the *Complete Folding Kayaker* came out in 1994, this genre of kayak was being largely ignored and sometimes maligned by publications and books as well as by newcomers and seasoned kayakers. The book made many cogent arguments against misconceptions, but it did more than just that. Previously, no kayaking manual had, among other things, looked in depth at paddling and rescue techniques best suited for folding kayaks; given detailed tips on activities such as sailing, camping, and travel with them; or detailed ways of modifying them.

Since publication of the book, its role in changing perceptions and giving folding kayaks legitimacy seems to have paid off. Most general sea-kayaking manuals published or revised in the intervening years have expanded their coverage on foldables in mostly positive tones (see Suggested Reading in the appendix). Also, the first edition, which sold close to 15,000 copies, encouraged a veritable army of disciples. These enthusiasts have not only bought folding kayaks and used them widely; they have been apostles for foldables, showing others that these boats are not toys but highly seaworthy, dependable vessels. When I wrote the first edition of the *Complete Folding Kayaker* I felt I was the proverbial voice crying in the wilderness, or as Paul Theroux said in his kind foreword to the book, I was a "solitary but resourceful evangelist." I no longer feel quite so alone.

Other developments have changed the perceptions and realities of folding kayaks. In the years since the first edition came out, folding kayak companies have been more responsive to changes in the demographics and desires of potential customers. For example, Feathercraft launched the Khatsalano, a boat that looked and acted more like the sleekest of hardshells, to appeal to paddlers who wanted a Greenland-style kayak. Nautiraid introduced the concept of two different grades of most of its models, with distinctions in materials, prices, and weight. The company also now has almost all its models assembled with the entire frame outside the skin, making the whole process easier. Folbot, along other manufacturers, introduced several more sizes of singles in recognition of the growing market for singles. Klepper made a complete reversal from its long tradition of wooden frames and introduced a lighter, less expensive single, the Alu-Lite.

These industry trends mean more choices for consumers. Years ago, no more than one new model would be introduced by the entire industry once every three years, but today new models are being introduced with much greater frequency.

Lastly, my own newsletter has had almost a decade more of intense study of folding kayaks and reporting on new developments, modification ideas, and ways of using the boats. I have learned more and shared this with readers, who in turn have reacted with ideas that they have fed back to me. The result is a mushrooming of information on folding kayaks, the best of which I've added to this second edition.

What's new in this second edition? Small and big things, in addition to those mentioned above. There are more boat reviews, and as you can see from chapter 4, the choices have grown.

There are also many more tips and suggestions in the Modifications chapter culled from the *Folding Kayaker* newsletter. When I went over back issues for purposes of this book, I was amazed how much was covered in the pages of the newsletter.

Through working with so many models over the years, I have learned much more about assembly, so I've added some underlying assembly principles that work for just about any foldable (see chapter 16). The book also contains more information on what to watch out for when buying a used boat, and the tips are very brand-specific

and cover minute parts of the boats. If you want to go camping, you will find very specific lists of gear and where to place it in three different sizes of folding kayaks (see chapter 13).

I hope this book helps you understand folding kayaks better and gets you to give one a try or enjoy the one you have more. If you have questions, do not hesitate to call or e-mail me (contact information is in the appendix). Thousands of readers have done just that since the first edition came out. They have learned—and I have learned—in the course of these exchanges.

Preface
to the First Edition

This book explores the many wonders of this special breed of seagoing vessel. It is based in part on my work as publisher of *Folding Kayaker*, a bimonthly newsletter about using and enjoying foldable kayaks. Over the years of producing the newsletter, I've been in contact with several thousand folding-kayak users who have shared with me what they've learned about their boats. I've lived closely enough with all of the major models to know how best to use them and to overcome any shortcomings an individual model may have. I've learned from the manufacturers all the intricacies of how their various models are constructed and how they should be taken care of. And I've visited with voyagers who embarked on epic journeys with foldable boats. They shared how their boats performed under extreme stress, what they might have wished changed, and the techniques that worked for their survival. The book is organized in three parts:

Part 1, What You Should Know, gives you an appreciation of the use of a folding kayak and helps you narrow your buying choices. It explains the advantages folding kayaks offer over rigid boats and their link to the skin-and-frame kayaks used by Northern peoples for thousands of years; the fascinating history of folding kayaks from the beginning of the century, when they launched a revolution in recreational small boating; what to look for when choosing the right one for you; the leading single and double folding kayaks in concise review; and tips about buying basic equipment and accessories that make for pleasurable paddling.

Part 2, Handling Skills for Foldables, offers practical advice on paddling and operating this unique breed of vessel. This part covers paddling and maneuvering techniques that work well in a foldable; landing and launching from docks, through surf, and under other conditions; confidence drills to get comfortable with the boats, and rescue exercises to practice just in case; and commonsense tips toward becoming a competent sea kayaker.

Part 3, Using and Enjoying, opens the door to this exciting world through its valuable, how-to advice, including packing a folding kayak for airline travel and other public conveyances to avoid in-transit damage; speeding the assembly time once you arrive; using a folding kayak for sailing, fishing, and camping; customizing your folding kayak with modifications and add-on products; and repairing and maintaining the various types of folding kayaks.

As you read this book, bear in mind that folding kayaks have a long, rich tradition of seafaring. For a century, hundreds of thousands of folding kayaks have been leaving their wakes on every waterway from the Arctic to Antarctica. They have crossed oceans and other major bodies of water, in frozen climes and in the balmy tropics. Family groups and rugged individualists have paddled these forgiving vessels under all kinds of conditions on the way to exploration and personal discovery.

The concept of the folding kayak is not just mystique; it has its practical payoff as well: if the day ever dawns when you and your foldable get into conditions that are over your head, you can remind yourself that boats just like yours have delivered many other adventurers out of harm's way.

Introduction

A touring kayak is the ideal boat to put you close to the water and the many wonders along shore. The participation sport of kayak touring, more commonly known as sea or coastal kayaking, has rapidly grown in popularity, gaining converts every day. And well it should. Unlike whitewater kayaking with which it is sometimes confused, sea kayaking offers its pleasures in profound adventure rather than a quick thrill. You can enjoy this pursuit for a few hours on a lake, a slow-moving river, or a nearby bay. Or you can stretch the experience into days and weeks along some interesting coastline far from home, a true antidote to civilization.

Young people don't have the corner on this market; you start kayaking at any age. Many people first put hand to paddle when they are older than fifty. And for those who obey its summons, sea kayaking quickly becomes a lifelong calling.

Sea kayaking is gender blind—nearly half the newcomers to sea kayaking are women. There's nothing macho about sea kayaking; it relies more on brains than brawn, placing a premium on judgment and stamina rather than muscles and reflexes. Under certain conditions sea kayaking can be hair-raising, but generally it doesn't attract daredevils and thrill-seekers. You don't have to be on a razor's edge to enjoy it. Sea kayaking's rewards are contemplative, to be drawn out and savored throughout the hours or days of exploration and discovery.

With the growing interest in sea kayaking, there are a number of new books that introduce the curious to the sport and help polish the skills of those already bitten by the bug. Among these sea-kayaking manuals are several fine works that are informative, enjoyable to read, and often inspiring. But they tend to have a serious flaw—their world largely ignores folding kayaks.

These manuals focus on the hardshell kayaks, which are made of fiberglass layups or molded plastic, or on developing the skills to use such rigid boats. If they do mention folding kayaks, they compress them into a paragraph or two, dismissing them as curiosity items. They advise that the only reason not to get a rigid boat is that you require the foldaway features of a folding sea kayak for storage or travel.

It is a myopic piece of advice—and dead wrong. Yes, folding kayaks have the unique advantage of disassembly into bags that can be stashed in the corner of a closet, and that can emerge like so many genies when called upon to do your bidding. And, in their bags, folding kayaks can be checked through airline ticket counters as ordinary luggage on a business trip or a flight to some exotic destination, where they'll spring to life in just fifteen minutes to open new horizons for you.

But foldability is just frosting on the cake, only part of their broader advantages and appeal. Contrary to the advice given in other sea-kayaking manuals, you should consider having a folding kayak primarily for its superior seaworthiness and reliability. Folding kayaks are inherently more seaworthy than their rigid counterparts. A folding sea kayak's underlying design features—flexible skin-and-frame construction, air tubes along each side—help keep you upright when conditions turn tricky. Under such circumstances in a rigid kayak, you would be calling on all your practiced skills to avoid going over. Folding kayaks flex with the action of the sea rather than fight it, as do rigid kayaks. Folding kayaks have more road feel—they hug the road, so to speak. They have proved time and time again that they are the quintessential open-water boat.

Stability and safety are their strong suits. You can rest inside your folding sea kayak, even take a needed snooze without fear of going belly up. A rigid kayak requires you to be alert to combat its fundamental instability. Folding kayaks are extremely difficult to capsize, and, if you ever do tip over, you can reenter easily, without the self-rescue aids needed to get back into a rigid kayak.

For basic versatility, folding kayaks have it all over their rigid brethren. To begin with, you can leave them assembled for long periods if you wish. Treat them as you would a hardshell kayak; i.e., store them already assembled in your backyard or on your car's rooftop, ready to head to a favorite paddling spot. Just because they can fold down doesn't mean you have to assemble and disassemble them for each outing.

You can easily sail a foldable kayak with a full upwind sail rig without the need for outriggers, which would be the only way you could sail a tippy hardshell. You can fish from a folding kayak with more stability for reeling in that big one than you would ever have in a rigid sea kayak. A folding kayak is voluminous, offering almost as much room for camping gear as you'd find in a comparable-size canoe. If faced with a portage on a river or between lakes, you have the option of knocking it down into smaller components to ease the carrying weight.

While folding kayaks are soft sided—they have decks and hulls made of fabric and coated materials—it would be wrong to think of them as delicate creatures. They tend to be long-lived. Skins can give thirty years of service before needing replacement, and frames last many decades more.

Folding kayaks can take plenty of punishment, a fact attested to by the military special-operations forces of several dozen nations. Such forces have deployed them for more than half a century for training, reconnaissance, interdiction, and softening up enemy shoreline defenses. Because of their strength and stealth, folding kayaks are at this very moment patrolling northern fjords and southern river deltas. These traits, imperative for military forces, make folding kayaks ideal vessels for close-up wildlife photography and observation in remote areas.

Part One

What You Should Know

Folding kayaks have more going for them than their ability to travel with you on a plane or be stored in small spaces. They're superb vessels to trust with your life. Foldables forgive those mistakes that most paddlers make at some point on the water. Stability and seaworthiness are inherent in their materials and underlying design features, which closely resemble the skin-and-frame construction of the kayaks used by Northern peoples for thousands of years. Foldables have built on that heritage to establish a tradition of their own in rugged use by noted explorers, the military, and everyday individual and family adventurers.

Picking the folding kayak that's right for you requires some thinking about how you want to use one. This section will help you decide what features are important to you and offers concise evaluations of the leading models by looking at the key factors that are likely to matter the most to you. There are also pointers about gear and accessories that will enhance the performance of your folding kayak and ensure your safety and comfort.

I

Chapter One

Why a Foldable Kayak?

The sea-kayaking world is divided into two schools of thought: either the *hardshell* kayaks made of fiberglass or plastic, or the *folding* kayaks. If your choice were based solely on the number of models available in each type, the figures are skewed toward rigid boats. One paddling magazine's recent annual buyer's guide showed nearly four hundred models of rigid sea kayaks being sold by some one hundred producers. By comparison, fewer than a half dozen major manufacturers make folding sea kayaks, and they offer fewer than forty models of double and single foldables.

Comparing the cornucopia of rigid boats with the relatively small bouquet of foldables, why in heaven's name should you consider a type of boat that has limited choices? The many solid reasons for picking a foldable sea kayak are covered in this chapter.

Going with the folding kayak crowd puts you in some pretty good company. These boats have been the choice of thousands of discerning individuals and families who have taken stock of their lifestyles and decided that folding kayaks provide the best all-around fit. Folding kayaks are the choice of the rich and famous,

Getting close to wildlife.
(Michael Skott)

Paddling the Big Apple.

too. You might be surprised to learn how many rock stars, jet-setters, politicians, authors, and professional people in the public eye have a folding kayak or two in their possession and use them to alleviate the stress of their celebrated lives. One author, Paul Theroux, has written some of his work from the seat of a foldable. He paddled a single folding kayak to gain his insights and observations for his *The Happy Isles of Oceania*. Theroux also has written several magazine articles on his reflections while solo paddling a single foldable in the Cape Cod area.

If you look very closely at articles in paddling magazines, you'll note that many of the long-range adventures described by contributors have been accomplished in folding kayaks. The magazines don't always note this, except perhaps with a quick passing reference, but the photos don't lie. They show mainly foldables with mountains of the gear that manages to get stored under their decks.

Just because there are more rigid models available than foldable ones doesn't mean that rigid kayaks are used more often. Plenty of rigid boats are being advertised, displayed, and sold, but this is a fairly recent phenomenon. Rigid sea kayaks didn't begin to surface in any significant number until the late 1970s and early 1980s. Before then, foldables dominated the market, and tens of thousands were sold each year. Because folding kayaks tend to last and last, many of the pre-1975 boats are still being paddled. You may not see them, because folding kayakers don't tend to run in regular sea-kayaking circles; they do their thing in splendid solitude, surfacing every decade or so to pick up a replacement part or repair item, then they paddle on again in their very much alive boats.

WHAT A FOLDABLE GIVES YOU THAT A RIGID WON'T

If you ask around about sea kayaks or read some of the introductory manuals, you're likely to run up against some strange ideas about foldables. The boats are supposed to lack performance and are considered vulnerable, constantly in need of maintenance. Some kayak dealers and several so-called experts even deny that foldables are sea kayaks at all. Before you rush to judgment and heed what these individuals have to say, please consider the following six points that distinguish foldables from their rigid counterparts.

1. Truer Descendants of the Eskimo Kayak

Look up the word *kayak* in *Webster's Tenth Collegiate Dictionary* and you'll find the following definition:

> **kay•ak** \ˈkī-ˌak\ *n* [Inuit *qayaq*] (1757) **1:** an Eskimo canoe made of a frame covered with skins except for a small opening in the center and propelled by a double-bladed paddle **2:** a portable boat styled like an Eskimo kayak

By that definition, folding kayaks are truer descendants of the Eskimo kayak than rigid kayaks. Foldables can make that claim because they adhere more closely to the design and materials principles of the kayaks developed by Northern peoples some 10,000 years ago. This association is far more meaningful than mere nostalgia; the underlying structures that Northern and folding kayaks have in common translate into some unique performance characteristics for both, characteristics that rigid kayaks cannot share.

If a Northern seal hunter of 2,000 years ago were suddenly to come to life and wander into the current sea-kayak scene, he would feel more kinship with the foldable kayaks than with the rigid ones. To the touch, the hulls of today's folding kayaks would be like those of the kayaks he hunted from. Their frame construction would be much more familiar to him than that of the rigid boats. The Northern hunter would be at home with how the folding kayak reacted to the water around it. He wouldn't get that same sense of the water when he tried out the rigid kayaks, despite hardshell designers' attempts to mimic the narrow beam and tight cockpit of his seaworthy kayak.

How our Northern time traveler would relate to the differences in boat shapes is anyone's guess. Upswept bows and sterns or flatter ends, narrow beams or broader ones, short or very long; they were all used by Northern people. There was a wide spectrum of hull shapes and sizes in those Northern kayaks, a spectrum as wide as the 5,000-mile arc of inhabited land and sea along the Arctic Circle, from Greenland to the Aleutians.

All Northern kayaks had three common features, three principles of construction that made them such splendid seafaring vessels. Two of these principles are readily apparent to the viewer, but the third is not. Folding kayaks enjoy the same excellent performance traits as the Northern kayaks because they inherited their three common design elements:

How many people can fit on a Klepper double? *(Walther/Klepper)*

1. The hull is made of pliable, fabric-type material.
2. The structure uses internal frames, which consist of crossribs and longitudinal long pieces.
3. The boat flexes because its frame members and pliable skin have a combined "give" to them.

The materials now used in folding kayaks differ from those of the earlier Northern kayak, but they perform identically. The kayak's skin once was made of actual animal hides, and animal fat was used for waterproofing seams and coating the hull itself. Now we rely on materials such as rubber, Hypalon, or urethane- or vinyl-coated polyester, and the decks are made of cotton canvas or a coated synthetic fabric, usually nylon or polyester. The Northern frames were bones and pieces of driftwood lashed together at crossing points with sinew and hide strips. The modern folding kayak has aluminum or wooden long pieces, and its crossribs are made of aluminum, polycarbonate, polyethylene, nylon, or wood.

Because folding kayaks are meant to disassemble, their joining points have fittings that have some flex to them. The amount of movement varies from one manufacturer to the next, but like the Northern kayaks, they allow twist and adjustment to the action of the surrounding water along the entire framework. In contrast, hardshell kayaks don't give with the action of the sea; they are rigid and inflexible.

The leaders of the revival movement of skin boats of original Northern designs recognize the link between foldables and the aesthetics they are trying to resurrect. George Dyson, the author of *Baidarka*, readily accepts the lineage, although he would not applaud the shapes currently used for foldables. John Heath, a noted scholar on Greenland kayaks and paddling techniques, feels strongly about the liveliness and flex of the skin-and-frame design. "Paddling a hardshell kayak is like dancing with a department-store mannequin, while paddling a folding kayak or skin boat is like having a real-life dancing partner."

2. Inherently More Seaworthy

John Heath's comment about foldables and skin boats points to a critical difference between them and rigid boats—the flex that underlies the performance of folding kayaks and their Northern ancestors. The flexibility built into folding kayaks, along with several other features, makes foldables inherently seaworthy and more stable than rigid kayaks.

Folding kayaks flex in several ways. First, they flex along their length. As they ride through swells or over the wake of close-passing ferries or tugboats, folding kayaks partly hug or shape themselves to the curvature of the water. Obviously, shorter folding kayaks have less of this flexing movement, and longer ones have more.

Second, they flex or twist laterally, or sideways. In confused waters, a folding kayak will twist slightly to absorb the collision force of waves coming from different directions. When the passing tug's wake hits you at the same time you're dealing with heavy swell, or when the tug's wake bounces back off a seawall and strikes you from an additional angle, that's when you'll appreciate this second type of flex. In addition, the soft sides of a folding kayak dampen some of the impact of these water forces.

Because a folding kayak blends with the actions of the sea, it isn't tossed around as much as a rigid boat would be, and neither is its paddler. Flexibility enhances seaworthiness.

Other characteristics also contribute to the folding kayak's seaworthiness and stability. If you watch a cross-section of a folding kayak as it moves through the open water, you would notice an interesting phenomenon. Water pressure from beneath pushes the hull in slightly between the longitudinal frame pieces. This causes shallow channels or indentations between the long pieces running the length of the boat. These elongated pockets help the folding kayak resist sliding or

Nautiraid Raid I and its bags. *(Nautiraid)*

rolling sideways due to the action of lateral waves and wakes. Some folding kayaks have more pronounced water-pressure pockets than do others, but they all have them and benefit from the phenomenon.

Width also adds to the stability of folding kayaks. As a genre, they tend to be a few inches wider than their rigid counterparts. For example, the average beam of a single rigid kayak runs about 22 inches. The narrow, so-called Greenland-style single kayaks are about 20 inches in beam, and Northwest kayaks run about 24 inches. Foldable singles average around 26 or 27 inches in beam. An average foldable double measures about 34 inches in beam, while its rigid counterpart would be around 29 inches.

Wider beam on foldables adds to stability not only because of these extra inches, but also because of the one particular feature that creates the extra width—air tubes along the sides. Almost all folding kayaks today have air tubes, called *air sponsons*, that run the length of each side. Air sponsons were introduced about fifty years ago to help the speed and ease of assembly. The frame halves go into a loose skin structure that is then tightened when the air tubes are inflated by mouth. But the air sponsons have the beneficial side effect of increasing stability. If a folding kayak is tipped onto its side while under way, the compressed air tubes will momentarily resist being submerged and thus help keep the foldable upright.

The seaworthiness of folding kayaks has been proved countless times on the high seas. They have crossed the Atlantic and Caribbean and been paddled over long stretches of Australia's coastline and the Pacific coast of South America. They have even seen their paddlers through hurricanes during long crossings between islands and continents.

During our more common trips of less epic proportions, the folding kayak's inherent seaworthiness pays off in several ways. Let's consider what its good sea manners give you.

Hiking out! Single Klepper with S-4 rig. *(Michael Skott)*

Faster learning curve. When venturing out in any sea kayak, you need paddling skills and the ability to read sea conditions. Make no bones about that. But folding sea kayaks allow you to progress faster in paddling; you can concentrate on developing an efficient forward paddling stroke without the need to be in a constant semibrace to keep your boat upright if seas are acting up. Folding kayaks are not tender; you can lean them more aggressively while making turns. Unlike in a hardshell, you can remain calm even when hit by beam waves and wakes as well as winds coming from the sides.

To get good at paddling a rigid sea kayak, you need to have lots of time in the saddle. Some of the narrow ones require constant honing of technique to get the most out of them. Folding kayaks deliver the goods earlier and require less time to acquire the skills needed to paddle them safely under varying conditions.

Better water feel. While some folding kayaks look clunky, they are sleek when it comes to unifying you with your surroundings. The flexible skins and frames provide a harmony with the sea that is both gratifying and inherently safer than having your boat fight the forces at play.

More forgiving of mistakes. When you combine the boat's stability with its flexible behavior on the water, you have a kayak that doesn't require you to always be at your best or most skillful. If you goof in going out through surf, for example, you have greater prospects of the boat seeing you through despite your mistakes.

3. As Tough and More Enduring

Contrary to what you might hear, folding kayaks are not delicate. Overall, their vulnerability is about on par with that of fiberglass rigid kayaks, but they will hold up longer and, like a cat, have several extra lives. Let's take each component, one at a time.

The hull. Basically, you treat a folding kayak hull as you would the hull on a fiberglass hardshell. Owners of fiberglass boats would never dream of dragging their vessels over barnacle-crusted rocks or along sharp gravel beaches. Such folly would quickly destroy the thin gelcoat layer that protects the bottom and expose the fiberglass layer to damage. You exercise the same cautions with the hull of a foldable.

The hull on plastic hardshells can withstand being dragged over such surfaces better than either foldables or fiberglass hardshells. Indeed, you see plastic-boat owners treating their boats in that way, but they do pay a price: The scratches leave loose plastic hairs and grooves that reduce speed on the water and ultimately shorten the life of the plastic hull.

Having said this about the hull of folding kayaks, it is surprising how much the skins can take. Punctures are very rare even in urban areas where "beaches" are mainly made of broken glass and jagged metal parts. Howard Rice, who circumnavigated Cape Horn in 1989 in a folding kayak, found himself at one point hemmed in on an island by a huge surf through which he had barely managed to land. The surf continued to build, stranding him. After exploring the island,

Rice found a beach on the other side with surf that was less imposing. The trouble was, this second beach was nearly a mile away, and he had to climb a high bluff to get off the first beach. He knocked down his folding kayak, carried everything up the bluff in several trips, *then using the skin of his foldable as a toboggan,* he dragged his gear to the other side in several trips. All this caused no damage to the hull.

One folding-kayak dealer loves to drag his boats on the kayak try-out beach at sea-kayaking symposiums. He demonstrates like this even when an outgoing tide has exposed scallop beds and sharp rocks, when his hardshell competitors are being very dainty about their demo boats.

The frame. The skin-over-frame construction of a folding kayak is quite strong and able to absorb plenty of punishment. It takes a lot to break a frame member. The conditions that would break some frame pieces, such as a huge dumping wave crashing a sea kayak onto a beach, are also likely to crack the hull of a rigid fiberglass kayak or create serious stress fractures that would compromise hull integrity. Such force could also dent or crimp a plastic boat.

The frames have proved their toughness for the military. One standard operating procedure for military special forces calls for dropping fully loaded folding kayaks from helicopters. The distance of the fall is often between 10 and 15 feet to keep the hovering helicopter above waves and swells. No damage is sustained by the boats despite the considerable stress created by the cargo and the distance dropped.

Folding kayaks have impressively long lives. Frames last and last. Wooden frames have been around the longest, having first been used around 1907 by the Klepper company for its folding kayaks. Some frames at the Klepper museum in Rosenheim, Germany, are nearly eighty years old and still capable of being used safely. Aluminum frames have been used for folding kayaks only for the last twenty-five years or so, but they show every sign of holding up well.

Hulls give long service as well. Hypalon, which is used for most folding kayak hulls, is good for about thirty years. Older natural rubber hulls lasted about twenty years. Some folding-kayak manufacturers are using other hull materials that also promise to have similarly long lives as Hypalon but are lighter and allow welding hulls to decks. By comparison, plastic rigid boats get brittle with age. Their hulls become suspect after around eight to ten years of service, and at that point they can't easily be patched. Fiberglass holds up well when used in power and sailboats, but the fiberglass layups in hardshell kayaks are relatively thin, especially compared with those on the larger boats. The trend in fiberglass kayak construction is toward ever-thinner layups to keep their weight down. Such light layups make fiberglass kayak hulls vulnerable to stress fractures, so they won't last as long as folding kayak hulls.

4. Greater Versatility of Use

Folding kayaks are much more versatile than rigid ones. The fact that you can fold them into bags raises all kinds of possibilities. A rigid boat is rigid in how you can use it because it's limited by that large bulk and size. To show just how versatile a folding kayak can be, take a look at the question of assembly.

Some people think foldable kayaks must be assembled and disassembled each time they're used. But, if you wish, you can leave your boat assembled, treating it just as you would a rigid boat. This means you can store a folding kayak, already made up, on a rack in your garage. Some models can be left that way for months and months, others for years. Many folding-kayak owners leave their boats assembled in storage buildings and garages, rarely knocking them down except for air travel. Ordinarily, they cartop their assembled folding kayaks to a put-in

THE BOAT THAT GOES BY MAIL

Shipping a folding kayak is inexpensive, and it's the only sea kayak you can order by phone and have delivered to your door by mail or private parcel carriers. For example, UPS charges around $60 for surface transport of a double foldable from one coast to the other. Shorter distances and smaller foldables travel via UPS or U.S. Postal Service for about $40. Folding kayaks that are packed in shipping boxes at the factory or distributor have a clean record in the breakage department.

Because rigid kayaks are much more bulky, shipping them is more costly and more of a hassle. Rigid-boat manufacturers have to find a bulk carrier traveling from the vicinity of the factory or distributor to somewhere in your area, and your wait can be up to six weeks or more. Unless your rigid kayak is handled very carefully, it is subject to breakage, especially if it's fiberglass. One large mail-order house in Maine stopped fulfilling orders for the fiberglass sea kayaks listed in its catalog because of breakage problems—too many boats were arriving with small cracks.

Tip: Be sure to save your folding kayak's original packing box. Whenever you go on vacation, you can use that box to ship your boat on ahead. This eliminates checking your kayak through as airline baggage, and it lets you use up your whole baggage allowance with all kinds of extra gear.

spot. Cartopping and storing assembled will do no harm to a folding kayak.

Rigid boats, on the other hand, don't usually break down into conveniently carried pieces. You can find some "take-apart" rigid boats on the market—i.e., fiberglass kayaks that have intentionally been cut into three or four sections that can be

Folbot Aleut arrives via UPS, New York City.

Looking it over at home.

Genie out of the bag, West Point, New York.

Laying out the parts.

Assembling a frame half.

Finishing touches.

Maiden voyage.

bolted together when needed—but these take-aparts have limitations. They are incredibly heavy because of the heavy-duty hardware keeping the parts together as well as added bulkheads and flanges. You have to be extremely careful not to strip the bolts or get sand into their threads, which would make joining difficult. The seals at the joining points are vulnerable to dents that will affect watertightness. The sections are quite bulky and require special handling and additional costs as checked luggage. Also, you can assemble and disassemble one only so many times before you have trouble with the bolts. Folding kayaks, in contrast, can be taken apart and assembled tens of thousands of times; that's the intention of their design.

If you plan to use the take-apart feature of a sectional fiberglass boat only a few times a year, you'll probably have little problem with it. However, if you intend to knock it down more often than that, you could run into difficulty.

Foldability works to your advantage in many ways. Storing a disassembled kayak is easy because it takes up far less room than a rigid boat. When it's stored in its bags, a folding kayak is safe from the elements, especially from ultraviolet sunlight, which damages any boat, rigid or folding. Even when you're moving a boat by car, foldability plays one of its strongest suits. When it's inside your trunk or in the back of your minivan, any kayak is much safer from thieves than it would be on your car's roof. Increasingly, kayaks are being stolen from roof racks because people often don't take the time and trouble to cable and lock them securely. There is a downside, though; cartopped hardshells get admiring glances from other travelers, much to the satisfaction of their owners, but with a kayak in your trunk, you won't be getting those envious looks!

You can take one-way trips almost anywhere in the world using public transportation. In the New York area, for example, the train that runs along the Hudson River has many stations within easy walking distance of the river. Board a train with your foldable packed away, get out at your favorite launching site, assemble and launch your boat, paddle along the river for a distance, take it out near another station, knock it down, and ride the train back home. In places like the Pacific Northwest, you can paddle to any of a dozen picturesque islands and then take a ferry back.

Sometimes one-way trips are unplanned but prudent. Many folding kayakers report being hit by bad weather that prevented them from finishing a paddling trip to their original destination. Knocking down the foldable boat and taking a ferry, train, or taxi back home proved to be the safer alternative to slugging it out on rough water. This is an important safety asset often overlooked about foldables.

Air travel is the advantage most people think of first. The ability to fly with your boat to a far-away destination opens up the possibility for all sorts of good paddling. On most major airline routes, the folded-up boat can be checked as ordinary luggage at no added charge. And it's easy to pack it well enough to prevent breakage. When you switch to smaller planes that drop you off in harder-to-reach spots, such as Alaska, you'll pay extra to carry your foldable with you. But you'd be charged much more for a rigid boat, if it could be carried at all.

Versatility doesn't end with foldability. Because folding kayaks are much more stable than rigid boats, you can do more with them. Superb stability means that foldables make good sailing boats. Almost all of them come with fixtures that will accept the manufacturer's mast-and-sail rig or one that you find in the aftermarket. Sailing rigs run the gamut—from downwind rigs to full-range sails capable of pointing into the wind.

Fishing is also possible from a foldable without too much worry about capsizing. Some foldables have cockpits large enough for you to easily cut up bait, handle fishing tackle, and land those tasty fish.

Foldables work well for scuba diving and snorkeling, too, because reentering is so easy. Even with air tanks, getting from the boat to the water and back again is no problem. This is one of the reasons why the military relies so much on these boats.

Camping with a foldable adds a whole new dimension. Camping gear packs away in the underdeck space in front and back, and you still have the space around your body for carrying gear you want to keep especially handy. The payload of the doubles runs between 700 and 800 pounds including the paddlers, and between 350 and 550 pounds in the large single folding kayaks. Even the mini-size foldables, those less than about 14 feet in length, have a payload in the 260-pound range, certainly enough for a week or so of paddling in most climates.

5. Easier to Repair

Into every paddler's life there comes the day when something goes wrong with the kayak. When that day comes, you'll find that your folding kayak is easy to repair, whether you're at home or in the field.

First of all, duct tape, the universal fixer-upper, adheres tenaciously to the hulls of folding kayaks, more so than it does to plastic hulls. A piece of good duct tape will stay on a folding kayak for months and months without working loose. You can even temporarily repair broken ribs or long pieces on a folding kayak with the handy stuff.

Folding kayaks really excel when you need to make permanent repairs under field conditions that are far from ideal. In temperatures below freezing, a Hypalon hull will accept a permanent patch, but not so with a plastic or fiberglass hull, because their repair material just won't function below about 45°F.

Because a folding kayak is made up of various components, replacing one or two pieces is easy. Getting an older kayak back to an almost-new state is also easy. You have the option to replace pieces, not repair, which becomes increasingly important as your kayak ages.

Rigid kayaks aren't made of components, so you don't have the replace-not-repair option. Plastic boats don't willingly accept repair patches after they reach a certain age. Plastic hulls grow brittle and inflexible with time, so the pliable patch material has difficulty adhering properly. How well a plastic kayak has been stored and treated determines the age at which it becomes too old to patch. Some experts advise that beyond about five or six years, a plastic hull cannot take a reliable patch. If you have to repair a five- or six-year-old plastic hull, they advise for safety's sake that you relegate the boat to light use from then on. On the other hand, fiberglass, like the hull materials on folding kayaks, should remain safely repairable as long as there is some surface for a patch to adhere to.

6. Safer at Sea

Safety is the most outstanding benefit paddlers gain from folding kayaks. In just about every aspect, folding kayaks are safer boats than rigid kayaks.

The risk of capsizing and getting dunked is far greater with a rigid boat than it is with a folding kayak, which is much more stable. Even under severe conditions, the average paddler with only moderate ability to *paddle brace* can keep a foldable kayak upright. In a rigid kayak, that same paddler would need greater bracing ability and other much more advanced stabilizing techniques such as *sculling*. (These techniques are explained in detail in chapter 6.) Your ability to *Eskimo roll* is considered your first line of defense when using a rigid kayak. It's generally harder to perform an Eskimo roll in a folding kayak, but then again, it's very hard to capsize one in the first place.

In the unlikely event that you find yourself overboard, foldables are far easier to reenter, whether they're singles or doubles. A double can be reentered when both paddlers are in the water without the need for outrigging a paddle float, which is normally required of a rigid boat. Under most circumstances, reentering a single foldable doesn't require a paddle float either; you can do a *cowboy* (over the stern) self-rescue (see chapter 10 for details). Even under the worst circumstances, a single foldable offers a far more stable platform for reentry than would any comparable rigid kayak.

Safety benefits reach beyond the getting-back-in issue. During a storm at sea, you can hunker down into the relative comfort of the cockpit of your folding kayak while you ride out the turbulence. Try doing that in a rigid boat, and you'll capsize for sure, because the rigid kayak requires you to keep paddling or sculling to stay upright under such severe conditions. If you wrench your shoulder and can't paddle, a folding kayak will continue to float along nicely. If food poisoning suddenly incapacitates you and you must lean over the side to vomit, your foldable will remain stable beneath you. In a rigid boat, you'd probably capsize without some helping hands alongside.

A capsized hardshell that is partially filled with water is almost impossible to paddle without capsizing again since the water swishing around inside makes the kayak quite unstable, like the swinging of a pendulum. However, a folding kayak in a similar condition remains stable and "paddleable" even though the paddler will be sitting in water, since the sponsons dampen the pendulum effect of the water swishing from side to side.

MISCONCEPTIONS UNMASKED

Like Rodney Dangerfield, folding kayaks "get no respect." Several bad images and misconceptions about foldables still float in and out of the kayaking world, but most of them have very little basis in truth. Let's examine the most common doubts people have about foldables, and let's allow the track record to respond to these notions and prove them true or false.

"They Lack the Performance and Efficiency of Rigid Kayaks."

That exact phrase has been used in several sea-kayaking manuals, so it requires some discussion. Exactly what the writers meant by "performance" was never spelled out, but in the context in which the statement was made it seems to refer to the ability of the paddler to perform his or her skills.

Indeed, given their stability, it is generally harder to perform an Eskimo roll in a foldable kayak, and you'll find that your ability to scull is

limited by your relative position in the boat. But Eskimo rolling and extreme sculling are less necessary in a foldable kayak to begin with.

"Efficiency" appears to have something to do with speed. Folding kayaks are considered slower than rigid boats and less efficient. That is partly true, but not to the degree that the statement implies. Folding kayaks are wider, which ordinarily tends to slow a boat, but the width differences between the two kinds of kayaks are not so great where it counts—at the waterline. Most folding kayaks taper down sharply from their decks to the bottom of their hulls, so although the average single foldable may be 5 inches more beamy than its rigid counterpart, the difference between them at the waterline is more likely to be about 2 inches. If foldables were inherently slow, then in any group trip all the folding kayaks would be toward the back of the pack. This doesn't happen in real life. Folding kayaks wind up positioned anywhere from front to back dependent on the skill and stamina of the paddlers. When water gets rougher they tend to move up in position because of their more stable paddling platform.

At cruising speeds—where most people do the majority of their paddling—folding kayaks move just fine. Folding singles are as fast if not faster than at least 80 percent of the rigid singles. In mixed recreational class races, foldables don't normally dominate first-place honors, but they come in ahead of many rigid kayaks. For example, in the Angel Island 8-mile Race in open water off San Francisco, a Klepper Aerius single has come in as high as third in a field of seventy kayaks made up almost exclusively of hardshells. In a special recreational class race that was part of the last leg of the 1993 Finlandia Challenge, one folding kayak beat out some twenty rigid boats on a 12.5-mile course off New York City, a course that headed into current and wind.

When sea conditions get rough, folding kayaks really enter their element. The folding-

FOLDING KAYAKS VERSUS HARDSHELLS: DRAG CONSIDERATIONS

There are some scientific arguments using fluid dynamics that suggest that in rougher sea conditions, a folding kayak's flexible structure and skin gives it a noticeably lower drag coefficient than that experienced by a hardshell kayak. Here is what happens.

First, let's consider the simple case of what happens when a hardshell kayak is moving smoothly through the water and the water flow around the kayak is laminar and even. On the front surface of the kayak an area of positive pressure will build up where the kayak collides with still water, resisting the forward progress of the kayak.

As the water passes around the kayak, an area of suction or low pressure will be generated on the aft wetted surface of the kayak. This happens for the same reason that air passing over the top of a rounded airplane wing generates an area of low pressure on top of the wing, thus creating lift. This area of negative pressure or suction produces a significant amount of drag on the kayak.

With a folding kayak, or any flexible skin-and-frame kayak, the situation is different. Its skin flexes in and out in response to chaotic sea conditions. This motion destabilizes the water flow around the kayak and produces turbulent water flow along the aft surface of the kayak if the speed and the length of the kayak are great enough. Contrary to common belief, this turbulent flow *reduces* the magnitude of the negative pressure on the aft section of the kayak. This reduction of negative pressure significantly lowers the drag on the flexible-skin kayak and makes it faster than its hardshell counterpart in chaotic sea conditions.

Without chaotic sea conditions, the in-and-out motion will cease, and laminar flow will return and increase the drag on the flexible-skin kayak so that it is equal to the drag on a hardshell kayak. With smooth, laminar flow of water around both types of kayaks, the drag on the kayak will be determined mainly by the cross-sectional area of the kayak. Because a hardshell kayak usually has a lower cross-sectional area than a folding kayak, the hardshell experiences lower drag and will be faster in smooth water than its flexible-skin equivalent.

If you're interested in racing in generally calm conditions, a hardshell kayak will be the fastest and most economical. If you want speed and ease of paddling under chaotic sea conditions, such as those that occur near windward rocky shores, on lakes, or in harbors with a large motorboat population, a flexible-skin kayak may be the better choice.

kayak paddler can put all his or her energy into moving forward, without having to devote some of that time and effort to semi-bracing and other strokes required for maintaining stability in a rigid boat.

"Foldables Are Not Really Sea Kayaks."

If seaworthiness is any measure of what makes a sea kayak, then foldables certainly are sea kayaks. Earlier, we discussed the many unique characteristics of foldables that contribute to their seaworthiness. Thousands of offshore and open-water trips have been successfully completed all over the globe in folding kayaks. Try telling those explorers and adventurers that their boats weren't sea kayaks.

Folding kayaks have weathered dangerous storms on the open sea, including hurricanes and tropical disturbances. Consider all the surf landings and launches made without upset in these boats.

When all these factors are tallied, folding kayaks must be recognized as sea kayaks. If not, then what are they?

"One May Accidentally Fold Up on the Water."

This imaginary vision arises from a misunderstanding of the term "folding." The misconception is: "If it's a folding boat, might it not fold up on me when I'm on the water?"

No, it won't. It's not as if one single fastener or device acts like a linchpin, holding the whole boat together. A folding kayak's rigidity relies on a series of such fasteners in a progression of overlapping layers, thus making them fail-safe, and all folding kayaks are structured with built-in redundancy. If one fastener fails, others are sufficient to keep the boat together. Even if several fasteners were to give up the ghost, the frame would maintain its integrity. A storm won't break the frame apart, nor will it come apart on its own. Some folding kayakers have arrived at a launch site only to realize that a part or two had been left at home, but they were still able to assemble the boat and paddle.

"Folding Kayaks Require Lots of Maintenance."

Not true. According to the instructions for folding kayaks with wooden frames, they should be varnished annually, but few owners do. Most never varnish their frames at all, and they have no problems. At worst, it means that their frames, instead of lasting eighty years, might survive for only thirty to forty years.

Folding kayaks that have aluminum frames need occasional attention, with some lubrication at joining points to make certain these don't stick. But it's a minor inconvenience and takes only minutes each year.

"They Are Costly to Purchase."

True. Generally speaking, folding kayaks do cost more than rigid boats, especially plastic ones. However, the price difference is not so great when comparing them with fiberglass kayaks, especially top-of-the-line models. The price range of foldables is wide, and their depreciation is far less than that of rigid kayaks, due partly to the foldable's longer life and utility.

A top-of-the-line fiberglass double costs about $3,000, and a similar folding double will run from about $3,200 to $4,500; altogether about a 30 percent price difference. In five years, you could sell that double foldable for anywhere from $2,800 to $3,500. The fiberglass double would be lucky to fetch $1,500. The rigid model would have depreciated some 50 percent, but the foldable only about 12 to 15 percent.

When pricing new single kayaks, you'll find that the differences are much narrower, especially since the recent advent of smaller foldables. A top-quality mini-single foldable runs from $1,600 to $2,200, which places it just a bit higher than comparable small fiberglass singles that cost from around $1,400 to $1,800.

Don't overlook the several less expensive folding doubles and singles on the scene. You can get a single for around $1,200 and several of the doubles for just under $1,900. In this price bracket, these foldables are very close to the prices of the least expensive comparable plastic hardshell kayaks. Though these foldables are relatively inexpensive, they are not shoddily made and have proved popular with many satisfied folding kayakers.

"Foldables Are Heavier than Hardshells."

People who say this, or write it in manuals, are comparing apples and oranges. They look at a sleek fiberglass single that weighs about 50 pounds and hold it up against a double foldable that may tip the scales at 75 pounds. The "heaviness" charge falls apart when similar boats are compared.

If you compare single kayaks, you'll find that most foldables are in the same mid-50-pound range where fiberglass and plastic boats generally reside. One single foldable does weigh in at 62 pounds, but several plastic singles are 65 pounds in heft! Doubles, both folding and rigid, generally weigh between 72 and 85 pounds. In contrast, the mini-foldables tend to be lighter than their rigid counterparts. The lightest mini-foldable, which can do sea duty, is just 20 pounds. Another popular model that is almost full-size weighs just 35 pounds.

"Assembly and Disassembly Take Forever."

Nonsense. Most models can be assembled in about fifteen minutes. Of course, the process takes a little practice. And, when you've just received your new folding kayak via mail or parcel post, plan to spend quite a while putting it together for the very first time. You'll be reading the instructions carefully, and no doubt you'll be a little apprehensive about the process.

You can even improve on the normal fifteen-minute assembly time, if you choose. In folding kayak races, non-factory teams (i.e., ordinary people) have speeded assembly times to about seven minutes, including rudder and spraydeck. The fastest assembly for a double folding kayak is around four minutes.

Still, even fifteen minutes is not a lot of time. Considering the time required to tie a rigid boat securely onto a car roof, handling a foldable doesn't take all that much longer. And, if you had to drive to a storage area to pick up your rigid boat, owning a foldable might actually save you time.

At the Heart of Sea-Kayaking History

Modern sea kayaking began nearly a century ago with the commercial development of the folding kayak. When present-day paddlers venture out in today's sea kayaks, they hardly comprehend the vast history of the sport because, like the tip of the iceberg, so much lies out of sight.

Today, if fifteen or twenty sea kayaks are on the water at the same time (other than at a symposium), it's a big event, a signal that sea kayaking is really taking off. But in the 1920s and 1930s, twenty kayaks would have been considered a small gathering, not uncommon. Then, hundreds if not thousands of kayaks, all foldable, dotted the immediate horizon on any weekend afternoon. Most of this kayaking boom occurred in Europe, but North America was also caught up in it. Folding kayaking was a small-boating revolution that in a world torn by unrelenting political and economic tension let people escape the madness for a while.

During the 1930s, more than eighty manufacturers thrived in Germany alone, and dozens more did business elsewhere. In that era, they were all folding-kayak companies. Today, sea-kayaking circles buzz whenever some daring voyage is made here or there in a hardshell. But between the world wars, major bodies of water were crossed as frequently as calendar pages were flipped; every one of the landfalls was made in a foldable sea kayak. Land masses everywhere were being circumnavigated, all ends of the earth explored, in the ubiquitous folding kayak.

HOW THE KAYAKING REVOLUTION BEGAN

Some people mistakenly believe that the kayak-touring movement started when Johann Klepper first began producing folding kayaks in Bavaria, in southern Germany, in 1907. Not quite. It's true that the Klepper company did touch off the commercial development of the boat, but for nearly half a century before, the basic designs for such a folding kayak—constructed of canvas skin over a wooden frame—were kicking around both Europe and North America.

There's evidence of such a design in the United States as early as 1850. Even the Lewis and Clark Expedition had a form of folding boat, although it wasn't a kayak. And during the latter half of the nineteenth century, England was in the midst of a budding love affair with the Rob Roy "canoe" made of canvas and wood lath; some of these home-crafted skin boats could be taken apart for transportation and storage. The first known patent was taken out in 1887 in Germany for a *faltboot*, or folding boat, but the boat was never produced, and the holder lost the patent due to nondevelopment.

Not until 1905 was a workable folding kayak first built by Alfred Heurich, a German architectural student. He paddled his creation on the Isar River near Munich and took out a patent on the design the following year. Heurich's folding kayak model, the Delphin, or dolphin, had a bamboo frame that, in a symbiotic relationship with its sailcloth hull, stretched out the skin and, in turn, was held in tension by it. This is the same principle underlying every folding kayak made since that date. Heurich's foldable went into three bags, each of which weighed less than 10 pounds. The rod bag was cleverly sized to fit in the overhead luggage racks of passenger trains.

Heurich's concept was revolutionary and practical. The Delphin was portable enough for one person to carry. By fitting in bags that could easily go on a train, his folding kayak opened up all sorts of possibilities for ordinary Germans—who were then getting their first symptoms of wanderlust.

Alfred Heurich with first foldable, 1907. *(Walther/Klepper)*

THE FOLDING KAYAK AS DREADNOUGHT

SBS crew, training exercise, 1992. *(Walther)*

Folding kayaks have a long military history that, by necessity, is shrouded in secrecy. Enough information has leaked out, however, to testify that these tiny vessels are capable of taking punishment and providing a stable platform for transporting soldiers and ordnance over vast distances through rough sea conditions.

Although they may have been deployed by German forces earlier, folding kayaks first surfaced publicly as a British weapon of war in 1940. The British Navy's elite special-operations unit started life in July 1940 as the Folbot Section. Its assignment: To employ folding kayaks for raiding and reconnaissance. The original name was quickly changed to the Special Boat Section (SBS) because it gave away too much about what the unit might be up to. The founder of the section was Roger Courtney, one of those many folding-kayak wanderers from the 1930s who had once paddled 3,400 miles down the Nile.

Throughout World War II, SBS units and similar folding-kayak warriors from other British services menaced enemy shipping and shore installations, and they scouted beach defenses for amphibious landings. The most famous SBS raid was Operation Frankton in 1942. Five double-kayak teams set out with magnetic mines to destroy vital enemy cargo aboard ships in Bordeaux, 62 miles up the Gironde Estuary. Folding kayaks provided the only means to crack the port's defenses unseen and to attack the shipping with pinpoint accuracy. The following year, the SBS's Australian counterparts used three folding kayaks to sink a half dozen enemy ships in Singapore; the Japanese defenders never suspected the raiders had come from the sea. As in Bordeaux, the folding kayaks had allowed their crews to approach targets undetected, so they could place their mines.

Folding kayaks remain a military "asset" for several dozen nations. For example, several Scan-

dinavian countries continue to patrol long stretches of sensitive coastlines with folding kayaks. The boats can cover long distances and, unlike motor patrol boats, are hard to spot. This keeps would-be intruders guessing about where a patrol may be at any moment and whether they are being observed. Similar patrols are deployed by both Iraq and Iran in the vast Tigris-Euphrates Delta, all the better to infiltrate and interdict each other. There is good reason to believe that, during Operation Desert Storm, U.S. and British forces used foldables to run long-range reconnaissance missions on these same rivers as far north as Baghdad.

Earlier, Britain used folding kayaks extensively in retaking the Falkland Islands from an Argentine occupying force. Foldables first transported reconnaissance teams to study defenses. Then, as the British fleet and troop carriers lay offshore, teams went in again to cut communications and clean out mines and shore installations.

The military continues to buy many Klepper and Nautiraid kayaks for its training and operations. The boats are often treated roughly, loaded beyond their intended capacities, manhandled from submarines and small vessels, dropped fully loaded from helicopters, and later winched back into the air with their crews and all their gear. Special-operation forces drag their boats over rocks, use them for prolonged periods in freezing and tropical conditions, and generally put more wear on them in one year than civilians would in twenty. Because these folding kayaks survive the torture, military procurement officers keep coming back for more.

Heurich had no real notion of how to produce the folding kayak on a commercial basis. He was having trouble with the materials for the hull and didn't have a clue how to set up a sewing shop, so he contacted Johann Klepper, an established tailor in nearby Rosenheim. Klepper had dreams of cashing in on the wanderlust that had fellow Germans passing through this Bavarian town in great numbers on their way to fabled Alpine lakes and mountains. Recognizing a golden opportunity, Klepper got a license from Heurich in 1907 to produce the boat commercially.

Immediately, Klepper began making improvements on Heurich's foldable. He changed the frame material to ash wood to achieve better strength and bend properties and to eliminate splintering. He increased the number of frame members to make the assembled boat less floppy, and he raised the cockpit coaming to keep water out. Klepper also improved the hull material, making it more waterproof. One thing he did not fiddle with was the packed size; Klepper knew that portability would sell the boat.

THE WANDERLUST YEARS

Klepper's production-model folding kayak was the right product for that time, the perfect getaway vehicle for a restless society. It hit Germany and the rest of the Continent in big and small ways.

Rugged individuals immediately began to embark on voyages that tested the toughness of the underlying design, first using foldables exclusively from Klepper and later from other producers as well. The English Channel was crossed in 1909 in one of those first Kleppers. In 1923, Karl Schott, paddling a double Klepper solo, went first from Germany to Cairo, and two years later he pushed on all the way to the Persian Gulf. Roald Amundsen took some folding kayaks on his North Pole exploration in 1926, and Admiral Richard Byrd did the same when he went to the South Pole in 1928. In 1929, Carl Borro Schweria used a single Klepper foldable to run the Frazer and Columbia Rivers, as well as the Colorado River through the Grand Canyon. A pair of intrepid folding

Folding kayakers on the Hudson River, New York City, circa 1936. (John Walther)

kayakers hopscotched from Germany to Hong Kong, taking more than six years to complete the journey. In 1933, Fridel Meyer paddled her Klepper halfway around the British Isles to win a long-distance contest.

These globetrotters were traveling billboards for folding kayaks. Accounts of their adventures stirred the imagination of newspaper and magazine readers back home. This led to more wanderlust and, of course, more purchases of Kleppers, Pioneers, and scores of other folding-kayak brands.

The voyager who most deeply moved the public was Captain Franz Romer, when he crossed the Atlantic in 1928 in a custom-made 19-foot Klepper. He managed to get to Puerto Rico despite being hit twice by hurricanes. Romer's transatlantic passage was the ultimate test of seaworthiness for a folding kayak, and his boat was only slightly different from the production models anyone could buy off the shelf. Romer's exploit made banner headlines on both sides of the ocean. In a poignant ending to his tale, Romer disappeared without a trace in another hurricane while crossing from Puerto Rico to the U.S. mainland. Pundits point out that he had added a motor to his foldable for that last leg of his journey, and it probably compromised the sea trim of his boat.

While these folding-kayak voyagers were almost bumping into each other as they crisscrossed the globe, ordinary people were creating folding-kayak traffic jams closer to home as they sought their own more modest adventures. Thousands upon thousands of wandering kayakers packed their folding kayaks for weekends and vacations, and they paddled every inch of water on the rivers, lakes, and coastlines of Europe.

Trains traveling south into the Alpine lake country would arrive in small villages to release an avalanche of folding kayakers from every passenger-car door. Kayakers by the hundreds would load boat bags and gear on two-wheel handcarts and roll down country lanes to the lakesides or riverbanks where their adventures would unfold. It was an impressive summer weekend sight that dwarfs anything we see today, even the sea kayak symposium at Port Townsend, Washington, that draws 800 participants annually.

It was not all touring. Folding kayaks quickly took to the whitewater during that period. Photographs of the day show narrow folding kayaks deep in the white foam of fast moving rivers, their paddlers expertly negotiating around rocks and bends, through chutes and over falls.

Folding-kayak racing events even became part of the Olympics. They were the only kayaks used in whitewater events until the late 1950s, when rigid boats were introduced. The ancient Eskimo roll was rediscovered by Edi Hans Pawlata in a folding kayak; one classic method of kayak rolling now bears his name.

THE POSTWAR ERA

World War II brought a hiatus to kayak wanderlust. Folding-kayak touring turned to folding-kayak warfare, and the boats participated in action on both sides of the conflict. They accounted for heavy toll in "enemy tonnage sunk" that is almost unbelievable considering the relative tininess of the kayaks doing the attacking. (See the Folding Kayak as Dreadnought sidebar on page 20.)

Most folding-kayak companies in Germany didn't survive the war's devastation, but Klepper and a handful of others literally rose from the ashes. Klepper's factory had been severely bombed, not because folding kayaks were a strategic target (they should have been), but because the building abutted the main marshaling yards for trains that crossed the Alps to support the German war effort in Italy.

Pope John Paul II, Kleppering in his student days. *(Walther/Klepper)*

Elsewhere in Europe, the industry thinned out. The United Kingdom, for example, lost its respected folding-kayak industry that had provided boats for the military during the war. Even with fewer makes to choose from, Europeans began hitting the waters again in folding kayaks. But because their need for economic recovery outweighed their need for recreation, the golden age of kayaking began to dwindle.

Meanwhile, the American scene turned dynamic. The manufacturer Folbot had moved to the United States from England just prior to the war, so by the postwar era, it was producing an inexpensive foldable that brought the sport within reach of most people. Thousands of Folbots were sold each year. In the Northeast, the railroads ran what were billed as Fold-Boat Trains, weekend specials that took hundreds of paddlers to the region's popular lakes and rivers.

Kleppers also began to sell vigorously in the U.S. market. A weak deutsche mark, in relation to the strong postwar U.S. dollar, allowed Klepper to export thousands of its sea kayaks to the United States at prices considered affordable by just about everyone. Several other developments helped sales.

In 1953, the company introduced its new Klepper Aerius model that for the first time in-

Hannes Lindemann's transatlantic Klepper.

A VISIT TO A FACTORY

Have you ever been curious about how a typical folding kayak like a Klepper is made? Forget those images of Bavarian craftsmen whittling out ribs, apprentices forging fittings, seamstresses with spectacles perched low on their noses sewing away by hand. It isn't like that, and never was, even in Hans Klepper's time. The process does include a great deal of skilled hand labor, but it all revolves around industrial machinery, templates, and jigs. Here's a glimpse of how the pieces are made and put together at the factory in Rosenheim, Germany.

The Rosenheim operation at one time did all its woodworking on the premises. Now all wooden parts are made at a lumber subcontractor's factory about a half hour away. The wood factory has an exclusive contract with Rosenheim, an arrangement that assures a steady supply of quality product to Klepper and steady income for the wood factory.

The process begins with careful selection of the wood—mountain ash for the long pieces that need to be flexible, and Finnish birch for the nine-layer plywood laminations used for ribs. The ash is aged three years, and the birch is cut and glued into marine-quality plywood.

The long mountain ash pieces are milled in fairly large automated machines that spit out the stringers and the rails used to form gunwales and keelboards. These are then cut to size, sanded, etc. The birch plywood is cut into ribs by a skilled worker using an industrial saw stand and template in which the centers are cut out and the outer lines formed. A similar process is used to form the bow and stern endpieces. Then the edges are beveled and sanded.

The gunwales and keelboards are put together at the lumber factory. The reinforcement plates for the gunwales are glued to the rails using jigs to assure precision in placement. The keelboards are glued together in a similar fashion on jigs to get just the right angles.

The wooden parts travel to Rosenheim every Monday. The pickup is a rush process because differences in humidity and temperatures can affect the dimensions of the wood, even minutely, and throw off the exact placement of fittings, and the precise alignment of the frame.

By late Monday, Rosenheim workers have drilled any holes needed for later placement of fittings and started the varnishing process. The machinery and jigs used for drilling represent some of the most costly equipment used in Rosenheim. The jigs are made of metal and allow up to a half dozen parts, let's say Aerius II #3 ribs, to be drilled at once. Worn jig parts have to be replaced often to assure continued precision. The costs are so prohibitive that Klepper is not quick to rush into new models with different ribs, gunwales, or other parts.

Varnishing is done in huge vats placed in the concrete floor. The parts are held on overhead racks, just so many parts to each rack. They are dipped in three baths of high-grade marine varnish; first one of a thin viscosity to assure deep penetration of the wood, then two more baths of a thicker viscosity to provide the needed protective layers. The dipping process is done at a rate of so many feet per minute to get the right amount of varnish on the wood. The varnished parts are then left to dry for at least twenty-four hours before going upstairs to receive fittings.

Fittings are made of a corrosion-proof aluminum alloy. If you've ever looked carefully at a Klepper frame, you know there are a lot of fittings, and each fitting is made of a number of parts—rivets, plates, springs—that all require precision fabrication.

All fittings are made by subcontractors, most of which are run by former Klepper employees. The main fittings are made in one factory very close to Rosenheim. It would amaze you to see how much equipment is needed to do all the work. One whole machine just forms the bend in the tongue fittings.

Klepper uses just-in-time inventory, which leaves it with only two weeks' worth of parts. It can do so because all the subcontractors are near by, and there are ways of backing up anyone who may run into a problem.

When the frame pieces get to the main factory floor, they go into a time-consuming process of fitting placement done by hand. Several skilled workers place the fittings by hammering rivets into the precision holes made earlier. The plastic holders for stringers are also hammered in with rivets at this point, and caps are placed on the stringers.

The next step is to test it all. Before a frame is readied for shipment, it's fully assembled from the parts bins. This assures Klepper that everything fits together. Because of the elaborate processes that preceded this step, very few rejects or parts ever need to go back to be fixed. In this test-assembly phase, the frames are also placed into boat skins to make certain they fit well within desired tolerances.

Klepper boat skins are made of cotton canvas joined to Hypalon hulls. All work on these is done in-house. Hypalon and canvas arrive from their sources in large rolls. Decks and hulls are cut on one huge table that is also used for cutting sails, spraydecks, and skirts. Working with patterns, the sewing staff cuts as many as four decks at a time, but hulls are usually done one or two at a time.

Several seamstresses work first on the decks. They sew on paddle pockets, deck D-rings and other such fittings, and the pockets that hold air sponsons. The air sponsons themselves come from a subcontractor, and to be sure they hold air, they're blown up and tested for a few days.

The seamstresses usually work on specific orders rather than just make decks for stock. The same sewing machines used for making the deck fittings sew the spraydecks, spray skirts, sails, and the bags used to store and carry the boats.

Klepper has a special proprietary process for attaching decks to hulls. First, using the heavy-duty sewing machines mentioned above, the seamstresses sew a ribbon binding to the perimeter of the deck. This ribbon binding, unique to Klepper, is about an inch wide and made of a specially blended material. Then the seamstresses haul the hulls and decks over to a very different sewing machine, one unlike any other in the Klepper factory. Here the hulls and decks are sewn together. The company's seam-binding process results in a seam that is absolutely watertight.

corporated air sponsons on a production folding kayak. This feature greatly helped assembly and disassembly of foldables. The skin fit could be designed to be looser, thus allowing easier insertion of frame halves; you then tightened the hull fit by blowing up the air tubes. Prior to this innovation, the fit had to be more taut, making assembly or disassembly a tricky chore.

Another boost to Klepper's postwar success, especially in the United States, came from another epic seafaring voyage that made news—Dr. Hannes Lindemann's 1956 crossing of the At-lantic, totally unassisted, in a stock Klepper Aerius double folding kayak. Dr. Lindemann was so independent that he bought his Klepper out of his own pocket from a dealer in Germany. He had the boat mailed to him in the Canary Islands, then set out for the Caribbean with some modified sails, a primitive outrigger, and 154 pounds of canned food, garlic, beer, and water. Seventy-two days and 3,000 miles later he emerged from a Caribbean rain squall to startle some onlookers on a beach in St. Martin.

He made the cover of *Life* magazine in 1957

and wrote a very popular book, *Alone at Sea*. He became a modern-day icon of sea kayaking, someone to point to whenever anyone doubts the seaworthiness of these small, vulnerable-looking craft. In the wake of all the publicity, the rush to buy Kleppers, Folbots, and other foldables created a boomlet for sea kayaking.

TO THE PRESENT

But lifestyles were changing. A society caught up in modern conveniences, television, and the automobile turned its back on the outdoor life. Camping, canoeing, bicycling, and exercise were not the way society wanted to spend its leisure time in the late 1950s and most of the 1960s. If people boated at all, it was in motor-powered craft, not muscle-driven ones. Reduced interest in physical pursuits prevented any resurgence to the level of sea kayaking seen earlier.

In the 1970s, commercial production of rigid kayaks began in earnest, forcing foldables to yield their exclusive hold on the world of sea kayaking. Fiberglass kayaks were relatively easy to make. The cost of starting up an operation was low, and production could begin in a barn or garage. Plastic sea kayaks, which came on the market during the late 1970s and early 1980s, required a sizable initial investment in equipment, but they could then be mass-produced inexpensively at a large markup.

Fiberglass and plastic boats both took advantage of new materials, a move that projected their image as modern and sleek. Foldables, because they were made of canvas and wood, were considered relatively old-fashioned and vulnerable.

One new maker of folding kayaks bridged the gap between these perceptions of modern and traditional. In 1980, Feathercraft began operations out of Vancouver, British Columbia, with a one-person folding kayak that offered an aluminum frame and synthetic deck. It even had a small cockpit opening similar to those on hardshell kayaks. These innovations helped Feathercraft buck the trend and draw customers.

Meanwhile, the Klepper conglomerate that produced folding kayaks had also taken on tents, clothing, sailboats, and car trailers. It became so overextended it went bankrupt and closed its folding-kayak production in 1978. Herman Walther, a retired international businessman from Germany, paid a chance visit to the dormant factory to get spare parts, and his subsequent involvement led to the revival of operations by 1981. Walther got a license to build boats from the thousands of warehoused spare parts and eventually bought the machinery and plant. He introduced new cost-cutting management methods, such as farming out many operations, and, to assure continuing quality control, much of this subcontracting went to former Klepper employees.

Folbot also had spread itself in too many directions, and production quality suffered when it offered dozens of models, including kits and hardshells. Then Jack Kissner, who had founded the company in London in the 1930s, died. Again, only happenstance brought Phil Cotton, a product design executive working in the same industrial park where Folbot was located, into the picture. Cotton bought the plant from Kissner's estate in the early 1980s, and then streamlined production methods, got rid of most of its models, and concentrated on a new design, the Greenland series, which had synthetic decks and aluminum frames à la Feathercraft.

WHAT NOW?

During the 1990s the major companies managed to hold their own against the many manufacturers of hardshell kayaks and kept the folding kayak niche strong and steady. They have done so by offering customers a wider choice of models as well as introducing models at the lower end of the price scale. A company such as Nautiraid, for example, has models that include a less expensive touring version as well as an expedition version. It also has some less expensive aluminum-framed models.

Feathercraft improved on its smaller boat, the K-Light, and then replaced it with the Kahuna, a model that weighs exactly the same as its predecessor but is 2 feet longer. Lighter materials allow this benefit. Feathercraft also introduced the Khatsalano in the mid-1990s, a long, skinny Greenland-style single that caught the attention of many hardshell kayakers. Whether they bought one or not, they wound up saying nicer things about folding kayaks. Folbot came out with a fuller-size single, the Kodiak, to augment its mini-kayak, and even an in-between-size boat, the Yukon. Klepper introduced its first aluminum-framed kayak, the Alu-Lite. This is all good news for anyone thinking of buying a folding kayak.

In weight, these lighter folding kayaks harken back to the early days of folding kayaks—the 29- to 42-pound range—which makes them lighter than most rigid sea kayaks. And they fit in a single bag. These new foldables are well suited for smaller people, particularly women, who make up more than 40 percent of new sea-kayak buyers.

People who aren't using sea kayaks for long expeditions don't need heftier boats. These lighter folding kayaks suit paddlers who mainly do day trips or outings of less than a week.

The companies also feel that the pendulum is swinging in their favor in other ways. There are so many look-alike rigid sea kayaks on the market that potential buyers get confused by all the choices. Lifestyles are changing, and home sizes are shrinking. More people are living in condos instead of houses with yards and garages. Apartments are smaller. The problem of where to store a 17-foot hardshell looms ever larger. With a kayak that can fold, the problem is solved.

Paddlers are being drawn to other benefits of foldables. The faster learning curve for safely using folding kayaks appeals to individuals who want to get out on the water fast, as opposed to spending months honing the skills required in hardshells. Conspicuous consumerism is giving way to greater appreciation of nature and the environment, a trend that's particularly favorable to foldables. They allow a wider range of travel for exploring great expanses of fresh and salt water. Paddlers can hop on a plane, bus, or train and get to new waters quickly. And, when they get there, they enjoy a greater degree of seaworthiness and safety that are required for exploring unknown areas.

Choosing the Folding Kayak That's Right for You

Here are three important points to remember when shopping for a folding kayak:

1. You have a surprising number of real choices. The differences between the leading models are fundamental divergences in designs, materials, and approaches. You're not dealing with dozens of look-alikes as you are with rigid boats, in which differences are often cosmetic.

2. You get what you pay for. This market doesn't support designer labels. Some folding kayaks cost more because they are better boats, not merely because they are imported or constructed of space-age materials. On the other hand, lower-priced models are not shoddily built and are proving satisfactory for many paddlers.

3. You'll never regret buying one. Owners of folding kayaks tend to hang on to their boats for decades, as witnessed by the scarcity of foldables on the used-kayak market. The boat you buy will give you long service and see you safely through your adventures, just as such boats have done for many thousands of paddlers.

As with any purchase, there are many factors to consider when selecting the exact folding kayak you'll be happy with. For one, you bring certain personal elements to the decision process: your size, interests, and skills. For another, the often radical differences between individual folding-kayak models in terms of assembly, the way they behave on the water, and other traits do require that you really think through how you'll be using your foldable. You'll see these differences in the next chapter, when we'll evaluate over twenty models.

SIZING UP YOUR NEEDS

Sea kayaking is a very personal sport. Needs differ. You should be wary of people recommending a particular model unless they have asked you some basic questions and then listed salient features that match your responses. The XYZ Walrus Hunter may be a great boat for one individual and lousy for another. The easiest way to lose a friend is to praise some model highly and insist that your friend get one—without sizing up whether it will fulfill your friend's needs.

When making a decision about a folding kayak you have more questions to answer than

you do with rigid kayaks. The questions posed below are intended to raise the key issues, but they are not necessarily the only considerations. Use them to get your thought juices flowing, so you'll find the best boat for you.

Do You Need a Single or a Double?

This question comes up for couples and for any individual who may be paddling at some point with a companion. If you're a couple, think through how you're likely to paddle. Will you want to be in the same boat for conversation, sharing the paddling load and the experience more intimately? Or will you want to move at different paces, one crossing from point to point, the other exploring the shoreline? Many couples start with a double and later pick up at least one single for the times one may want to go alone. This opens the option of bringing along another person, perhaps someone new to the sport. The novice can paddle in the double with one half of the couple, while the other goes in the single.

For a couple, costs may complicate this decision of buying one double or two singles. Two

Solo paddling a double. *(Michael Skott)*

WHAT TO HAVE ALONG WHEN BUYING A USED BOAT

Assembly instructions. Get these from the factory or dealer. The instruction sheet reveals if any parts are missing. The seller may have inherited the boat—without instructions—and not know how to assemble it.

Price list of replacement parts. You will want to factor in the replacement costs for broken or missing items. Making a list of these items and showing this to the seller may help to lower the price.

Repair costs. The factory, for example, can tell you the cost of restringing bungee cords inside tubes or for sewing parts of deck seams.

Folding Kayaker **newsletter contact information.** Having doubts? Get in touch with a trusted resource (see the appendix).

singles are almost always more expensive than a double of the same quality.

Some individuals buy doubles with the thought that they may want to have a friend along. They feel that they can paddle the double alone the rest of the time. Don't do that to yourself unless you are very certain you'll have company enough of the time—about 70 percent—to warrant the less-than-optimum paddling you'll experience in a double by yourself.

Solo paddling is best done in single boats. All doubles paddled solo are a compromise. However, if you plan to sail a good amount of the time, a double will have the advantage of greater stability and no particular disadvantage for the person going off alone since the boat will be mainly wind powered. Also, if you are planning to paddle in remote areas for weeks, possibly months at a time, a double will carry all the gear you're likely to require.

If you're absolutely determined to buy a double that you'll be paddling alone most of the time, get the best solo-paddling model you can. Some models are not too bad when paddled solo, but others are dogs. Look into how conveniently the boat can be set up for solo paddling, which usually involves moving one seat into a better trim position. Solo seats for some models can be costly. You may also want to have a solo

spraydeck, which costs more money. You could save the extra expense by making your own solo seating arrangement and deck. On a temporary basis, you could also put some weight in the front seat to improve the kayak's trim a bit and keep the nose from being pushed around by the wind.

Certain paddlers can manage solo paddling a double quite well, and it doesn't necessarily correlate to muscle mass. Some of these paddlers stand about 5 feet, 8 inches and don't appear exceptionally strong.

Will You Need to Assemble It Regularly?

Remember, we are talking about *foldable* boats. So, if you won't be leaving it set up most of the time, consider how fast and easily a particular model assembles and takes apart. Some foldables can normally be assembled in ten to fifteen minutes. Others take closer to twenty. Still others require thirty to forty minutes even after you become totally familiar with the assembly process. Notice the assembly times in the evaluations of different models in the next chapter.

If you plan to use the boat mainly for weekend camping and weeklong trips, longer assembly times are not critical. If you'll be paddling for a few days before knocking the boat down to go home, what difference does an extra fifteen or

Author assembling Nautiraid Mini-Raid, 10:00 A.M.

10:02 A.M.

10:06 A.M.

10:09 A.M.

10:14 A.M.

twenty minutes make? But if you only have time for day trips or just an afternoon, then the long assembly time will probably discourage you from going paddling at all.

Where Do You Intend to Paddle?

Be realistic. If you plan to remain on calm lakes and sheltered coastlines, if you'll never venture out in anything but clear weather, give serious consideration to a lighter-duty model that will save you money and weight. "Lighter duty" does not mean flimsy; such models have proven more than satisfactory for many paddlers.

It's similar to buying a tent. A Eureka three-person dome tent will cost you less than $200. By comparison, a North Face three-person, double-wall expedition tent runs about $500. Of course, the North Face expedition tent will handle heavier winds and weather than the Eureka, but the Eureka is probably all you need. It's the same with foldables.

But if you'll definitely be paddling under severe conditions, then you would be better off with a more substantial foldable. In fact, your life may depend on it. Similarly, if you're pretty sure of encountering sharp obstacles or having to make many rough landings, the same rule holds true. A more substantial boat, one with thicker skin and keelstripping, will resist punctures and stand up to excessive wear.

This durability is even more important if you're buying a single. If you paddle alone, you'll have to drag your kayak a few boat lengths to clear the surf or crashing waves. (An exception are singles weighing about 35 pounds or less that can be easily lifted by most people.) In a double, there would normally be two paddlers who would carry—not drag—the kayak to a more secure spot.

How Will You Use It?

Folding kayaks offer plenty of versatility, but be careful not to choose one just because it offers more possibilities. If you're definitely planning to sail, you'll need a model that can handle a full-range sailing rig, and some models are better natural sailing vessels than others. But, if sailing is something you just *think* you may want to do someday, don't buy a particular foldable just to have this sailing potential. If the sailing bug hits you later, you can always sell the model that isn't easily sailable and not lose much money since the boat is likely to retain most of its value.

The same goes for fishing. The best fishing boats are extremely stable, enabling you to cast or pull fish confidently, and they have wide-open cockpits that let you get at all your fishing gear.

If you plan to do many extended camping trips, bear in mind how all your cargo will fit. But do think this through as you may not need a full-

Folding kayak in the Arctic. *(Walther/Klepper)*

size boat. Mini-foldable kayaks can carry quite a load, easily enough for a weeklong camping trip (see pages 176–77).

What Are Your Skill Levels?

All folding kayaks are more stable than their rigid-boat counterparts, but some foldables are more tippy than others. If you think you'll be uncomfortable in one of the more tippy models, then opt for a foldable that feels more stable.

Some single foldables have lots of rocker in their hulls, which makes them easier to turn. But rockered boats also tend to turn into the wind and waves more easily, a trait that makes them difficult to keep going in the right direction. If you don't have the paddling skills to keep a rockered boat going straight, you'll need a rudder. Most double-boat owners consider a rudder crucial, but single paddlers often find them a nuisance. A rudder adds to the weight you carry—they can weigh up to 4 pounds—and increases assembly time. It also creates drag, slowing you down.

Be wary of buying a boat that you'll need to "grow into" in order to handle it well. In many cases, individuals who do this wind up hating the boat and not using it because they feel so insecure paddling it. The used market in hardshells often is glutted with such boats. The folding-kayak market doesn't have many such models, but you do occasionally see people selling off such boats because they proved to be too much to handle.

How Strong Are You?

If you're looking for a single, your strength should be your first consideration. If the single boat you're eyeing is too big or heavy for you, you'll never enjoy carrying its bags or hefting the assembled boat down to a dock or beach. Sea kayaking is supposed to be fun and liberating, not a chore.

Some of the singles are heavy, make no mis-

take about it. One model weighs around 62 pounds, which puts it in a weight class with the heaviest plastic boats around. That's a lot for a small person to deal with. This particular foldable may be a terrific boat, but do you really need it? Instead, go for one of the mini-foldables that will make you a lot happier in the long run.

If you don't have the necessary upper-body strength but are absolutely determined to get a heavy-duty, sea-crashing boat, be prepared to use a boat cart. And when your boat's being hit by wake or surf, you'll need to work out a way to get it away from the water's edge.

If you're buying a double, you don't face quite as much demand on your strength. The weight of a double foldable is generally the same as a hardshell double. The lightest model weighs in at a little less than 70 pounds; the heaviest is up around 85 pounds. These weights have proved manageable for just about any two people.

WHAT ARE THE BEST MATERIALS?

When you start to investigate folding kayaks, you'll soon hear comparisons of the materials that go into their frames, hulls, and decks. One manufacturer may claim its frame material is superior to that of other folding kayaks, while another company says its decks are the best.

Experience with many hundreds of folding kayaks through years of service has shown that each material has its advantages and disadvantages. Compare materials to suit your particular needs, but don't think for a moment that any particular material used for a frame or hull could be best in every way.

Wood Versus Aluminum

Several of the major manufacturers—Klepper and Nautiraid—continue to use wood for most of their frames, including the long pieces and crossribs. However, in some of their models they now use aluminum long pieces and synthetic materials for crossribs, as Folbot and Feathercraft do for all their boats.

The wood-versus-aluminum arguments seem endless, not unlike the sleeping-bag controversy. Some people would rather give up camping than switch from their down-filled sleeping bags, while others swear their bags filled with synthetic fibers give them many extra advantages. On a cold night, either material is sure to keep a person warm, so neither is "superior" to the other.

It's really a matter of preference rather than objective analysis. Some people like the modern, up-to-date associations aluminum gives them, while others like the tradition and aesthetic sense they get with wooden frames. If the modern-versus-traditional point is important to you, follow your heart.

But beyond that, don't worry about wood-versus-aluminum arguments unless the way you plan to use your foldable will make one material work better for you than the other. For example, if you paddle frequently in cold weather, you may find that nonconductive wood is more pleasant to handle while assembling the boat than cold aluminum. It's a minor point, but it may be critical to your enjoyment of your kayak.

Be careful about the claims that are made in the wood-versus-aluminum argument, because they don't hold up in the real world. Here are a few of the most common:

"Aluminum frames are no good; if they break in the field, unlike wood, they are impossible to repair, so you'll be stuck." Not true. Repair kits provided by the manufacturers often contain aluminum sleeves of a diameter slightly larger that regular frame members. You slip a sleeve over the two broken ends of the long piece, tape or tie the repair sleeve tightly in place, and you're free to paddle on. You can get a replacement part when you're back from your trip. Also, there is no rule that says you can't take a tree branch to repair or replace an aluminum tube the way you would with a wooden frame piece. Repairs do require thinking out of the box, and such approaches will be discussed in chapter 17.

"Aluminum frames are better than wood, because they need no maintenance, unlike wood, which has to be varnished regularly." This is not true. It's amazing how little varnishing many people do and get away with it. Aluminum, on the other hand, does require attention at the points where tubes connect. These points should be lubricated several times a year and washed every so often. Wash and lubricate especially if the frame has been lying on sand or been kept assembled with salt water sitting in the bilge. If you don't maintain the aluminum, you may find the frame very difficult to disassemble later.

"Wood is no good because it's fragile and breaks easily." It takes a lot to break a wooden frame member. Under ordinary use, it won't crack or split. There are many forty-year-old wooden frames around that have been used regularly and show no breakage. Even extraordinary abuse of wooden frames causes only minor damage. For example, the Aussie Challenge expedition that covered some four thousand miles along Australia's east coast suffered little damage to the frame of the Klepper double it used. The foldable landed through the country's famous rough surf during some one hundred days of the voyage, a tough test for any kayak.

"Wood is better than aluminum in the tropics because it's less susceptible to corrosion and therefore holds up better." Actually, both materials suffer equally under tropical conditions. Several touring services use Feathercrafts for all their Caribbean and Baja trips, and they've had no particular problem. And the boats stay assembled for long periods at a time. Kleppers and Nautiraids

are used by other touring services in the same way. Both types of material need maintenance to hold up. Wooden frames should regularly be taken out of the hull and allowed to dry thoroughly to prevent rot. With aluminum, take the precautions mentioned earlier; i.e., lubricate and wash tube ends when you can.

Deck and Hulls

On decks, it's Klepper versus the rest of the pack. All Klepper decks are made of cotton canvas. The other major manufacturers use synthetic materials, albeit with differences in weights, coatings, and methods of waterproofing.

Cotton has the advantage of breathability. The environment under the closed decks of a Klepper is considerably less humid than under decks with synthetic coverings. Cotton canvas has another unique property: It doesn't require coatings to be waterproof. As in old canvas tents, the material is tightly woven. Individual threads swell when they get wet, so the openings between them close up, rendering the entire surface waterproof. When wet, the cotton deck also tightens up, giving you the benefit of a tauter skin fit when under way.

But cotton has its downside. Because cotton is less abrasion resistant than synthetics, cotton decks have to be thicker to compensate. Cotton canvas is heavier than synthetics of equal thickness; even when it's dry, you have a lot more weight to contend with. The weight problem is compounded when a cotton deck gets wet and absorbs water as part of its natural waterproofing process. The boat gets even heavier. Finally, a wet cotton deck takes longer to dry than a synthetic one.

Synthetics are stronger than cotton, but they do require coatings to achieve watertightness. At one time all the boats with synthetic decks varied in the number of coatings and the surface upon which the coatings were applied—the underside

or the top. Increasingly companies have started coating their boats' decks in different ways. For example, Feathercraft now has Poly-Tech decks that have embossed application of urethane coatings to a nylon core on both sides that enables the seams to be welded between the deck and a Duratek hull (polyurethane on nylon core) rather than stitched. Others such as Nautiraid now use PVC vinyl coatings on both sides of the deck and either Hypalon- or PVC-coated hulls.

Then there's the question of which synthetic to use. Companies have been moving away from nylon and Cordura nylon decks in favor of polyester. Nylon is particularly susceptible to UV damage; that's why nylon decks require UV inhibitors. Nylon becomes stretchy when wet, as much as 5 percent. This forces manufacturers to compensate by making their nylon deck skins on the tight side. Some expensive new processes now allow integral coating of both sides of nylon skins so that they aren't exposed to possible stretching. Polyester is somewhat more UV-resistant than nylon, but it still requires some added waterproof coatings. Polyester has little stretch, assuring a consistently taut skin.

UV light, by the way, harms all material used in kayaks, soft or hard. Like folding kayaks, rigid kayaks also should be kept out of direct sunlight as much as possible when not actually out on the water. UV dries out both plastic and fiberglass decks, making them brittle and more susceptible to hairline stress fractures.

The hulls on folding kayaks are mainly made of Hypalon, a synthetic rubberlike material, bonded to a textile core material. Hypalon-covered hulls have an advantage over those covered with natural rubber, which was the main material used previously. Hypalon lasts much longer—thirty years under normal use. Natural rubber, which has not been used in decades, tends to last about twenty years before it gets scaly. Again, some companies, such as Feathercraft with its proprietary urethane-coated hulls, have started using different hull materials. You will also see PVC-coated hulls, which are lighter and cheaper to make.

Hypalon hulls vary in several respects, such as their thickness and the types of adhesives used to bind the Hypalon to the core material inside. For example, all of Klepper's hulls, even its nonexpedition boats, are thicker than those of its competitors. When Feathercraft used a Hypalon, the coating was molecularly denser than Klepper's Hypalon. Polyester has replaced cotton as a core material since cotton absorbs water and tends to rot from within. Adhesives are a complex subject. You'll hear esoteric arguments about which works best to bind Hypalon to its core material, but generally all you need to know is that Hypalon works well.

Keelstrips are a critical consideration for any hull. These protective strips, made of materials similar to those used in hulls, absorb a lot of the abuse of landing on gravel beaches and the like.

STRATEGIES FOR BUYING A NEW FOLDABLE

As mentioned in chapter 1, folding kayaks generally cost more than rigid kayaks. So it's good to have a strategy for getting the best buy if you're in the market for a new boat.

How Much Leverage Do You Have?

You don't have a lot of play with prices because of the relatively small markups folding-kayak dealers and distributors have to work with. In plastic hardshells, dealers have as much as an 80 to 100 percent markup over the price they pay for their stock; fiberglass retail markups are generally about 40 to 60 percent, depending on the dealer's own leverage with the supplier. Folding kayak prices run 25 to 35 percent over what a dealer or distributor might pay for the supply, so dealers selling plastic boats can be very generous in discounting their prices. Folding-kayak sellers don't have much leeway.

But don't give up. Here are several tactics that will increase your leverage, depending on which make you're looking at.

Folbot has regular sales that bring down the prices of its boats as much as 20 percent. If this is the brand of foldable you want, and if you can wait to get it, a simple inquiry for information will get you on the company's mailing list so you'll receive notice when these sales are running. (See the appendix for major manufacturers' addresses.)

The other companies generally don't discount their prices, nor do they have any regular sales. But if you buy a Feathercraft at the factory, you may save something if you buy with Canadian dollars. Then there is the issue of Canadian provincial and federal taxes. Some rebates are available for goods bought by foreigners who take the items out with them. But you are legally liable to pay duties on reentering your home country.

You can save some money by buying a Klepper in Germany. Your savings come in the rebate of the value-added tax when you leave Germany, minus import duties when you reenter your own country. But getting this savings is neither quick nor easy. Kleppers are made to order, so they have scheduled deliveries and waiting lists. The boats aren't sitting around on shelves at the Klepper factory or at the various dealers. If you plan to be in Germany over a summer or for a year, then you can probably sit out any delays in production and delivery. But if you're there only for a quick business trip or a two-week vacation, you may be unable to get your hands on a boat in time to bring it home. To avoid hurting its overseas distributors, the company will not sell directly to you outside Germany. And only as an exception will Klepper make a direct sale at its factory.

The Cost of Accessories

Here are a few pointers about paddles, spray-decks, and rudders that you might want to buy at the time you are purchasing your new boat.

Accessories for folding kayaks can sharply add to the total package cost because not all makes come fully equipped, so be aware of what is included when you compare prices. Feathercraft, for example, includes the price of the spray skirt and sea sock and usually a basic rudder in its larger boats. Klepper varies; at one time it included just a set of wooden paddles but now it includes some key accessories such as spraydecks.

Folbot sometimes throws in an accessory such as a paddle in the basic price, particularly during its special sales. If you already have a paddle or plan to buy a better paddle later, you usually can get the factory to let you use the credit from the Folbot paddle toward the purchase of some other items, such as a rudder or spraydeck. Nautiraid includes several accessories in the basic price, such as a rudder and a spray skirt.

You may be able to bargain. The price margins on accessory components are generally much higher than on the basic boat; some of the items are marked up 50 to 100 percent. If you're buying a fully equipped package, you may get something thrown in for free. Do whatever bargaining and finagling you can before you purchase the boat; you're less likely to get a break later.

Less-Expensive Alternatives

From time to time, folding kayaks from nontraditional export sources come into the market, such as foldables from the former Soviet Union and other formerly socialist countries. Generally these boats are offered at substantial savings over what is available from the Big Four (Feathercraft, Folbot, Klepper, and Nautiraid), but you'll have to make tradeoffs. Many of these boats are not well made and will give you trouble in the long run,

nor can you count on receiving any warranties or follow-up service. An individual gets his or her hands on, say, ten Russian boats at some bargain price, resells them for a quick profit, and is not around a year later if you have a problem.

If it were merely a matter of *buying* a rigid kayak from such a source, there would be no problem, assuming you were happy with the boat to begin with. With a foldable, however, you have to contend with the possibility that down the line you may require a spare part and, much later, even a new skin to place on the frame. If the source is gone, you may be stuck.

New Companies

Then there is the matter of new companies coming on the scene. If you plan to buy from one of them, you need to ask yourself some questions. The biggest point to consider is that the company may not be around in a year or two—after you've bought your foldable. Several companies that started up in the North American market in the late 1980s stopped producing foldables soon after.

In some cases, you don't have to shy away from purchasing from a startup company. If you're considering buying one of these foldables because it seems a good fit for you, take a careful look at the frame. Does it have exotic fasteners for its crossribs and long pieces? Are the pieces made of unusual material? If the answers are yes, then the boat would be difficult to deal with if anything ever were to go wrong. If the answers are no, then you may be able to remedy any later problems.

For example, with a wood frame, you can probably get a carpenter to replicate the shape of a crossrib if you ever damage one. If the means of fastening the part to the rest of the frame is fairly simple, you'll be OK. The same is true for aluminum ribs and tubing, because you can get a metalworking shop to replace a part should it break. Again, the key is how simply it attaches to the rest of the frame.

The hull is another matter. If the source of the boat has disappeared, it's unlikely you'll find anyone who can make a satisfactory hull for you. Even if you got one sewn up by some local source, it's not likely to hold up and will probably create assembly problems for you. Don't kid yourself. The major manufacturers are not going to do one up for you.

WINNING AT THE USED-BOAT BUYING GAME

Used rigid kayaks are cheap to buy. They depreciate 50 percent or more within just three to five years of the initial purchase. Folding kayaks, on the other hand, hold their value for decades. It's not unusual to see a twenty-year-old foldable, one that cost its buyer $500 when new, easily resell for $1,200—more if its accessories are intact. The seller is basically pegging the selling price to what it would cost to buy a new boat. For a used foldable of more recent vintage, the owner can usually get what he or she paid for it new, minus sales taxes and a slight depreciation factor.

Still, you can do nicely on the used market if you have a strategy.

Sources for the Best Used Buys

By the time someone places a used foldable boat into the regular sea-kayaking pipeline, the person is likely to be asking top dollar. The seller will know what he or she can get for it, based on other ads and advice from knowledgeable individuals. This means club newsletters and paddling magazines are not the places to look for bargains. Here are some better sources.

Penny Savers and other local buy-sell tabloids. Generally people who list folding kayaks in these publications have little or no inkling of what they can ask. These sellers are more likely to look at that twenty-year-old foldable that cost them $500 (and can fetch $1,200) and ask just $100 or $200 for it. This happens often enough that such publications are a viable source.

Nonpaddling friends and relatives. You'd be surprised how many individuals bought foldables twenty or twenty-five years ago when they seemed fairly cheap and, after using them a few years, carefully stashed them away in an attic. Ask around, and you may find one of these. A number of happy paddlers have done just that. Most were giveaways.

The Internet. Folding kayaks are regularly offered on eBay and other such sources. Some people have done well by such purchases, but be careful. Often a seller on eBay asks for a fairly hefty price (sometimes more than the original price), and people bid it up higher still even when the boat's true value is actually much less.

Outfitters. Several dozen outfitters and touring services regularly use foldables for their trips and instruction. You won't get a terrific price, but it's generally less than what an individual seller will ask. The boats will have some wear, however, which is why they come on the market at a price that's lower than other used foldables.

Out-of-town sources. Your immediate area may be very competitive for would-be buyers of foldables, but the situation may not be as tight in other regions. For example, a folding kayak for sale in a large coastal city is likely to bring a higher price than one being offered in a smaller town located well inland. You can arrange an out-of-town sale in various ways. For example, if you have the kayak sent to you COD, you will be able to examine it before paying up. It may seem risky to buy a foldable sight unseen from a stranger thousands of miles away, but this arrangement has worked well for many buyers.

Looking Over the Used Boat

In buying a used foldable, you're buying a boat made of parts, so don't be put off if every part isn't perfect. You can repair or replace any parts that are in poor shape or that may temporarily render the boat unusable. Here are some specific areas to consider regarding materials, brands, and models when evaluating a used boat. (See the sidebar on page 30 for suggested items to have on hand.)

Deck Materials

Decks are the first area to deteriorate on most folding kayaks, so this is worth checking out first. While it may take twenty to thirty years for a deck to go, poor storage methods and other factors may bring on advanced age a lot sooner.

Cotton canvas decks. These are the most susceptible to wear. All the major brands except Feathercraft have used cotton decks at some point; Klepper and Pouch continue to do so. The cotton canvas is strong and will last a long time, but it is susceptible to dry rot. Earlier Folbots and Nautiraids used cotton or cotton blends. If in doubt, get in touch with the manufacturer to find out when such cotton material was used.

The easiest way to detect dry rot is to tap hard on the deck after the boat has been assembled (you may not detect much if the skin is not under the stress of being on the frame). Do so along the seam lines and the area alongside the cockpit, *but* the area most likely to experience rot would be at the bow and stern. These deck ends are often the slowest to dry because they don't get as much drying air on their underside as other spots. Using a cheap ballpoint pen, the kind with a separate cover that goes over the point, really tap hard with the covered end. It won't damage anything, but it will quickly determine if there is rot. When you snap a good deck with your finger, you should hear a "ping" sound.

Coated synthetic decks. None of these materials are subject to rot like cotton-based ones, but there are still things to look out for. When looking at a boat, keep in mind the materials used by different manufacturers. Feathercraft has used coated Cordura nylon for most of its existence, although coated polyester was used on early versions of the Khatsalano, and the company's new decks are made of an embossed coating on a nylon core. Folbot has varied its decks but basically uses coated Cordura. Nautiraid went from cotton to coated polyester and now uses PVC-coated polyester.

The strongest of the materials is Cordura. Its weakness and that of all the coated materials is loss of coating. The coating is on the underside in the older Feathercrafts and all Folbots, so it is difficult to see what condition it's in. On the Nautiraids the coating is on the outside, where you can see areas that may have lost their coating.

The first thing to look for is any abrasion that has worn the material thin. This is quite obvious with Cordura as it tends to lose color in worn areas. Areas that could get such wear are on top of the deck bars. Unlike cotton, where rot spreads and is hard to repair, abraded spots on coated synthetic decks can be fixed with Aquaseal, small patches, or even good duct or other tape. Next check the coating by turning the skin inside to see if the coating has flaked or rubbed off. Worn areas can be recoated.

As a general rule, polyester is more susceptible to abrasion than Cordura nylon, which is why the manufacturers that use it have placed protective strips over high-wear areas. You can see this on Nautiraids; they have a strip of Hypalon along the deck bars and big swatches of Hypalon at the deck ends.

Deck seams. Another area to inspect carefully on any used boat you are considering buying is the deck seams. With the skin on the frame, look carefully at the entire seam that connects the hull material with the deck material as well as any deck seams and seams around paddle pockets, hatches, etc. If the stitch seam is visible, go along it carefully to see if any stitches have pulled. Nautiraid's seam stitches are visible, and it's easy to detect any abrasion. However, Nautiraid has reduced the chance of abrasion by placing the Hypalon up over the outside edges of the boat so the seam and deck edges won't rub against docks and rocks and be damaged. If the stitches are not visible, such as on Feathercrafts, just see if any separation or pulling away at the seams has taken place.

Years ago, Klepper used cotton thread, which rotted away over time, but now all folding kayaks use polyester (or similar material) thread, which resists rotting. If you find any lifted stitches or separated seams, you may have a hard time fixing this yourself. A small spot may be fixed adequately with some Aquaseal, which would cover the gap or frayed material and prevent the damage spreading.

Hull Materials

Most folding kayaks have hulls made of Hypalon, a tough material that should last twenty-five years or more provided it has not been overly abused.

In inspecting a used boat, look for wear spots. Folding kayaks with keelstripping on high-wear areas (along where long frame pieces run at the keel and the lower chines) are best at resisting abrasion. Hypalon unprotected with keelstripping will show definite signs of abrasion along the hull where these long pieces touch.

Folbot doesn't keelstrip its models, and the Klepper Classic or Magic models do not normally have keelstripping either. When looking at these makes and models, you have to decide whether the abrasion is problematic or acceptable. If you see that the Hypalon has worn away enough to show the weave of the core material (almost always polyester these days), those areas

need attention. You may want to put keelstripping on these boats; however, the material is expensive and hard to put on yourself. Factor in this need when considering the asking price for the used boat.

By the way, you can tell a lot about how well the boat has been cared for if there are any patches on the hull. Accidents will happen, and a hull may have gotten gouged. If there are any patches, see how well they have been put on. If the patch edges are squared, not rounded, and lifting off, it tells you something about how well the owner took care of the boat. A patch, if well attached, is a favorable, not a detrimental, sign.

While looking at the hull, consider the protective material used to cover the very ends of the hull. On Kleppers, the bumper caps at the bow and stern do tend to get cracked and peel. They will need replacement if they reach that state. The synthetic materials used at the ends of Feathercrafts and Nautiraids are not generally Hypalon, but rather a more abrasion-resistant material that would be too heavy to use on the entire boat but is excellent for protecting the ends. Still, see if it is lifting or getting worn thin. Folbots have metal rails at the end, which are unlikely to ever wear thin, but do see if they remain well attached.

Another hull consideration for Kleppers is that prior to the early 1980s, the hulls on Klepper doubles had a seam in the hull itself alongside the cockpit, and its position made it subject to wear on docks and shorelines. So if you are looking to purchase a pre-1980s Klepper double, make certain the hull's seam is not rotting or fraying away.

Frame Materials

Frames generally hold up better than decks and hulls. If you have time, you may want to assemble the entire frame first outside the skin. This will show you parts that may be a bit off in how they connect, and it will also reveal the condition of the wood and the aluminum frames as well as crossribs made of other materials such as polycarbonate and polyethylene.

Wooden frames. Klepper still uses wooden frames for its boats, except for its latest single, the Alu-Lite. Used Nautiraids are almost always wooden framed, while aluminum-framed models are a relatively recent phenomenon. Some older Folbots have wooden frames or wooden crosspieces alongside aluminum longerons or tubes.

If there's any damage on a used Klepper, it will likely be at the bow and stern end pieces. If bilge water has sat in the boat for long periods, there may be some warping of these end pieces. Other areas of damage on a Klepper would be along the keelboard rails.

While it is best that the frame along the keel rails have a pristine, varnished look, don't be too disturbed if the wood is a bit blackened, especially around metal rivets. The frame of a used boat will have plenty of service left in it even in this condition.

On Kleppers pay particular attention to the snap fittings to see if they fit and snap together snugly without popping apart. If they don't, however, this can be easily fixed by carefully using needle-nosed pliers to bend the tongue into a position where it will engage with the snap portion of the fitting. If the snap fitting is loose, it is easy to remedy with a rivet. If the snap fitting is slack, it may mean it needs a new spring. Such repair materials are readily available at any Klepper dealer.

If a stringer is cracked, you should still be OK—just tape it together. This frame part has little stress. Replace it for aesthetic purposes if you like. The stringers fit to the crossribs through holders that previously were blue rubber and are now black plastic. You may want to replace them if any are missing, but the boat will do just fine without them.

With a used Nautiraid, examine the wood for warping and black spots the way you would a Klepper. Unlike Kleppers, where the wood is never in direct contact with other wood, Nautiraids have numerous spots where wood touches. The result is that varnish there can wear thin or rub off. It is fairly easy to revarnish, so don't write off a used Nautiraid because of this.

A spot to look at carefully is around the many hinges that hold Nautiraid frame subassemblies together. If the previous owner has not been careful with assembly some of the wooden stringer ends may be cracked and loose where they connect to the hinge. This can be a slight problem to repair as the tolerances are tight, but it can be done by anyone who is handy with glue. Nautiraid doesn't use snap fittings and instead has an open fitting approach. The crossribs are preconnected to the top bar and keelbar with screwed brackets. Check the brackets to see if any screws are loose.

For both makes, look at the crossribs closely to determine if they are seriously warped or cracked. You can live with a bit of warping. If it is a problem, however, you can always use plastic ties or Velcro strips to help hold the crossribs in contact with long pieces. A cracked rib can easily be repaired with epoxy or glue and reinforced with a splint.

Aluminum frames. Feathercraft and Folbot use aluminum frames. In some ways they resemble each other, but they also differ significantly in how the frame halves are extended inside the skin.

Feathercraft and Folbot are alike in that in many places aluminum tubes connect via male and female tube ends and that such parts are kept together with internal bungee cords. With both of these makes, look to see if these male and female connections are smooth and fit together well. Watch for burred ends in the tubes and for cracks.

It is OK if the tubes have a slight bend to them. Sometimes the aluminum has a slight bow instead of being fully straight. You may also see some discoloration or pitting, which means that the anodization is failing a bit. Don't worry about this unless it is in certain areas. For example, in Feathercrafts look for such corrosion in the parts that involve overlapping tubes that are lengthened to extend the frame inside the skin. You have these in the keelbar of the singles and also in the gunwale and chine areas of the Kahuna, Khats, and K1. Also check for corrosion where you have sliders in the K-Light, as well as the slider areas in Folbots on the longerons that form the chines.

For aluminum frames, check that the bungee cord on the bungeed tubes is still elastic enough to keep the ends snug together. If not, you can still assemble the boat, but watch out for the male and female connections pulling slightly apart when the frame halves are inserted into the hull. You may want to have the bungee replaced at some point, either by the manufacturer or at a dealer familiar with this.

Aluminum-framed folding kayaks have cross-ribs made of either polyethylene or polycarbonate for the most part. The polyethylene ones can sometimes warp out of their flat configuration so that they wobble if you set them flat on a table. Don't worry about that—it doesn't make the frame any weaker. If the distortion is great, however, you may want to straighten such crossribs out. One way to fix this is to put them in an oven, but this is a tricky solution. A better way is to lay the crossrib on a black surface in strong sunlight until the crossrib relaxes back to a true flatness.

Polycarbonate is strong and not easily warped. Look for chips and any enlargement of drilled holes that may lead to cracks.

With any of the crossribs, you can always duct tape any damage, and the boat will be more than serviceable. Later on you could seek a replacement. If crossribs are damaged, you may want to get the used boat seller to reduce the price a bit with the replacement purchase in mind.

Evaluating the Leading Doubles and Singles

Chapter Four

There is a folding kayak for everybody, but not all are suitable to everyone. Some are expensive; some are less costly. Some are very well made; others less so. Some use high-tech materials and design; others resort to traditional materials and proven shapes and features. Some can be put together very quickly; others are more tedious to assemble. Some should probably not be used under certain conditions; others can safely handle the widest range of activities.

This chapter will help you wade through the uncharted waters of the buying decision, to get you beyond the general model specifications and advertising hype. To find the boat that's best suited to your needs, you need to know the specifics of the leading single and double foldables, so we'll look at eight crucial factors of each one (see the sidebar). These key factors are the outgrowth of questions raised in the previous chapter.

The boat evaluations avoid assigning numerical scores or rankings. You'll never come up with your "perfect" boat just by adding up columns of numbers. One factor may be so pivotal to your own needs that it outweighs most of the other factors. Other people might value different factors more highly for their needs. For that reason, you won't find an overall recommendation of any particular boat.

The best way to benefit from these boat appraisals is, first, to make certain that you've narrowed down your personal requirements by reviewing the points in chapter 3. Then, zero in on those aspects among the eight factors that match your individual needs. Finally, look over the remaining factors to see if

43

EIGHT KEY FACTORS IN EVALUATING A FOLDABLE

1. Assembly and Portability. How long do assembly and disassembly take? This factor is crucial if you must assemble and knock down your boat each time you paddle. If the process takes more than fifteen minutes, even after you get the hang of it, the evaluation will note this. Portability becomes a factor when you have to carry the disassembled boat aboard trains or ferry boats, through airports, etc.

2. Stability and Seaworthiness. Stability tells you how much the boat will resist tipping. Seaworthiness assesses the boat's ability to deal with the conditions of open seas and high winds.

3. Tracking. How good is the boat at going straight ahead without a rudder, despite cross seas and wind? This is especially important in the single foldables. In a double, two paddlers normally need a rudder to offset the difficulty of coordinating their paddling strokes.

4. Maneuverability. How easy is it to turn the boat by using paddle turning strokes, body lean, or both?

5. Speed and Efficiency. What is the top speed of the boat? This is important when you want to cover long distances quickly. How efficiently does it move at lower speeds? How much effort is required to get up to and then sustain its cruising speed?

6. Versatility and Access. What can you do with the boat besides paddle it? Can you sail it upwind, attach a rowing seat, cut fish bait in it? Can you customize the boat to meet any particular need? If it's a double, can it easily be paddled solo? Can camping gear and belongings be loaded and unloaded easily, or is the access restricted?

7. Quality and Durability. What is the workmanship like? How long is the boat likely to last? What kind of punishment can it take? For example, can it stand up to the demanding use of expeditions or outfitters?

8. Cost and Depreciation. How much does the basic boat cost? What other items are included as standard equipment? How much do the needed accessories add to the price tag? What can you sell the boat for later?

---

any create a problem for you. These remaining traits should register a "neutral" or a "no big deal" as far as you're concerned. Voilà! You've probably identified the folding kayak that you'll be most happy with.

DOUBLE FOLDING KAYAKS

Doubles are considered the "coin of the realm" in the folding-kayak world. They traditionally have accounted for 80 to 90 percent of sales for three of the leading manufacturers, Folbot, Klepper, and Nautiraid, but these figures are changing as the companies introduce leaner and lighter new singles. Feathercraft's double represents a smaller business, about 10 percent of its sales in the North American market.

This is in sharp contrast to plastic and fiberglass sea kayaks. Tandems are just a sliver of the rigid-boat market, accounting for 2 to 5 percent of rigid sea kayak sales. Rigid doubles are an anomaly; you don't see very many around.

Not so for foldables. Doubles are the defining element for folding kayaks, not just in the number of sales. Doubles are what most people conjure up as the image of a foldable: two people carrying some bags to the water's edge, miraculously creating a craft of integral frame and skin, throwing in mountains of gear, and taking off without too much concern about conditions, because they're confident the resulting vessel will see them through.

Now let's look at a number of the leading models produced by the major folding-kayak companies.

Feathercraft K2

First introduced in the early 1980s, this model is the longest and narrowest of the folding doubles. The K2 is unique among folding doubles because it has individual cockpits, and it appeals to paddlers who want a foldable that seems most like a rigid boat.

The frame consists of aluminum long pieces and high-density polyethylene crossribs. At one time decks were made of Cordura nylon, with the coating applied on the underdeck surface. The K2 now uses Poly-Tech decks (urethane embossed on both sides of a nylon core) and Duratek hulls (polyurethane on both sides of nylon core), which allows the seams to be radio-frequency welded. The boat has keelstrips at the chines and keel.

Assembly and Portability. The K2 takes at least forty minutes to assemble, even when you get proficient at the process. It has lots of parts and can be tricky to put together. The boat is on the heavy side, due mainly to its greater length. However, Feathercraft carrying bags with full backpack harnesses, including padded shoulder straps and hipbelts, make the K2 somewhat comfortable to carry.

Stability and Seaworthiness. Although it is narrower than the other folding doubles, the K2 is quite stable largely because of the added length. Its frame is on the flexible side because the boat lacks floorboards, so many of the joining points are meant to give. This makes the K2 a highly seaworthy vessel in rough conditions when the boat must shape itself to the turbulent surface of the sea. The K2, as well as Feathercraft's Klondike, are the only doubles that include an important safety feature, *sea socks*, which fit over the cockpit coamings to keep water from filling the boat. The K2 provides a stable reentry platform, but it's slightly harder to get back into than other foldables because of its relative height and smaller cockpits.

Tracking. The boat tracks well even in crosswinds. The assumption is that, as in any double, you'll normally use a rudder to help you go straight. The rudder is top quality; Feathercraft supplies rudders for a number of hardshell manufacturers.

Maneuverability. The boat will turn even without a rudder, especially since you can easily and safely lean it on its side.

Speed and Efficiency. The K2 is fast, giving what is probably the highest potential top speed of the folding doubles. It has some slight inertia on the first paddling stroke or two because of its weight, but once under way, it's very efficient to paddle. Its cruising speeds are easy to maintain with minimum effort.

Versatility and Access. The K2's individual hardshell-like cockpits limit the number of ways you can use the boat or customize it. The K2 is

Feathercraft K2. *(Courtesy Feathercraft)*

meant mainly for paddling. It does not come equipped to take an upwind sail rig, just downwind sails and spinnakers. The K2 can be fished from but doesn't have a roomy, move-around cockpit for cutting bait, as do most other doubles. You can't easily paddle a K2 solo, because you can't get yourself into a better trim position; you're stuck paddling from the rear cockpit. Access to underdeck areas is superb. The K2 has watertight hatches through which you can store gear or reach through to adjust loads, thus maximizing your use of underdeck space.

Quality and Durability. Workmanship on Feathercrafts is excellent, as is the quality of the materials that go into them. The K2 stands up to rough landings and expedition use. Since the hull and deck materials have been used only since 2000 or so, no long-term durability record exists, but these should hold up well.

Cost and Depreciation. The K2 is near the top of the price ladder, but it comes standard with rudder, spray skirts, and sea socks. Because relatively few K2s are made, used ones are hard to find and they command top resale prices.

Feathercraft Klondike

The Klondike is Feathercraft's entry into the world of open-cockpit double boats; i.e., there are not individual cockpits for each paddler. However, the Klondike's spraydeck's refinements make the boat seem more like it has individual cockpits when you want them.

Feathercraft Klondike. *(Courtesy Feathercraft)*

Its profile is lower than the company's K2 and may be a better choice for anyone who is not looking for maximum payload.

Assembly and Portability. The Klondike takes a while to assemble, possibly the longest of any of the folding doubles. Its secondary frame (similar to that on the Khatsalano) adds to assembly steps, and the coaming also takes time to get into place. Portability is fine because of the way the two-bag carry system divides the load; both bags are well designed for comfortable carrying.

Stability and Seaworthiness. The Klondike is both stable and seaworthy. This is a boat that is meant to take you safely through rough water, which is a hallmark of Feathercrafts.

Tracking. The Klondike tracks very well and will not wander off your chosen course. It will not be thrown off by turbulence and side winds.

Maneuverability. It is amazing how easy it is to lay this boat on its side for sharper turns without a rudder. In this regard it is better than other doubles.

Speed and Efficiency. The Klondike is a fast double in the hands of capable paddlers who can take advantage of its low profile and narrow beam. It is a rigid enough boat to be efficient in translating your paddle stroke into forward motion.

Versatility and Access. There isn't any provision for an upwind sail for this boat yet, but with its open cockpit, you could probably rig one for it more easily than for the K2. It is versatile for fishing and other nonpaddling activities. You can even fit a third seat in the cockpit for a child or small adult. Access is superb through hatches and the open cockpit.

Quality and Durability. The Klondike is superb in both these departments as befitting the reputation of Feathercraft. It is a top-of-the-line boat.

Cost and Depreciation. The Klondike is costly but competitive with Klepper. Depreciation is minimal on this kayak.

Folbot Greenland II

The Greenland II has proved to be a very popular boat since coming on the market in 1989. It is lightweight and inexpensive, and it performs well in a lot of activities. Many folding kayakers report they are happy with this model and the service they're getting from it. The Folbot company has gained a solid reputation for customer service and for standing by its products.

The Greenland II has an aluminum frame with polycarbonate cross members and a Hypalon hull. The decks are now made of urethane-coated polyester, coated on the underside surface.

Assembly and Portability. The Folbot double assembles in a jiffy—no difficult moments—thanks to some subassemblies and easy-to-manage connecting points. It is one of the fastest doubles to assemble. There is only one small fitting part that you have to be careful not to lose, the turn knob at the apex of the washboards or cockpit coaming. Although it's the lightest of the double foldables in this review, its storage bags are awkward to lug and lack padding in the carrying straps.

Stability and Seaworthiness. The Greenland II has plenty of initial stability because of its width and air sponsons. Its seaworthiness has been greatly improved due to some subtle changes in the frame at the gunwales and keel and the increased stiffness provided by cast-aluminum washboards (what Folbot calls its coamings), making it stiffer in heavy seas, waves, and winds.

Tracking. The Greenland II will go quite straight on its own without a rudder in most cross seas.

Folbot Greenland II.

Maneuverability. The boat is a bit more difficult than others to put on its side for carving turns. As with other doubles, you'll want to use a rudder, but the rudder is awkward to attach and is troublesome.

Speed and Efficiency. This model is slower than others at top speed. It's also somewhat less efficient, requiring a bit more effort at cruising speeds, but it will get you where you want to go.

Versatility and Access. The Greenland II is a very versatile boat that lends itself to full-range sailing and fishing, thanks to its high stability and open cockpit. You can easily customize a Greenland II as many users do. Full deck zippers are reliable, and they help when you're assembling the boat and loading gear. However, once the air sponsons are blown up, getting at that gear becomes more difficult because you can't unzip without releasing some air. The boat is easy to paddle solo, especially when the inexpensive solo-seat setup is added.

Quality and Durability. Workmanship is good, but not like that of its pricier competitors. What Folbot does offer is a lot of value for the money and an ironclad lifetime guarantee against breakage; i.e., free replacement of parts. The Greenland II will hold up to normal family and individual use, but it's not generally up to the consistent hard abuse dished out by outfitters and long-range, remote-area expeditions.

Cost and Depreciation. The Greenland II is the least expensive of the doubles and is occasionally on sale at substantial savings. Generally, its accessories are sold separately, but they aren't costly. Depreciation won't bring down the resale value of the Greenland II as quickly as it would a comparable rigid boat. But since you can buy a new Folbot so cheaply, this model won't hold its value as well as some of the other folding boats.

Klepper Aerius II

The Klepper Aerius II has seen more paddling miles—under the widest and wildest conditions—than any other sea-kayak model—rigid or foldable—currently in production. Although it's undergone some one hundred modifications, its underlying design has not been tampered with since it was first introduced in the 1950s. You'd be hard-pressed to spot the differences between the boat you can buy today and Hannes Lindemann's 1956 transatlantic Klepper, which is on display in a Munich museum. The frame and hull on his boat are virtually 100 percent compatible with Aerius IIs currently being built.

The Aerius II has a cotton deck and a thick

Klepper Aerius II.

Hypalon hull. It comes in two models: the basic Magic (formerly known as the Classic) and the Expedition, which has added deck fittings and a thicker hull that includes keelstrips. (The Quattro is a separate version of Aerius II, so we'll look at it separately; see next review. There is also a new longer version of the double that has just been introduced, which is not reviewed here.) Depending on which country you buy your Klepper in, accessories such as rudder and spraydecks may or may not be included in the price.

Assembly and Portability. The Aerius II practically assembles itself, despite having no subassemblies. It's the fastest of the foldables to assemble on a consistent, troublefree basis under any conditions. The boat varies in weight from around 75 pounds for the Magic to about 85 pounds for the Expedition model. Carrying bags have padded straps, and they allow the crew to share the load fairly comfortably, although not quite as well as the Feathercraft K2.

Stability and Seaworthiness. The Aerius II is highly stable in both initial and secondary stability. It takes a lot to capsize this boat, and the Aerius II is at home on the open sea. It is impervious to side swells and flanking waves, and it rides up them as well as the best of the narrow, rigid sea kayaks of the British.

Tracking. This model tracks well through open water without being blown or thrown off course by anything. A rudder is needed mainly to even out the different paddling styles of the two paddlers.

Maneuverability. You can lay this boat on its side to carve turns. It responds well to its rudder, which has a large bite.

Speed and Efficiency. The Aerius II does not have the top speed of the Feathercraft K2, but it paddles efficiently at cruising speeds despite the drag of the large rudder. In capable hands it can cover long distances quickly and safely.

Versatility and Access. The Aerius II is capable of handling the widest range of uses of any foldable; you can even mount an electric or gasoline motor if you wish. It performs well under sail. Solo paddling is easier now that Klepper has placed the seats on rails so they can be adjusted forward and backward and even raised with an inexpensive option. Although deck zippers are available, gear access is possible through the cockpit area, but you have to push the gear over and past ribs that tend to catch it. But the Aerius II will hold a lot, and you'll have well-designed space around you in the cockpit to strap or tie in additional gear.

Quality and Durability. Quality is top-notch in every respect. The boats are extremely durable, as attested by their military use. Even the wooden frames of boats that came off the assembly line in 1953 are still going strong. The hulls have proved to be tough and long-lived.

Cost and Depreciation. The Aerius II is generally expensive, but the Magic model is very close to the price range of top-of-the-line hardshell doubles. Depreciation is absurdly low on all the models, reflecting the long life expectancy and utility of this craft.

Klepper Quattro

The Klepper Quattro is an extremely heavy-duty Aerius II designed to meet increasingly stringent military demands of a number of nations. It differs enough from the rest of the Aerius line in several key factors to warrant a separate evaluation.

The Klepper Quattro is based on the Aerius II Expedition, but it has an extra set of air sponsons. This feature distinguishes the Quattro from every other kayak, double or single. It allows you to change the shape of the hull's cross-section, and it raises the boat's effective weight payload through the added buoyancy. The Quattro comes equipped with military-specified features, including many lifeline D-rings along the entire perimeter of the craft and raised markings for identifying ribs and other parts in pitch darkness.

Assembly and Portability. With the exception of the fact that the Quattro is a bit heavier, these factors are rated the same as the regular Aerius II Expedition.

Stability and Seaworthiness. When the extra sponsons are inflated, the Quattro rises to a stability league all its own. It's virtually impossible to flip the Quattro except under the most extreme conditions. With all tubes fully inflated, it can be paddled even when it's filled with gear and water and being pounded by heavy waves. This is a feat any other boat would be hard-pressed to match.

Tracking. The Quattro tracks as well as other Aerius IIs.

Maneuverability. With *all* its tubes inflated, the Quattro is slightly less maneuverable, but you have the option of only partially filling the extra tubes or leaving them deflated.

Speed and Efficiency. Inflating all tubes will rob you of speed and make the boat harder to paddle, unless it's very lightly loaded.

Versatility and Access. In this factor the Quattro is the same as the Aerius II Expedition, except that it does have a higher weight payload.

Quality and Durability. The Quattro offers the same top-notch quality and durability as the Aerius II Expedition model.

Cost and Depreciation. The Quattro lays claim to being the most expensive production sea kayak on the consumer market (Nautiraid's military double is more expensive). It will depreciate slightly more than the rest of the Aerius line because of its high initial price and competition from new boats of less costly Aerius II models.

Long Haul Mark II

This double is made by Long Haul Folding Kayaks, a company previously known as the U.S. Klepper Repair Service Center. It is similar to the Klepper product in many respects, including complete compatibility of hull and full frame (but not individual parts). It differs in that many parts of the frame are stronger or are meant to avoid perceived weaknesses in the Klepper based on repair experiences.

Assembly and Portability. The Mark II generally assembles as quickly as a double Klepper. It uses the same form of expanding the frame halves inside the skin; i.e., overlapping horseshoe and block connections at the keelboard and gunwales. Changes in the coaming, the way the seats are placed, and use of cotter pins instead of snap fittings mean it's slightly slower to put together. Portability is somewhat less because of the additional weight of the boat and the way the carrying bags are designed.

Stability and Seaworthiness. Identical to the Klepper double.

Tracking. Similar to that of the Klepper double.

Maneuverability. The Mark II employs a different rudder system from that on the Klepper. It has a balanced rudder that has 20 percent of its surface forward of the pivot point. This creates less drag and is better for sailing purposes. The foot pedals are also easier to work.

Speed and Efficiency. This kayak is slightly faster than the Klepper due to a more rigid frame, especially at the gunwales. Also, the rudder creates less drag. Its efficiency is on par with the Klepper.

Versatility and Access. All the activities suitable for the Klepper can be done in the Mark II. The Mark II comes standard with deck hatches that are watertight, which permit easier placement of larger items pushed in through the cockpit area as

Long Haul Mark II. *(Courtesy Long Haul)*

well as placement and retrieval of small items while under way, something not possible with deck zippers that require deflating the sponsons in order to close up.

Quality and Durability. While there isn't a track record for this new model yet, its quality is at least equal to the Klepper. Durability is likely to be better because of the heavier materials and parts design intended to avoid repairs sometimes needed in the Klepper.

Cost and Depreciation. Model for model, late 2002 prices for the Mark II run about $800 less than the equivalent Klepper. It's too early to tell what the depreciation record will be.

Nautiraid Raid II 500 Expedition

Nautiraid designates all its models according to approximate length, which is the model's length in centimeters. This boat was previously known as the Raid II. The company makes two other somewhat longer and slightly narrower, the Grand Raid II 520 Expedition and the Grand Raid II 540 Expedition.

The Raid II 500 Expedition is a jack-of-all-trades because of its size and performance features. This French boat is supplied to the military of a number of nations, as are its larger sister kayaks.

The frames on all the expedition doubles are made entirely of wood, and decks are all PVC coated. Hulls are all Hypalon and come standard with keelstripping.

Assembly and Portability. The Raid II can take longer to assemble than might be apparent since you'd expect its numerous subassemblies to speed up the job. However, the boat has external sponsons, which figure only minimally into the skin-tightening process. This means that fitting the frame halves into the skin is more exacting since tolerances are tighter than on foldables that have internal air sponsons. The Raid II weighs less than some of the other boats, and the bags are moderately easy to carry.

Stability and Seaworthiness. The Raid II is extremely stable thanks to its external air sponsons, which form channels that cup the water and resist sideways sliding and tipping. Seaworthiness is good, although the relatively flat bottom tends to make the boat a bit bouncy in heavy seas.

Tracking. The Raid II will go straight and does not get sucked into beam seas or crosswind action.

Maneuverability. The Raid II is very maneuverable, as befits the shortest of the foldable doubles. It has a rugged rudder that works well.

Speed and Efficiency. The boat has a light, nimble feel when on the water. Its sides are relatively low compared with several other folding doubles, so you can reach the water better, which makes it easier to paddle. As far as cruising speeds, the Raid II is about in the middle of the pack.

Versatility and Access. For solo paddling, the Raid II is arguably the best of the double folding

Nautiraid Raid II.

hard to find. Improvements in distribution and the availability of a repair service should help bolster the resale value of older Nautiraids.

SINGLE FOLDING KAYAKS

Single folding kayaks offer you a world of personal discovery. They have all the seaworthiness of folding doubles but are generally more responsive than their bigger cousins. The single foldables bring you into closer contact with the elements around you than any double, whether rigid or folding. The single-seat folding kayaks come in two classes: full-size craft that generally average from 15 to 16 feet in length, and mini-foldables that average 12½ to 13 feet. These two classes share many attributes but are different enough to be examined separately.

FULL-SIZE SINGLES

The foldables in this class are every bit as good as their rigid counterparts at providing that sports car feel of the sea. And they have the added advantages of foldability, stability, and inherent seaworthiness.

Contrary to popular opinion, these foldables are not slow. If you're on a demo beach at some sea-kayak gathering, you can count on any of these being as fast as, if not faster than, at least 80 percent of the single rigids being demonstrated. In competition, and in capable hands, they come in toward the front, especially if the water is choppy and the distance long.

Feathercraft K1

This model is long and fast. Like other Feathercrafts, it has a rigid kayak–type cockpit rather than a more open one. The K1 has a nice feel on the water, especially since the company elongated

kayaks because of its smaller size. The company provides a way to use the existing seat to achieve a good paddling trim at no extra expense. Again, arguably, the boat is one of the best natural sailing vessels of the folding-double crowd. It can be heeled over radically while sailing with little danger of a capsize. Access is like that of Kleppers, although you must push cargo through smaller rib openings.

Quality and Durability. The quality of workmanship is about on par with that of Feathercraft and Klepper. Durability is good, as befitting a boat used by the military, although its fittings do not hold up well.

Cost and Depreciation. The Raid II is priced between the Folbot and the top-of-the-line foldables. Depreciation has been a bit less favorable than for other foldables because spare parts were it by half a foot, made the bow sharper, and added other refinements in 1998.

The K1 has an aluminum and polyethylene frame. It's available in the same array of hull options and deck colors as the K2.

Assembly and Portability. Assembly requires some strength and leverage. Assembly times will exceed twenty-five minutes for most people. The K1 comes in one backpack with a full load-bearing harness.

Stability and Seaworthiness. The K1 is narrow but has decent initial stability. Its seaworthiness is superb as the K1 clings beautifully to the contours of the sea. For greater safety, the K1 comes with a sea sock.

Tracking. The K1 has little rocker and tracks as straight as an arrow in flight. It will not be pushed around by side winds.

Maneuverability. The K1 lacks rocker, so its turns tend to be wider unless you're skilled at body lean and turn strokes. The rudder works well and, as an advantage, can be pulled out of the way onto the deck when not in use.

Speed and Efficiency. The K1 scores well on both counts. It moves out fast with your first paddle stroke with little inertia and can cruise efficiently at high speeds.

Versatility and Access. Versatility is limited because of the cockpit arrangement. It also lacks customizing potential. Underdeck access, however, is great because of the Feathercraft deck hatches that allow you to insert gear and shift it around for optimum use of space.

Quality and Durability. The K1 shows top-notch workmanship and great attention to detail on the deck layout of tie-on points, grab lines, and similar features. The hull is made of Duratek, a polyurethane on nylon core that should hold up well. Hull and deck are radio-frequency welded; i.e., no sewn-through seams.

Cost and Depreciation. The K1 is high on the singles price list, but it comes standard with just about everything. Depreciation is generally low except for the few times that the company has made major changes (such as lengthening and refining the frame and changing deck and hull materials), in which case earlier models did dip some in resale value.

Feathercraft Khatsalano-S

The Khatsalano is a long, skinny foldable built on Greenland-style lines. When it came out in 1995 it caused quite a stir and made many hardshell enthusiasts eye folding kayaks in a different way. The Khats or Khats-S, as it is known, has gone through many refinements. It now has two versions, one with small sponsons, which you can choose to inflate or not inflate, and another with regular sponsons. The width difference is about 2 inches. The Khatsalano-S, with the bigger sponsons, is more popular and easier to handle by most paddlers.

Assembly and Portability. It takes at least forty minutes to assemble the Khats-S because of the many parts of the frame and the numerous steps needed. It also has a secondary frame, which is necessary to keep such a long boat stiff, and this adds to the assembly time.

Feathercraft K1. *(Courtesy Feathercraft)*

Feathercraft Khatsalano. *(Courtesy Feathercraft)*

Stability and Seaworthiness. Initial stability is low, but skilled paddlers can take advantage of the boat's good secondary stability. It calls for more skill from the paddler to keep upright than other singles, including its sister ship, the K1. But in the right hands, seaworthiness is superb.

Tracking. The Khats-S tracks well in most situations. The high swept ends can catch side winds that affect tracking, especially if the boat is lightly loaded.

Maneuverability. The boat will respond to lean turns quite well. You can easily carve turns with just a slight edging of the boat.

Speed and Efficiency. The Khats-S is a fast boat that ranks up among the top five or so production sea kayaks, hardshell or foldable. This boat is meant for swift passage over long distances with minimal effort.

Versatility and Access. The Khats-S is limited in versatility in terms of sailing; it is a paddle boat, period. Although it is designed mainly as a day-trip boat, it can carry a large load. (See the table on pages 178–79 for how to load a Khatsalano for a two-week camping trip.) Hatches give you access, but you may find that some secondary frame members will hinder placing bags and determine their size.

Quality and Durability. The Khats-S is well made with top-notch materials and workmanship. The aluminum frame is tough. The deck and hull materials are fairly new and differ from what the rest of the industry uses, but they should hold up well.

Cost and Depreciation. Khatsalanos do very well in the used market and are in high demand. The initial cost is high—it's the most expensive of the singles—but almost all accessories are included except a paddle.

Folbot Kodiak

The Kodiak is Folbot's first excursion into fuller-size singles and has proven to be a very successful kayak with high customer marks. In many ways it resembles the Klepper Aerius I, but it has traits that are more user-friendly, and the price is amazingly low for such a well-built boat.

The frame is aluminum with synthetic cross-ribs, the deck is synthetic, and the hull is made of Hypalon.

Assembly and Portability. Folbots are some of the easiest folding kayaks to assemble, and the Kodiak is no exception. The zippered decks help, but the frame practically makes itself anyway. Portability is not as good. The two packing bags, while tough as nails, are not easy to carry for any distance as they lack padding and a backpack harness, and your loads are quite heavy.

Stability and Seaworthiness. Stability is very good, even though the Kodiak is narrower than the company's Aleut. The boat has a solid feel to it on open water, with lots of bouyancy to pop over oncoming waves.

Tracking. Folbots have always been good at tracking straight, and the Kodiak is no exception. Just point the bow, and you go where you want to go, with little bother from beam- or rear-quarter waves and seas.

Maneuverability. The Kodiak does not turn easily. You can lean it somewhat for a turn, but it still will take a lot of turning paddle strokes to get you around.

Speed and Efficiency. The Kodiak is not a speedster, but it will keep up with most hardshells. You need a place to brace your feet in order to transfer more of your paddling effort to forward movement of the boat.

Versatility and Access. With such a stable boat, you can set it up for sailing and fishing and the like. Underdeck access is excellent because of the zippered decks, and you have plenty of room in the cockpit to get at things you may want while paddling.

Quality and Durability. The quality of Folbots is just as good as their durability. Parts will certainly hold up to normal use, and the company has a terrific warranty policy with no real time limit. Break a part, and you will get it replaced or repaired free.

Cost and Depreciation. The Kodiak is a lot of boat for the money. Folbots depreciate somewhat

faster than other foldables, partly because new ones are inexpensive.

Fujita 480

Fujita has been making folding kayaks in Japan for half a century, but they seldom have been seen outside the domestic market. Now imported into North America by FoldingCraft, this model and the slightly larger Fujita 500 offer an interesting choice for consumers. The boats are much better built than what was rumored about them.

The boats have wooden crossribs and fiberglass long pieces. The decks are urethane-coated synthetic, and the hulls are PVC coated on a polyester core.

Assembly and Portability. The Fujita 480 assembles intuitively and easily. Major sections of the frame consist of preassemblies that can fit together only one way, resulting in fairly fast assembly times. Portability is top-notch, with a carry bag that is very similar to a real backpack with padded shoulders and a hipbelt. It carries well and can also be put onto an ordinary luggage cart, which you can easily stow in the assembled boat.

Stability and Seaworthiness. The 480 is rock-solid stable, with good initial and secondary

Folbot Kodiak.

stability. You'll feel secure and relaxed in rough water as it is highly seaworthy.

Tracking. The 480 has excellent tracking, and goes where you point without being pushed around by side winds, and even following seas offer little problem.

Maneuverability. While it tracks well, the 480 also turns well in response to turning strokes. It also responds well to leaned turns, which you can easily do because of rods in the cockpit area that allow you to brace your knees.

Speed and Efficiency. The 480, at just less than 16 feet long, has enough waterline to allow for good speeds, and it is not as beamy as single folding kayaks can be. The deck is low, allowing even shorter paddlers to reach the water easily with a paddle.

Versatility and Access. Since neither the coaming nor the cockpit area would support a mast, this boat is not suitable for sailing. There is plenty of room at the bow and stern areas for camping gear. Gear can be loaded through the small hatches, but most people will insert larger gear through the cockpit area.

Quality and Durability. The boat has good workmanship, although some seams appear coarse. All frame parts are well finished, and the wooden ribs are heavily varnished. The frame is quite strong. There are some fasteners holding some of the subassemblies together that look skimpy, but they could be easily fixed if they failed. The hull does have keelstripping.

Cost and Depreciation. The price is very competitive, which should attract buyers looking for a longer single.

Depreciation is unknown at this time, as the boat has no track record yet in North America.

Klepper Aerius I

This kayak has been with us almost as long as the Aerius II, and it enjoys a similarly long track record of achievement and owner satisfaction. The Aerius I has been around Cape Horn and been paddled on nearly every waterway from pole to pole. This stellar performer is capable of delivering broad service.

The Aerius I comes in two models, the lighter-weight Magic (formerly known as the Classic) and the heavier-duty Expedition.

Assembly and Portability. Assembly is slightly more difficult than for the Aerius II because added torque is needed to form the frame's radical lines. But the Aerius I has the fastest assembly time in this class, ten to fifteen minutes. Its two carrying bags have padded straps but require some juggling, especially if you're porting lots of other gear.

Stability and Seaworthiness. The Aerius I defines stability and seaworthiness for single boats of any kind, rigid or folding. It is amazingly at home in the sea under any conditions.

Tracking. Because of its considerable rocker, this boat has only fair tracking ability. Many paddlers prefer to use a rudder to keep the boat straight,

Fujita 480. *(Courtesy Fujita)*

Klepper Aerius I.

especially in beam winds and waves. But if you work at developing good technique, you'll need a rudder only for sailing.

Maneuverability. The Aerius I will turn on a dime and has been used in Class III whitewater because of this quick-turning ability. You can lean it on its side in open water and carve some very sharp turns to maneuver through the waves.

Speed and Efficiency. The Aerius I has some inertia on takeoff, so you need a few strokes to get it up to speed. Once at cruising speeds, it doesn't take much to keep it going. This boat has proved itself in a number of open-class races, where it has beat out numerous fiberglass and plastic sea kayaks.

Versatility and Access. Almost as versatile as the Aerius II, the Aerius I offers the best sailing ability of any of the singles. Access to underdeck cargo space is adequate, and you have room for plenty of gear around you in the cockpit area.

Quality and Durability. This model is top-of-the-line in both areas. The quality of its workmanship is flawless. For durability, even the lighter-weight Aerius Magic I will hold up well.

Cost and Depreciation. The Aerius I is expensive, especially the Expedition version, and accessories add to the cost. However, its depreciation is very low, thanks to its high demand on the used-boat market. This isn't a kayak you find at garage sales, where you may find used doubles.

Nautiraid Greenlander 500 Expedition

The Greenlander has a pleasing appearance due to its good lines. This model is one of the Nautiraids that comes in either an all wooden frame or aluminum frame with synthetic crossribs. There is a slight weight savings in the aluminum frame version, and the cost is somewhat lower.

Assembly and Portability. Assembly is easy because this model's frame is entirely put together outside the skin. It is then slipped into the skin via a wide-open zippered rear deck, and the frame is extended within the skin by a simple built-in levering device. The boat comes in two bags with nonpadded shoulder straps, but they are not hard to carry because of the separation of the load.

Stability and Seaworthiness. The Greenlander is quite stable, as Nautiraids tend to be. It has a very solid feel in rough seas, and you won't be bounced around much.

Tracking. The Greenlander tracks quite well without the use of a rudder or much in the way of paddling finesse. You basically point it, and it goes where you want it to.

Maneuverability. This boat is not as agile in turning as its slightly shorter fellow model, the

BOAT	LENGTH	BEAM	WEIGHT	PRICE	KEY FEATURES
FOLDING DOUBLES					
Feathercraft K2	19'3"	33"	87 lb.	$4,985	highly seaworthy expedition boat
Feathercraft Klondike	17'10"	31"	75 lb.	$4,380	open-cockpit boat with fine performance
Folbot Greenland II	17'	34"	68 lb.	$2,145	versatile family double
Klepper Aerius II	17'	34"	75 lb. / 83 lb.	$3,390 Magic / $4,700 Expedition	enduring performer with fine track record on open-water expeditions
Klepper Quattro	17'	34"	85 lb.	$5,179	2 sets of sponsons allow conversion to various configurations
Long Haul Mark II	17'	34"	90 lb.	$3,515	extra-strong frame, hatches
Nautiraid Raid II 500 Expedition	16'6"	35"	73 lb.	$3,195	double that functions well as a single because of its size
FOLDING FULL-SIZE SINGLES					
Feathercraft K1	16'6"	25"	51 lb.	$4,125	workhorse expedition single
Feathercraft Khatsalano-S	17'9"	23"	49 lb.	$4,295	Greenland-style–sleek and fast, expedition capacity
Folbot Kodiak	15'	28"	52 lb.	$1,545	well priced, good single
Fujita 480	15'10"	24"	37 lb.	$2,495	fast, light, stable, easy assembly
Klepper Aerius I	15'	28"	55–60 lb.	$3,239 Magic / $3,995 Expedition	reliable with a long track record of accomplishment
Nautiraid Greenlander 500 Expedition	16'6"	28"	52–58 lb.	$2,250 aluminum / $2,495 wood	easy to assemble, fast, feature-filled
Nautiraid Raid I 460 Expedition	15'3"	28"	50–53 lb.	$2,150 aluminum / $2,395 wood	very stable, solid boat, easy to assemble
Pouch E68 Touring	17'	23"	68 lb.	$2,670	fast, well built
MINI-FOLDABLE SINGLES					
Feathercraft K-Light	12'10"	25"	29.5–34.5 lb.	discontinued; top seller on used market	combines light weight, easy assembly, good performance in highly portable boat
Feathercraft Kahuna	14'9"	25"	35 lb.	$2,300	comes close to being the all-around "best" boat
FirstLight 420C	13'9"	22.3"	19.6 lb.	$2,395	lightest folding kayak
Folbot Aleut I	12'	30"	42 lb.	$1,345	easy to assemble, stable
Folbot Yukon	13'	30"	45 lb.	$1,445	large, open cockpit, big payload
Klepper Scout	12'6"	26"	48 lb.	$2,600	smaller version of Aerius I
Klepper Alu-Lite	13'	28"	39 lb.	$2,106	lightweight, aluminum frame
Nautiraid Raid I 416 Expedition	14'	28"	48–50 lb.	$1,995 aluminum / $2,295 wood	choice of wood or aluminum
Nautiraid Raid I 416 Touring	14'	28"	37–40 lb.	$1,550 aluminum / $1,750 wood	lightweight, PVC hull
Nautiraid Raid I 380 Touring	26'6"	29"	37 lb.	$1,500	lively, light weight

Raid I 460. It does have inflatable hip pads, however, which will help you transfer the power of a lean to get the boat around.

Speed and Efficiency. Due to its length and slightly narrower profile, the Greenlander is faster than the Raid I 460. The sponsons are large, however, and will slow you down some.

Versatility and Access. This boat is not all that versatile beyond being used for paddling, and there is no easy sailing arrangement. Access to gear in the rear is fine since you have the zippered deck.

Quality and Durability. The quality of this boat is good, but with the wooden-frame version you need to be careful that the rear cockpit crossrib and the wood around the hinges don't break. The hull and deck are strong and will take lots of punishment.

Cost and Depreciation. The Greenlander is relatively inexpensive for an expedition-class kayak. Depreciation is steeper than that of other makes since new Greenlanders are not costly.

Nautiraid Raid I 460 Expedition

The Raid I 460 comes in either an aluminum or wooden frame and has a PVC-coated deck and Hypalon hull. It differs from the Greenlander in several respects.

Assembly and Portability. The Raid I 460 is quick to assemble since the frame is put together entirely outside the skin, including the coaming, and inserted via a wide-open rear zippered deck. The frame is then extended within the skin with a simple built-in levering device. The boat comes in two bags that are manageable to carry, although the carry straps are not padded.

Stability and Seaworthiness. The Raid I 460 is highly seaworthy, thanks to the added stability of its flexible frame and external sponsons. It is a boat you can relax in.

Nautiraid Greenlander.

Tracking. The Raid I 460 is only fair in tracking compared to the Greenlander. To track well, you'll have to develop paddling finesse or use the rudder.

Maneuverability. Although its width and external sponsons don't allow much body lean for turning, the Raid I 460 turns better than the Greenlander with just a few turning strokes.

Speed and Efficiency. This kayak's sleek look doesn't disappoint when you paddle it. The Raid I 460 will accelerate fast but is not as fast as the Greenlander. It does, however, respond efficiently to your paddling stroke.

Versatility and Access. This boat has limited versatility; it does not come ready to accept an upwind sail. Access to the rear cargo area is relatively easy because of the zippered deck. Its payload is somewhat greater than the Greenlander in both weight and volume because of its greater width.

Nautiraid 460.

Quality and Durability. This boat's quality is quite good. You do have to be slightly careful, however, that the wooden frame doesn't break at the hinges and at the crossrib in back of the cockpit.

Cost and Depreciation. The Raid I 460 is quite inexpensive for its class. The boat does depreciate due to the relatively low cost of a new one.

Pouch E68 Touring Single

The E68 has sleek, modern lines. With this model, Pouch breaks from its tradition of an open-cockpit design and introduces a cockpit similar to hardshells. The E68 combines elements of Pouch's

Pouch E68. *(Courtesy Pouch)*

traditional wooden frame technology with a new generation of strong stainless steel fittings.

Assembly and Portability. Assembly involves putting together the frame outside the skin and inserting it into the skin via a rear deck opening. It is then extended with a lever and sliding plate, and the deck opening is sealed with a special watertight slit tubing. The process is relatively quick. The E68 fits into a single large bag with shoulder straps, useful for carrying the boat short distances. For longer distances, a boat cart is recommended because of the boat's weight.

Stability and Seaworthiness. Unlike most traditional-style folding kayaks, the E68 has tender initial stability and thus is not suitable for novices when lightly loaded for day use. When you load the boat down with touring gear, however, its initial stability increases rapidly. The boat is quite seaworthy for more experienced paddlers.

Tracking. The E68 tracks well without a rudder.

Maneuverability. The E68 is a long touring boat and therefore does better at tracking than turning. However, the ease with which you can edge it allows a small turning radius.

AN ANOMALY: FEATHERCRAFT AIRLINE SERIES

Is it a folding kayak, a sit-on-top kayak, or an inflatable? The Feathercraft Airline models are a little of each. By using an inflatable base, you can create the ultimate enclosed hull. By adding a frame, you can avoid one of the downsides of an inflatable: lack of stiffness or rigidity.

Feathercraft's Airline models share several features. The hull consists of four gigantic air chambers inside welded urethane Duratek hulls. Assembly, which is mostly pumping, is lightning fast. The frames are shock-corded aluminum like in other Feathercrafts. While the boats are all self-bailing, the drains are set deep down between air chambers so very little water comes through, unlike many sit-on-tops. They all include a very efficient hand air pump and a carry bag.

The four models include a double, the Gemini, which is 18 feet long with a 30-inch beam and weighs just 48 pounds, a lot less than most sit-on-tops. The singles range in size. The Uno is just over 12 feet in length with a 30-inch beam and weighs 25 pounds. The Java, the next one up, is pretty much a standard sit-on-top size, but it's a lot

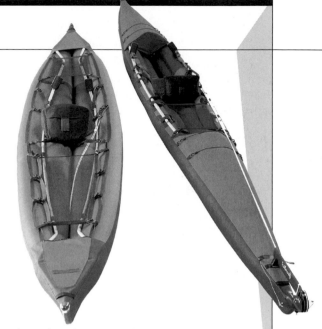

Feathercraft's Airline Java and Jet Stream. *(Courtesy Feathercraft)*

lighter—33 pounds—than hardshells. The pièce-de-résistance of the fleet is an honest-to-goodness surf ski, the Jet Stream, which is 19 feet, 3 inches long with a 20-inch beam.

Speed and Efficiency. The E68's long waterline length makes it a fast, efficient touring boat.

Versatility and Access. The boat's standard reach-through hatch in the foredeck is very helpful when manipulating gear forward. Cargo in the rear section can be easily accessed through the aft split deck. The E68 is solely a paddling craft with no provisions for sailing.

Quality and Durability. The E68 shows good workmanship. Pouch's PVC hulls have stood the test of time since about 1950. The new Bretex decks, introduced for the E68, have not been in service long. The color of the red ones does seem to fade, but there have been no reports of impaired function.

Cost and Depreciation. The price of a new E68 represents a good value at the lower end of the price range for comparable performance kayaks. There is no track record yet on relative depreciation.

MINI-FOLDABLE SINGLES

During the late 1980s, hardshell manufacturers began to introduce shorter versions of their most popular boats to meet the needs of the growing women's segment of the market. They've been dubbed women's kayaks but don't be turned off by this gender-specific term. At least in the folding kayak field, the smaller kayaks, called *mini-foldables*, are a good choice for virtually anyone. Even strapping 6 foot, 2 inch, 220-pounders will be comfortable in any one of several models of mini-foldable singles.

The new folding minis can keep up with the traditional-size foldables under most situations and, in some instances, actually will cruise with less effort. The mini-foldables have much more to offer than the small rigid kayaks. They weigh about the same as their fiberglass counterparts and are lighter than the plastics. In waves and wake, the mini-foldables seem to thrive playfully and are much more stable than their short, rigid counterparts.

The typical folding mini packs into one bag that is manageable by virtually anyone. The minis can generally be assembled more quickly than their larger counterparts because the radical lines of the larger boats create tension and torque resistance that must be overcome in the assembly process. Once assembled, the minis are easier to put on a roof rack and carry down to the water. Also, the minis tend to cost less. All of the minis make good day-use boats. And, if you know how to pack small and light for camping (see pages 176–77), they will see you through weeklong and longer camping trips.

Feathercraft K-Light

This model has been discontinued, but it was so popular that many are available on the used market. Weighing 29 to 34.5 pounds (depending on the year of manufacture), the K-Light is unbelievably light. The aluminum tubes are lighter than other Feathercrafts, and the crossribs are polycarbonate, not polyethylene. You can lift the assembled boat with what seems like just one finger, and the bagged boat hefts easily onto your back and carries well in its backpack bag or on an easily stowed cart available as an accessory.

Assembly and Portability. Assembly is easier than in the K1 because leveraging is called for in only one place; however, there is a step that involves sliding parts that some people find difficult. The K-Light takes portability to a new level.

Stability and Seaworthiness. Under most sea conditions you're likely to encounter, the K-Light resists tipping. It allows that nice one-with-the-water feeling.

Tracking. The K-Light tracks well. Only the most severe of beam winds is able to nudge it a bit off course.

Maneuverability. This mini-foldable responds well to leaned turns. It doesn't require a rudder.

Feathercraft K-Light.

Speed and Efficiency. The K-Light has a nimble feel and will cruise almost effortlessly. Like other minis, its top speed is not as great as that of regular-size foldables, but, since few paddlers can maintain their boats' potential top speeds, the K-Light won't leave you behind.

Versatility and Access. The K-Light is on par with its larger brothers. Access to gear underdeck is through the cockpit area and is no more difficult than in other minis. You will find some K-Lights with hatches in either deck or both.

Quality and Durability. The K-Light involved less hand-crafted labor, which was a departure from Feathercraft's norm, but it is still a quality product. You're never likely to drag such a light boat on land, so that factor should enhance its durability.

Cost and Depreciation. The K-Light's original price included accessories, so look for a used one that comes fully equipped—except for a paddle. (If you need to replace accessories, try the Kahuna's; they're basically the same.) On the used market you can find K-Lights for around $1,100 to $1,200. The version made in 2000, however, can demand a premium price since it has radio-frequency-sealed seams, newer materials, and is a few pounds lighter than the version with a Cordura deck and Hypalon hull.

Feathercraft Kahuna

The Kahuna is classified as a mini-foldable mainly because of its weight, but its length makes it an anomaly. It is just 2 inches or so shorter than models that are considered regular size, such as the Klepper Aerius I and the Folbot Kodiak. When looking at the Kahuna, consider it a regular-size kayak in terms of performance and other features.

Assembly and Portability. The Kahuna is a bit more difficult to assemble than the K-Light due to extra steps that involve leveraging to extend the frame; however, assembly is somewhat more predictable. The superb Kahuna backpack has a paddled hipbelt and lots of adjustment for comfort and distributing the load. A cart that fits the bag is also available.

Stability and Seaworthiness. This model is more stable than the K-Light and has a solid feel. It has many of the seaworthy traits of its bigger fellow model, the KI. In a way it is a poor man's KI.

Tracking. The Kahuna tracks very well. It does not require a rudder, although one is available as an accessory.

Maneuverability. All this boat needs for making fast turns is a quick sweep stroke and boat lean. The latter can be done with confidence that you will not tip over.

Speed and Efficiency. The Kahuna is fast, with good acceleration from a dead stop. Its cruising speed will definitely keep up with kayaks that are much longer, and it is easy to maintain a good clip.

Versatility and Access. Other than paddling, there's not much more you can do with this boat. It's not amenable to a sail, and the cockpit is fairly small for fishing, although you can fish from it if you want to. Cargo access is possible from the cockpit area, but if you plan to do a lot of camping, you may want to order the extra rear hatch. You may also opt for the Big Kahuna version, which has a slightly larger cockpit opening.

Quality and Durability. Feathercrafts are all well made. The Kahuna has lighter-duty aluminum and synthetic ribs than other Feathercrafts, but they do hold up well.

Cost and Depreciation. The Kahuna may be the finest performing folding kayak for a boat of its price. Depreciation should be as good as it was for K-Lights during most of the years the latter were produced.

Feathercraft Kahuna. *(Courtesy Feathercraft)*

FirstLight 420C

This model (see top photo, opposite) is made by a nontraditional folding-kayak company, FirstLight Kayaks of New Zealand. The 420C is included in these reviews because it incorporates many innovations and new materials, plus it weighs less than 20 pounds for a 13-foot, 9-inch boat—the lightest folding sea kayak available. (The company also has introduced a 15-foot, 9-inch kayak that weighs around 22 to 23 pounds.)

The frame's long pieces are made of carbon and Kevlar fiber; the crossribs are a nylon material. Both have lots of flex, which figures into the assembly of the boat and the adjustments one can make to trim and rocker. The hull material is a solid urethane sheet. This is totally unlike all other hull materials in folding kayaks that consist of some form of coating on a core fabric. It is highly flexible yet quite strong and abrasion resistant.

Assembly and Portability. The 420C's unique assembly differs from all other foldables. It takes practice, but assembly times are quick after you become proficient. The portability depends on the aftermarket bag you purchase since a bag is not provided.

Stability and Seaworthiness. At just 22 inches of beam, this model is narrow and lacks sponsons. It gains stability, however, by the way water pressure indents the skin and by having a two-rail keel that creates a somewhat flat bottom. The 420C handles seas as well as any light boat will.

Tracking. The 420C tracks very well because of its relatively long waterline. It turns into the wind and waves slowly so you can keep a true course.

Maneuverability. This boat turns very easily with a slight body lean and sweep stroke. You also have thigh braces that will help you control turns.

Speed and Efficiency. With such a narrow beam and long waterline, the 420C is quite fast and seems to move almost effortlessly across the water.

Versatility and Access. The 420C cannot take a sail and is not good to fish from. You have full access to both the rear and front compartment via zippered decks.

Quality and Durability. This is such a new model that durability is hard to gauge. The quality is good overall, but finishing details are rough.

Cost and Depreciation. Again, the model and company are so new that no track record has been established for how well the boat will depreciate. The price is competitive with Feathercraft's minifoldables but does not include the cost of a bag. It does come with a spray skirt and sea sock.

Folbot Aleut I

The Aleut is the least expensive foldable kayak on the market today. Like the double in the Folbot family, the Aleut is designed for the mass market, for people who aren't performance-minded but simply want to enjoy paddling without much fuss. For that market, the Aleut I delivers the essentials of any folding kayak—foldable convenience and stability.

The Aleut's frame consists of aluminum long pieces and polycarbonate ribs. Its hull is Hypalon, and its deck is coated polyester.

Assembly and Portability. Assembly is a snap; the Aleut has only three ribs and only about fourteen parts. Some parts are already held together in subassemblies. You can get the Aleut either in one or two bags, but take the convenient two-bag option because the single bag is awkward to carry.

Stability and Seaworthiness. The Aleut's stability cannot be overstated. No kayak can be termed untippable, but the Aleut goes a long way in that direction. It handles well in open water, and its nose refuses to dive in all but the highest waves and wake.

Tracking. The Aleut tracks extremely well. It refuses to turn into any wind or water force on your beam. In following seas it resists broaching or being turned sideways.

Maneuverability. This is the downside of the Aleut's terrific tracking ability. The boat is hard to turn because it wants to go straight. Turns require lots of stroking on one side and plenty of body lean.

FirstLight 420C. *(Courtesy FirstLight)*

Speed and Efficiency. The Aleut is the slowest of the foldables. It's hard to get moving, and effort is required to keep its speed up.

Versatility and Access. The Aleut's versatility rating is high because of the great underlying stability of the boat. Access to underdeck areas is not especially restricted because the rib openings are big and, in this short boat, there isn't much deck to begin with.

Quality and Durability. Quality and durability are on par with the Folbot Greenland II; i.e., good enough for most purposes—but not normally for heavy-duty use.

Folbot Aleut.

Cost and Depreciation. This is the least expensive foldable you can buy. Depreciation suffers because of the low cost of buying a new Aleut.

Folbot Yukon

Folbot created the Yukon to fill the niche between its two successful singles, the Aleut and Kodiak. Basically it is an elongated Aleut with a much bigger payload, which makes it appealing to budget-minded paddlers who may not be comfortable in a standard-size boat. Because of its elongated cockpit, it doubles nicely as a boat in which to take a child or large pet.

Assembly and Portability. Assembly is speedy, on par with the Aleut. It comes with two bags. The bags are awkward to carry for any distance, but they are virtually indestructible.

Stability and Seaworthiness. Stability is top-notch. It is somewhat better than the Aleut in open water because of its length. Folbot now makes the coaming of aluminum, which adds stiffness and makes the boats behave better. The Yukon does have a large cockpit, and you should use the spraydeck with it to keep out waves.

Folbot Yukon. *(Courtesy Folbot)*

Tracking. Like all Folbots, the Yukon tracks as if on rails.

Maneuverability. The boat is hard to turn. It wants to go straight, and it is not easy to lean with such a wide cockpit.

Speed and Efficiency. The Yukon is surprisingly fast—quick enough to keep up with an average group of kayakers in hardshells. It seems to maintain cruising speed well.

Versatility and Access. You can sail this boat. It has lots of room for camping gear both underdeck and around you. Access is fine through the large crossrib openings.

Quality and Durability. Folbots keep improving in both quality and design. Changes to the frame of these boats, all of which are used in the Yukon, have improved durability through added strength in the component changes.

Cost and Depreciation. Folbots are among the least expensive of folding kayaks. Given the low cost of a new boat, depreciation on old ones tends to be high because there is less incentive to buy a used one—especially considering the lifetime warranty that comes with a new one.

Klepper Scout

The Klepper Scout (formerly known as the 2000) is a no-compromise, shorter version of the time-proven Aerius I (see review pages 56–57). It is lighter by far than its larger sibling but just as tough. If anything, it feels more solid because Klepper basically compressed the Aerius I's frame to form the Scout's frame. The Klepper mini also seems to have inherited all of the good sea manners of the Aerius I and developed some unique performance virtues of its own.

Assembly and Portability. The Scout can be assembled more quickly than the Aerius I because it has less torque and fewer parts. The Scout is Klepper's first one-bag carry, and it works well. The single bag incorporates a full backpack harness that can be detached and checked as airline baggage.

Stability and Seaworthiness. The Scout has an initial stability that may feel a bit "tender" to some paddlers, but its final stability is excellent; i.e., it won't easily capsize. It handles beautifully in open water and has a lively, responsive feel.

Tracking. The Scout tracks better than the Aerius I. It will go as straight as you want without being affected by beam seas and winds.

Maneuverability. It won't turn quite as quickly as the Aerius I but will respond to body lean to get around in a hurry.

Speed and Efficiency. The Scout is fast off the mark and has phenomenal glide. It keeps going and going even after you stop paddling. This trait makes the Scout a delight to paddle at normal cruising speeds.

Versatility and Access. The Scout has a provision for a sail mast, but the boat may lack the stability needed for aggressive, full-range sailing. None of the minis is as good a sailing vessel as a regular-size foldable. Its below-deck access is on par with the Aerius I.

Quality and Durability. Klepper did not compromise anywhere when making the Scout. Frame dimensions and specifications are identical to the rest of the model line. The hull is expedition quality.

Cost and Depreciation. The Scout is slightly above the price range of the other mini-foldables. Depreciation is remarkably low.

Klepper Alu-Lite

The Alu-Lite represents a major departure for Klepper, its first foray away from a long tradition of all wooden frames. It feels totally unlike any of the traditional boats that Klepper has produced.

Klepper Scout.

Its strong points are ease of assembly compared to Feathercraft, which it aims to compete with, and it's relatively lightweight compared to other Kleppers.

Assembly and Portability. Most of the assembled frame can be slipped into the skin via the zippered rear deck. This process is somewhat easier than for Nautiraids that have the same assembly system. The aluminum tubes sometimes come apart, however, and you need to watch out for this. The boat's weight helps in portability, but the carry bag is somewhat awkward.

Stability and Seaworthiness. The Alu-Lite has so-so initial stability and takes getting used to. Its secondary stability is good. The boat handles nicely in rough seas.

Tracking. The Alu-Lite tracks well, and it won't broach in following seas. It does not come with a rudder, nor is there provision for one.

Maneuverability. This boat turns easily because you can lay it on its side and come around quickly with a sweep stroke.

Speed and Efficiency. The Alu-Lite feels speedy and accelerates well. Paddling it is pretty effortless.

Klepper Alu-Lite.

Versatility and Access. This boat can be paddled and not much else. Access is excellent through the zippered rear deck.

Quality and Durability. The quality and durability of the skin are that of any Klepper—which is to say a lot—because of the make's proven track record. Although the aluminum frame and synthetic crossribs are new for Klepper, they are well made and should hold up well.

Cost and Depreciation. The Alu-Lite is competitively priced compared to other mini-foldables. Depreciation should be minimal on this relatively new model.

Nautiraid Raid I 416 Expedition

This model, also known as the Nautiraid 14, comes with either a wooden or aluminum frame. There is a marginal difference in weight between the two since they both have Hypalon hulls. (For a lighter version, see the review below of the 416 Touring.)

The following review is for the wooden frame version, although it is not much different from the aluminum.

Assembly and Portability. Assembling the 416 Expedition is relatively easy since the frame is put together entirely outside the skin and slipped in through the zippered rear deck. The extension process then takes place and is simple to do. The boat is heavy considering its short length and comes in one bag that is hard to manage.

Stability and Seaworthiness. The 416 Expedition has very large sponsons that add stability and thus is good for a beginner. The boat is very forgiving in open-water paddling.

Tracking. The 416 Expedition tracks quite well and does not turn into beam winds or wakes.

Maneuverability. The boat can be turned easily by a simple lean and a sweep stroke.

Speed and Efficiency. Speed is not this boat's strong suit. Width and big sponsons mean some drag for such a short length, and paddling it can feel sluggish.

Versatility and Access. The boat is set up for paddling and not much else. However, the boat's stability lends itself to other pursuits such as fishing and photography. Access to the rear is ample since the 416 has a zippered rear deck, while access to the front does require a bit of a reach through the cockpit.

Quality and Durability. The Hypalon hull will provide many years of use and take abuse well. The quality of Nautiraids is generally good, but sometimes there are small mixups in packaging and accessories.

Cost and Depreciation. The price of the boat is competitive with other mini-foldables, but a few hundred dollars more will get you a bigger model such as the Greenlander or Raid 460 Expedition. Depreciation is moderate.

Nautiraid Raid I 416 Touring

The touring version of the 416, this boat uses a much lighter PVC-coated polyester hull material, which brings it in at about 10 pounds lighter than the expedition version. So, a buyer who does not plan to kayak in extremely rough conditions may want to consider this model. It comes with either an aluminum or a wooden frame. Its lightness is also a selling feature of the 416, especially the aluminum version; there's about a 3-pound difference.

Assembly and Portability. Assembly is as easy as for other Nautiraid singles. Portability is much better than on the 416 Expedition version since the single carrying bag is easier to handle.

Stability and Seaworthiness. Large external sponsons make this a stable boat that one can relax in during rough conditions. This is a good boat for a beginner.

Tracking. The 416 goes straight and is well behaved in all but the strongest side winds. You won't need to do much to keep it on track.

Maneuverability. The boat is easy to lean. When you do lean it, the boat turns quickly because of the radically wide center of the boat in the cockpit area.

Nautiraid 416 Expedition.

Speed and Efficiency. The boat can accelerate fast due to its light weight, and it has a lively feel in this regard. There is a good place to brace your feet in order to transfer power to the boat's forward motion.

Versatility and Access. The zippered rear deck makes getting at cargo easy. The boat is stable enough for many activities.

Quality and Durability. The quality is OK. The PVC-coated polyester hull will not take the abuse of the expedition line of Nautiraid models and will not last as long, especially since it lacks keelstrips.

Cost and Depreciation. The price is quite low and affordable. Depreciation is moderate.

Nautiraid Raid I 380 Touring

This model, formerly known as the Mini-Raid, offers a tight, personal fit and is extremely responsive. This model, one of the first mini-foldables, has a wooden frame. Its deck is a PVC-coated polyester, and its hull is reinforced PVC-coated polyester.

Assembly and Portability. The 380 is quick to assemble because the frame is put together entirely outside the skin and slipped into the hull via the zippered rear deck. The frame is then extended within the skin with a simple built-in levering device. This kayak is so light that it is very easy to carry in its one bag, despite the lack of padded carrying straps.

Stability and Seaworthiness. External sponsons make the 380 a very stable sea kayak. In open water, the boat gives you a secure feeling, and its responsiveness allows you to take on all but the most severe conditions.

Tracking. This model does not track well. It has lots of rocker, which tends to make the boat turn into anything beyond a beam breeze. It has no provisions for a rudder. To keep it going straight, you'll have to learn good paddling technique or rig up your own rudder substitute.

Maneuverability. The 380 turns on a dime; you don't even need much body lean to coax it around a turn.

Speed and Efficiency. The 380 has a fast, nimble feel on the water. Paddling it requires very little effort, and at cruising speed, it will paddle efficiently.

Versatility and Access. This kayak is meant to be paddled and nothing much else. For pushing gear inside, its access is tight because the decks are low and the ribs small.

Quality and Durability. Nautiraid's quality is quite good in general, but because the 380's hull is made of a PVC-coated polyester, it is likely to be less durable than other models in the company's line.

Cost and Depreciation. The 380's cost is low in the price range for mini-foldables, and it comes complete with spray skirt. This boat depreciates more than other models.

OTHER CHOICES

Your choice of folding kayaks does not end with the boats reviewed above. There are other options on the market.

Some folding kayaks are produced by large companies but aren't marketed outside of their home country. For example, of the handful of Japanese folding-kayak manufacturers, only Fujita (imported by FoldingCraft) is available in the United States (see review pages 55–56). Pouch, a German company, makes a line of singles as well as a double, but it has no dealer network in the North American markets, although an individual currently is importing them directly (see review pages 60–61). There are also folding kayaks available from former Soviet bloc countries, including Russia.

Some folding kayaks come from small operations with little if any dealer network. An example is Seavivor in the United States, which has a very limited production run. It makes a single and double that resemble German folding kayaks of the 1930s. Whalecraft is another small U.S. company that makes a double folding kayak.

Also, the folding-canoe companies are getting into the folding-kayak field. Pakboats, a U.S. maker of quality folding canoes with a great reputation for toughness, sells a folding kayak that is somewhat of a decked canoe. Ally Folding Canoe, based in Norway, now has a folding sea kayak (not reviewed).

All of these kayaks have their good points. Sometimes it is price; sometimes some design feature. Their presence enlivens your choices.

Equipment and Accessories That Work Well in Foldables

Chapter Five

Folding kayaks can make good use of most of the equipment and accessories made for hardshell kayaks. But foldables differ enough from hardshells that you should use special care when selecting some of these items, and you may want to consider a number of products that are made just for folding kayaks.

As you read through this chapter, keep in mind that you don't need to purchase everything at once. You can stock up on items as you get accustomed to your boat and your horizons and needs broaden. It's better to start off slow, go easy on your pocketbook, and keep things simple.

BASIC EQUIPMENT FROM FOLDING-KAYAK MANUFACTURERS

Some decisions about add-ons will already have been made for you. How so? A manufacturer may have only one option for a specific item, and your foldable's requirements in that area may be so specialized that there simply aren't any aftermarket alternatives available to you. Your only other choice might be to make your own substitution. Several suggestions for do-it-yourself options are covered in chapter 15.

Here are the key pieces of equipment that your folding-kayak company is likely to offer.

Spray Coverings

Spray coverings (spray skirts, spraydecks, or both) keep out ocean spray and rain, but you'd be surprised just how dry you can remain in some folding kayaks, especially doubles, without such covering.

It's not unusual for a paddler to go out without any spray covering for a few hours into the middle of a large bay that's being churned up by wind and powerboat wakes and find that only a few cups of water have gotten into the open folding kayak. Much of that water is kept out by higher sides and the flare-out overhang created by the air sponsons. However, if that paddler were in a hardshell without a spray skirt in such conditions, he or she would be taking on enough water to be in danger.

In warmer weather, the little water that does splash in from chop or drip off your paddle can feel refreshing on your body. Many folding kayakers, especially in boats with large cockpits, never use spray coverings.

But a spray covering is a wise investment. Not only will it keep you from getting chilled in cold weather, but you should be concerned in a general way about having an open boat in open water. A large, breaking wave could dump gallons of water into your foldable, potentially getting you in trouble; that same wave would very easily be deflected by a spray covering.

When shopping for a spray covering, you'll find yourself hemmed in by proprietary equipment that is difficult to find substitutes for elsewhere. The spray-covering options differ by company. Here are your options.

Feathercraft. All of this company's folding kayaks have individual cockpits designed to be covered by spray skirts that attach to the paddler. (An original version of the K1 came with an integral spray skirt built into the boat; you may see one in the used market.) Feathercraft's own spray skirt is top quality and worth your consideration. There is a standard version as well as a combination version with a nylon tunnel and a neoprene deck and an all-neoprene version. Many aftermarket spray skirts fit the Feathercraft coaming,

and you may want one with features such as a chest pocket. (Feathercraft also will offer a chest pocket if you ask for one.)

Folbot. You have little choice but to buy Folbot's own spraydeck and spray skirt setup. No aftermarket company makes the spraydeck, and the skirts are of a peculiar size for the cockpit hoops in the Folbot spraydeck. And Folbot's setup is so inexpensive that making your own custom substitute would cost almost as much as the original spray equipment.

Klepper. This company offers you some variations in spraydeck and spray skirt arrangements for both singles and doubles. The options offered for the doubles, described below, are good representations of the singles options as well.

The least expensive double, the touring spray cover, is a one-piece affair with chimney-type openings for each paddler. It comes standard with new boats. You wrap the chimney material around yourself and secure it with snaps. The touring cover connects to the coaming via a Velcro connection that mates a Velcro strip on the hem of the spray cover with a strip glued to the outside of the coaming. This covering is not advisable for serious open-water use because a dumping wave conceivably can knock it off the boat, and if you ever capsize, the cover would be hard to get back on.

The preferred Klepper spray covering is the Expedition tuck-under. It has a spraydeck and two spray skirts. The latter is worn like any ordinary spray skirt. The connection is via a tuck-under feature rather than Velcro strips. The hem of the deck has a bead that tucks under the coaming and into a groove on the hidden side. To attach the tuck-under spraydeck, you partially inflate the sponsons with a few puffs of air, tuck the bead into that underside groove—making certain to get the entire hem into place—and then finish inflating the sponsons. The cover stays tucked so tightly you can almost lift the boat by the spray cover alone.

Klepper also offers a zippered spray skirt that allows access to things around you. This military-derived option costs more and is probably overkill. If you have to reach things, you can just pop the regular spray skirt to find what you need, achieving the same effect as a zipper.

You do have an aftermarket option on spray covers for Kleppers. Long Haul Folding Kayaks, which has several kayaks that compete with Klepper, offers a tuck-under version of the large spray cover similar to Klepper's Velcro-connected one. It provides the best of both worlds of the two versions of spray covers offered by Klepper. Long Haul also has a three-piece tuck-under spray cover with spray skirts like that of Klepper but made of heavier materials.

Nautiraid. Like Folbot, Nautiraid has only one offering in the spraydeck department for its doubles, and it is peculiar enough not to be found on the aftermarket. If you want features like easy-release suspenders and handy stash pockets as described above under Feathercraft options, you could use commercially available substitutes for the Nautiraid skirt used in its singles or in conjunction with the spraydeck in its doubles. A variety of such aftermarket spray skirts will fit Nautiraids.

Rudders

Most of the manufacturers don't offer you much choice here. Folbot, Klepper, and Nautiraid offer only one rudder option for their boats, both singles and doubles. You could make your own rudder but would probably have to buy a component or two to complete the job (see chapter 15).

Feathercraft offers a top-notch rudder. Feathercraft is a major supplier of original-equipment rudders to numerous hardshell companies, so it has a good reputation in this department. Its flip-

up surf rudder is a classic and comes as standard equipment on most Feathercraft models. It is easy to operate and comes with a device for lifting it out of the water from your cockpit. Once lifted out, the rudder lies securely out of the way in a holder on the rear deck. This is a distinct advantage, because although the rudders on other foldables can be lifted out of the water, they aren't stowed on deck and out of harm's way. Instead, they hang a few inches above the water where they can get slapped around by waves and provide unwanted windage.

The other Feathercraft option available is a strap-on skeg, basically a nonturning rudder meant to help keep a boat tracking straight when hit by beam winds and waves. It will fit any of the Feathercraft singles. The strap-on skeg is made of soft materials and can be easily adapted to most single folding kayaks. You can also make one, but it may not be worth the effort since the factory model is so inexpensive.

Sails

Generally, folding kayaks are good sailing vessels. All the manufacturers underline this fact by listing sails in their catalogs. Except for Klepper's and Folbot's, the sail offerings are downwind rigs, but for your convenience some manufacturers are happy to point you to outside sailmakers who can provide a full-range sail.

For example, Folbot has an excellent upwind cat rig sail. Its sail area is 30 square feet, and it comes with inflatable outriggers and a leeboard. The outriggers snap on easily, which takes advantage of the fact that you can also just sail without them as Folbots tend to be quite stable anyway. The Folbot sail can be reefed by rolling it around the mast to reduce sail area when winds get too high to easily manage.

The big advantage of buying your sail rig through your folding-kayak manufacturer is that you'll know for certain that the rig works on your

WHAT SHOULD ALWAYS BE IN YOUR BOAT

You may get away with bringing along very little. Just jump in your foldable with a can of soda and a couple of sourballs in your pocket, and on many of your outings you'll be OK. But what about other times? Sourballs and soda can't repair anything, won't help you find your way if you're lost in fog, and make lousy signaling devices—unless you can make enough noise by rattling the sourballs in the soda can.

To meet all of the vagaries of kayaking, you'll either have to carry the essentials listed below or travel with someone who does.

Some items need explaining. First are the **absolute essentials**. The assumption is that, in a variation of the old American Express card slogan, you should never leave your launch site without them. These are the items that keep your boat floating and moving, and the water on the outside. They keep your internal engine fueled and lubricated, and let you know where you are and where you're headed.

All items on this list that could be damaged or compromised by getting wet should be packed in whichever form of watertight bags or containers you prefer. The special side bags mentioned on page 81 are a handy place to carry these absolute essentials. Or, if you want to put them in a large fanny pack, you can keep the pack either strapped around you or very accessible and easily removable. Or you could thread the strap of the fanny pack through the arm holes of your personal floatation device (PFD), thus keeping the pack on your back.

In the **repair section**, the Leatherman tool is an unusually important component. Much better than a Swiss Army knife, this multitool has real screwdrivers, pliers, wire cutters, a functional file, and a knife. For any folding kayak—with all kinds of fittings and brackets—the Leatherman is an all-in-one must.

Gerber makes a similar device, as does SOG.

Other spare parts listed in the repair section will depend on which model of folding kayak you have and which of its components has the greatest probability of breaking. Your dealer or distributor may help you with this. The dental floss isn't just for your nice smile, and the leather laces aren't just for your shoes. Both these items can be used with duct tape to secure or repair broken ribs, stringers, and more (see chapter 17).

Extra clothes are a must, even in the blazing days of summer. If you've ever been caught in a July hailstorm, when you're chilled to the bone by plummeting temperatures, you'll understand why extra clothes are essential.

It's a big list—thirty-nine items altogether—and that's just for ordinary day trips. Major crossings might require running lights and other additions. The items listed weigh as much as 5 to 8 pounds, not counting any of the absolute essentials. This adds to the heft of what you need to carry with your folding kayak, so it's easy to say, "Why bother?" But consider this. In the fickle environment that is the sea, these items will give you an edge and make an uncomfortable situation more tolerable. And at some point in your paddling adventures, they may make the difference between life and death.

Absolute Essentials

- ❑ PFD
- ❑ spare paddle or paddle leash
- ❑ extra flotation
- ❑ water
- ❑ food
- ❑ chart and compass
- ❑ pump, bailer, sponge
- ❑ spray skirt
- ❑ marine VHF handheld radio

Extra Clothes

- ❏ bandanna
- ❏ wind or spray pants
- ❏ wind or paddle jacket
- ❏ socks
- ❏ shirt
- ❏ warm top
- ❏ gloves or *pogies* (special mittens that attach to the paddle)
- ❏ hats—wool and rain
- ❏ sunscreen, lip balm
- ❏ sunglasses
- ❏ toilet paper
- ❏ weather radio

Emergencies

- ❏ windproof and waterproof matches
- ❏ fire starter

- ❏ small tarp
- ❏ energy bars
- ❏ space blanket
- ❏ signal mirror
- ❏ flares
- ❏ flashlight
- ❏ whistle
- ❏ first-aid kit
- ❏ knife

Repair

- ❏ boat repair kit
- ❏ spares for break-prone parts
- ❏ Leatherman tool
- ❏ parachute cord
- ❏ dental floss
- ❏ leather shoelaces
- ❏ duct tape

boat. If you buy it aftermarket, you'll have to make sure the supplier has fittings to adapt the sail to your particular boat. Check on this before going through the expense.

Klepper's sails give you a stepped-up approach to sailing; you can buy increasingly complex components as you build up toward a full-range sail rig capable of beating (going into the wind). The system revolves around one common mast and leeboard setup. You'll need the leeboard to do any beam reaching and beating. You can buy a jib, which will give you the ability to reach and to run downwind comfortably. Better upwind performance comes with the large mainsail. The full sail rig is called the S-4 (S-1 for singles).

The S-4 is a classic gaff-rig sail with a jib. Many thousands have been sold, especially years ago when the cost of buying both the boat and sail rig was so little that it made sense to go all the

way. The S-4 is the most widely used kayak sail in recent kayaking history. It's a good sail that, like any rig, has its tricks (see chapter 12). The S-4 has recently faced some stiff competition from the aftermarket (see Other Sail Rigs, pages 85–86).

Klepper now makes an interesting proprietary sail called the Freewind. It's basically a small downwind rig that can broad reach. Its key advantages are that it uses half of a paddle for its mast and is simple to set up. The sail area is small, but it's large enough to give any Klepper, even a loaded double, a boost when the wind is cooperating.

Nautiraid has a sail that resembles a paper fan. It tends to be a rarity as there are few actually on the market. Feathercraft offers a Genoa sail that basically acts like a spinnaker for downwind sailing. If requested, the company also will put on a bracket to accommodate the aftermarket Spirit downwind sail.

Carts

All the manufacturers offer boat carts that can be used either to move the assembled boat for long distances and/or to cart around the disassembled boat in its bags.

You'll probably need a cart at some point in your folding kayak's lifetime. This type of cart is made to knock down quickly and stash away in your boat until it's needed again. It's especially handy for moving a cargo-laden folding kayak, and when you're traveling by train, a cart allows you to walk long distances through train stations with minimum effort. (See chapter 11 to learn how to make best use of a cart for this, and chapter 13 for how to avoid damaging your assembled boat when carting it.)

Even with mini-folding kayaks, which are quite lightweight, you may want to use a cart, especially when traveling by public transportation. Feathercraft has a cart that attaches to sewn-in tabs on the boat's carry bag (the company will add the tabs free of charge to older boat bags that lack them). It operates very much like a luggage cart and allows you to roll your bagged K-Light or Kahuna. Unlike a luggage cart, it can be flipped to allow you to roll the assembled kayak as well. The cart works on the K1 bag and on an empty assembled K1.

Boat cart, compass, anchor. *(Walther/Klepper)*

You're probably best off buying the cart offered by your folding-kayak manufacturer because you can be confident it will work with your boat. Some aftermarket carts may not function as well, and they may not withstand salt water. Carts designed for canoes are primarily meant for freshwater environments.

ESSENTIALS FROM THE AFTERMARKET

Some of the essential equipment you'll need for paddling your foldable is best purchased in the aftermarket. While most of the folding-kayak companies offer paddles, you're better off getting them from other sources because they'll likely perform better.

However, if you deal with sources for nonfolding kayaks, be aware of the differences between hardshell kayaks and foldables. Their advice about essential equipment may not always be the best for your foldable because such advice is mainly geared to the requirements of hardshell paddlers.

Paddles

After purchasing your boat, which paddle you choose is your next most critical decision. Your paddle is what will put you in contact with the water and move your boat. Just as you would want the best hiking boots you can afford for the kinds of terrain you're likely to traverse, you shouldn't be too thrifty when it comes to purchasing your paddle. A good paddle can make the difference between a pleasant day out on the water, covering great distances effortlessly, and a miserable time, getting nowhere and hurting at the end of the day.

Paddling a foldable narrows your range of choices of this essential piece of equipment. First, obviously, you'll have to go with a take-apart paddle. It's no use having an 8-foot, one-piece paddle when you're planning to carry your boat in bags that measure half that length or less. Next, you'll have to select a slightly longer paddle than you would for a rigid boat, especially if you're not tall.

Paddle-length choices. Since foldables tend to be a few inches wider than their hardshell counterparts, you'll need a paddle that's a bit longer in order to clear your deck. For example, a typical single hardshell might be paddled with a 7½-foot paddle, perhaps even a smidgen shorter, while a folding single will require several inches more. Double rigid kayaks rarely need 8-foot paddles, which is what a folding double would likely need.

Paddle length for foldables hinges on how much of the paddle is blade and how much is shaft. For example, Klepper's standard wooden paddles for its doubles are 8 feet in overall length. The Camano is a great paddle, made for the aftermarket by Werner. But to use the Camano effectively with a double Klepper, you'll have to get one slightly longer than 8 feet. The reason is that the blade portion of the Camano is not only narrower, but, more critically, it's longer. So all that extra blade length will hit the side of the Klepper—unless you get a longer Camano paddle.

One way to know how long an aftermarket paddle should be is to measure the shaft length of the paddle sold by the folding-kayak manufacturer. As long as the shaft lengths match, you can be sure to get the right length of paddle from an outside source.

You may find some shortcomings when using a longer paddle. You might not be able to keep up as great a stroke rate as you could with a shorter paddle because you have to swing through a wider arc. (Because of this, the more recent trend even with foldables is to try to use shorter-length paddles than recommended in the past.) The longer paddle will also put more stress on your forearms. To compensate for both arc and stress, you'll have to develop some good paddling technique, which will be described at length in the next chapter.

With a double you may want to have two different lengths, one for the front paddler (shorter) and one for the rear paddler (slightly longer). If you can, borrow several paddles of different lengths from friends so you can try the different lengths and see what length may be best for you in your specific boat.

What about paddles from folding-kayak manufacturers? With the exception of Feathercraft's paddle option, you'll probably want to avoid what the manufacturers have to offer. Let's take these one at a time.

Klepper's wooden paddle is made by an outside source, and it's been used by many thousands of paddlers. But a Klepper paddler who tries one of the better aftermarket paddles usually buys one despite the high cost. Why? The Klepper paddle is heavy. About a decade ago the shafts were round and on the fat side, making an awkward grip for your hand. Their shafts are now slightly more oval, but if you choose to feather your paddle, it will still be awkward and troublesome. (More about this in the next chapter.) The feathering angle built into the Klepper paddle is 90 degrees. This forces you to crank back excessively with your control-hand wrist to get the opposite blade in position, more so than you would have to with a feathering angle of 65 to 75 degrees.

Folbot's paddle shares some of the same handicaps. It is heavy and feathers at 90 degrees, not the wrist-saving 75 degrees or less you'll find in better paddles.

Feathercraft's optional paddle is significantly better than what the other folding manufacturers have for their customers. Made for Feathercraft by a well-respected Canadian paddle maker, it is light, has a better feathering angle, and breaks down into four pieces. Since Feathercraft's storage bags are shorter than those of other foldables, this paddle's shorter take-apart length is important. Also, you may not find as reliable a paddle as you will with the Feathercraft offering. The company has extensive experience with four-piece paddles. Another paddle manufacturer may offer to cut a four-piece for you, but you can't be absolutely certain this would be done in a manner that will hold up as well as the time-tested Feathercraft one. So get the Feathercraft one or find out which manufacturer is making the former's paddle and buy a four-piece from it.

Which are the best of the outside sources? You can spend a lifetime trying out what's available from the many manufacturers, but your best bets are the few that have proved to work well with foldables.

The Camano by Werner, mentioned above, is the proven choice of folding kayakers who want the best in performance and rugged durability from their paddles. It also happens to be one of the top choices for hardshell paddlers as well.

The Camano is not inexpensive, but it's worth it. It has a fiberglass shaft and reinforced fiberglass blades that are asymmetrical so they don't pick up water when being lifted out at the end of the stroke—as a more rounded or squared-off blade end would. The shaft's springiness helps put more power into your stroke. The shaft is oval and slim, which helps your paddling technique and promotes a more relaxed grip on the paddle. It is also available in Kevlar for greater weight reduction, albeit at equally greater cost.

Another top choice in paddles is the Eddyline, either the Sea Swift, which is 8 inches wide, or the Wind Swift, which is 5 inches wide. Both are lighter than the normal Camano. The shafts have gone through some changes and are now round instead of oval, but they're still choice paddles for foldables. Be careful about the length. Ordinarily you can't get them in anything longer than 8 feet. The Sea Swift works slightly better with a double boat than the Wind Swift because its blade is slightly shorter. Aqua Bound also offers good paddle choices, and it has a reliable four-piece as well.

Personal Flotation Devices (Life Jackets)

Next to your paddle, your personal flotation device, or PFD, is your most important boating accessory. It may well save your life someday— *but only if you're wearing it*. It's an essential piece of safety equipment. Regardless of the nature of the water you're paddling, always wear your PFD. Otherwise, at that critical moment, it can't possibly work.

Unfortunately, paddlers who think of their folding kayaks as invincible don't always wear their PFDs. Why? The sensation of stability one gets in a large foldable lulls them into thinking that nothing can happen. Some paddlers will wear a PFD in a hardshell kayak but insist they don't have to wear it in a foldable. *Not smart.*

Though foldables are certainly more stable than other sea kayaks, they can tip over. And, though folding kayaks are easier to climb back into than rigid ones, why not gain the extra boost a PFD's buoyancy gives to your reentry effort?

PFD, a must. *(Ian Giddy)*

If you were injured in a capsize, wouldn't you appreciate that extra measure of protection keeping you afloat?

The common excuse some people give for not wearing a PFD at all times is that they can be uncomfortable in foldables. Folding kayaks have higher spraydecks and higher seats than rigid kayaks. When you wear a spray skirt in a folding kayak, your PFD will often ride up uncomfortably.

The choice of fine PFDs has grown over the last decades. At one time it was hard to find a PFD that fit well and had pockets large enough for gear. Now many companies have such models as a matter of course. Among the favorable features are as many as six or eight adjustment points, including several pairs of side straps, a waist strap, and adjustable shoulder straps. There also may be two or more pockets configured to carry various things such as a marine radio and emergency gear. Some even have a back shoulder tab for a strobe light and webbing tabs on the back that allow you to attach to a small emergency pack or hydration system. Some have reflective tape sewn into various spots to help make you easier to spot. Among reputable companies are Extrasport, Lotus Designs, Stohlquist, and Serratus. Any visit to a paddling shop will present you with a wide variety of the latest designs with the greatest improvements. When choosing a PFD, pick a color that stands out—such as yellow or orange. This may help you avoid getting run over by other boat traffic if you capsize (but still be vigilant around other boats—see chapter 9, Sea Savvy, for tips on paddling in traffic). If you pick another color, you can improve your visibility by wearing a bright hat, taping reflective strips onto the vest, or using paddles with brightly colored blades.

Flotation Bags

Flotation bags, or air bags, are a *must* for any folding kayak. Foldables do not have bulkheads,

Adding flotation to a Folbot Aleut.

which are underdeck walls that create watertight compartments in the fore and aft areas. Fiberglass kayaks generally do have bulkheads and therefore don't require flotation bags. Even so, some hardshell paddlers use them as a backup. In plastic boats, flotation bags are also a must because their bulkheads tend to come loose and compromise the integrity of their supposedly watertight compartments.

In the event of a capsize, a boat equipped with flotation bags takes on much less water. The upright boat will ride higher and be more buoyant, and emptying it will take a lot less time and energy. A single foldable can fill up with more than 80 gallons of water; a double can take on 150 gallons or more. That's a lot of pumping.

Many people don't use air bags because of their naive belief that the air sponsons are enough. They are not. (Read chapter 10 for the details about rescue drills and dealing with a swamped boat.) The only time you can safely venture out without air bags is when you have the underdeck areas so completely loaded with camping gear that the gear will displace any water that may enter the boat in a capsize. Of course, the gear can only do that job if it's stowed in waterproof storage bags.

Some manufacturers sell air bags for their boats, but they tend to be of marginal use. Folbot's are simply too small; they wouldn't displace much water. Klepper's are also on the small side. Both are constructed of lightweight vinyl that appears flimsy. Feathercraft has excellent ones, which is interesting. The company at one time relied just on its excellent sea sock, which comes standard with all models. However, the company now recommends the use of both the sea sock and air flotation bags, adhering to the suspenders-and-belt safety theory (i.e., two systems are better).

There are many choices of flotation bags on the aftermarket. Some are sold as store brands such as REI. Others that are reliable include Dagger, Perception, and Voyageur, among others. These air bags, which are often labeled with such descriptions as Sea Kayak Standard Flotation Bags, generally work well in double and single folding kayaks. They won't fill all the underdeck area, but they're large enough to reduce the amount of water that would need to be pumped out after a capsize. Remember that the indicated size is generally of the uninflated bag. When inflated they are effectively shorter and less wide. Go for a bag that will fill as much of the length of your underdeck area as possible. Don't worry if the bag may be wider than your underdeck width, because you can compensate by not quite filling it.

Bailers and Pumps

Bailers and pumps are necessary safety items for any kayaker. They're doubly important in a foldable because, in the event of a capsize, the relatively large interior space could fill with a huge amount of water. If the flotation bags covered above are "preventive medicine," then pumps and bailers are your "first aid" or remedial measures. They should always be on board.

A bailer is a handy way to extract water quickly, but you won't find a single one on the market. Make your own from a pail, plastic bleach bottle, or almost any large, unbreakable beverage container made for refrigerator storage.

Hand pumps are available on the aftermarket and are inexpensive. Look for one with a cylinder large enough to do some good, about 2 inches in diameter. The hand pump should also have a flotation collar in case it falls overboard. Perception makes a good one that is available just about everywhere.

Electric pumps are sold in marine-supply stores as electric bilge pumps for small craft, and they cost more than hand pumps. Operating on flashlight batteries, an electric pump is good for getting rid of several hundred gallons of water—that is, until its batteries need replacement. The pumping rate is less than you can do by hand, but because it requires no effort on your part, an electric pump will work while you paddle for shore. Like anything electric or electronic around a small boat, electric pumps can fail. Some cynics store them in their bailing buckets.

Klepper makes a hand-operated bilge pump that fits into a special cut in the keelboard of a double, just in front of one of the paddlers. This is a military-specification item. If you feel you absolutely need one, you can probably coax it out of the company as a special order.

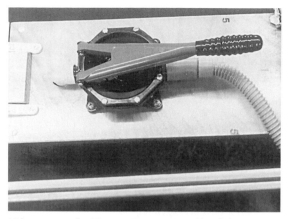

Military pump for Klepper Quattro. (Walther/Klepper)

HANDY-TO-HAVE ITEMS

The wise paddler would never venture out without the basic gear discussed above. But, depending on what you are doing, you might also want to include some of the handy items discussed below.

Side Bags

One advantage of a folding kayak is that you have accessible storage room around you for things you might want to get at while on the water—without having to land to dig them out from underdeck areas. The crossribs in the cockpit area are ready made for attaching specialty side bags that can keep such needed items handy.

Good side bags are available on the aftermarket that can attach to the crossribs alongside you. You can keep handy a rain jacket and pants, rain hat, a wool hat, socks, and gloves, plus a medium-weight polypropylene top, bottom, and gloves. You'll probably want a pair of these side bags so you can keep the second bag filled with sunglasses, sunscreen, repair kit, lunch, flashlight, flares, toilet paper, first-aid kit, and other items from the thirty-nine essentials you should always have in any sea kayak (see sidebar on pages 74–75).

Cascade Designs (www.cascadedesigns.com/sealline), in their SealLine products, offers a deck bag that will work. It's made of vinyl and has a zipper that's almost waterproof.

With its boats, Klepper issues small canvas bags that fit on special hooks built into the cockpit area. At best, these small bags can carry some sunscreen, sunglasses, and a pair of gloves. Long Haul Products also offers such bags but with a much larger volume than Klepper's.

Use your imagination as you look for good side bags. Some fanny packs will fit alongside you with the belly strap wrapped around gunwales or crossribs. You can also use bags in Feathercrafts and some other singles that you attach to the deck bar in front of you. Bring it into your lap when you want to retrieve something, and slide it forward when it's not in use. Accessory bags sold by backpack companies as side pockets work well for this. Make certain that the bag won't trap you in the event of capsize.

Dry Storage Bags

All the camping gear you take on a trip should be placed in watertight storage bags. This is true not only of folding kayaks, which have no waterproof compartments, but also of hardshells, which invariably let in some water—no matter what their manufacturers claim.

PROTECTIVE CLOTHING FOR WINTER PADDLING

Paddling in northern climates can always involve the possibility of hypothermia unless you're equipped to be immersed in cold water. All too often folding-kayak paddlers who somehow feel immune to the forces of nature don't prep for cold water—don't even wear PFDs—on the theory that nothing bad can ever happen in a folding kayak because of its great stability.

Not true. Folding kayaks go over. Perhaps it's only infrequently, but if it happened to you, you'd certainly wish you'd been prepared.

Canoeists have long been fond of wearing woolens and rain gear during cool-weather paddling. Some of this gear has a long history behind it. Shackleton's expedition survived several years of Antarctic travel after its ship was crushed in polar ice. The explorers wore heavy woolens and Burberry rain gear.

Even if you are as hardy as a polar explorer, don't bet your life on rain gear and wool fibers. When the water is cold (experts vary on the precise cautionary level, but below 50°F to 55°F), you've got three choices:

Don't venture out.

Wear a neoprene wet suit.

Don a dry suit.

Wet Suits and What They Do

A wet suit is your cheapest and most basic survival alternative. It is made of 3-millimeter-thick neoprene. Farmer John–type wet suits generally cost about $100–$120 and come with a front-entry zipper. They allow a thin layer of water to penetrate the material and be held close to your skin, where the water is warmed by your body heat and insulated by the neoprene.

A wet suit must be tight to keep the layer of water thin. How tight? You should be unable to gather the material when you clasp the suit with your hand, except in the crotch area and behind the knees. But it shouldn't be so tight that your breathing is severely hampered.

For comfort, wear a thin polypropylene or polyester (Thermax, Capilene, etc.) shirt underneath the top portion of the wet suit. Don't wear long-john bottoms underneath, because they won't help insulate very well and also will make it harder to put on the wet suit in the first place. Slick Lycra tights will work OK if you feel a need for an extra layer. To keep warm while paddling in cold weather, wear insulation layers, such as a fleece jacket, over the wet suit. Over that wear a paddling jacket (waterproof material, neoprene neck and wrist gaskets) or a dry top (waterproof material, latex gaskets). For comfort when on land, wear pants that are windproof or waterproof. Neoprene has a chilling effect when wind blowing across its surface rapidly evaporates any water or sweat.

The Dry-Suit Phenomenon

Dry suits work on an entirely different principle—they keep the water out. They're made of loose-fitting waterproof material with tighter gaskets at the neck, wrists, and ankles. In one-piece suits, access is generally through a waterproof front zipper. A two-piece suit has a means of mating the top and bottom, usually overlapping latex material that is rolled tightly for waterproofing.

Some water may enter a dry suit, but you're more likely to get damp from your own sweat than from the half cup of water that will creep in during a day's outing. You are insulated from contact with the cold by your layers of insulated clothing. Synthetic tops and bottoms worn inside the dry suit can be of varying thickness, depending on the water's temperature.

Dry suits cost about $350 each, but they're worth the expense for at least two reasons: They are more comfortable to wear, since they're less restrictive than neoprene, and they will protect you longer if you're exposed to cold water.

You may tend to build up sweat within the suit, but you won't feel cold or clammy because no air can pass over you to cool you down. You hit what dry-suit paddlers call "a relative, happy humidity level" within the suit. One fabric that seems to work well as an underlayer to keep you feeling drier is Polartec 100 or 200, depending on water temperatures. The fabric, which is available in a number of brands of clothing, does a fantastic job of wicking moisture away from your skin surface to the product's outer layer. The layer next to your skin will always feel dry.

Dry suits also come in Gore-Tex, which is breathable and theoretically will keep you drier. Some comments: It's more expensive, about $600 per suit. Salt water has long been thought to contaminate Gore-Tex, rendering it useless. The manufacturer claims this problem has been solved but instructs you to rinse it with fresh water after each use. Your PFD will reduce the advantage of Gore-Tex by reducing its breathability, as would your spray skirt. Gore-Tex works by letting moisture out through microscopic membrane holes that are too small to let water molecules in. But it takes heat to drive the moisture through the membrane, your precious body heat. You'll chill faster unless you have more insulation than someone in a non–Gore-Tex suit.

Light Scuba Suits

You have another option beyond wet and dry suits—one of the miracle products that are being sewn into special suits for scuba divers. The material is made by Polartec, as well as others such as Watersports.

These special diver suits are sometimes called tropical diving suits to distinguish them from those meant for cold-water dives. Don't let that throw you off. The suits are equivalent to 2 millimeters of neoprene in the protection they provide and can be brought up to the same 3-millimeter protection as normal wet suits by adding special vests, bought separately. Your PFD also adds insulation. Companies offering these include Henderson, O'Neill, and Body Glove, among others.

The specialty suits have several advantages over wet suits. They are less restrictive, virtually windproof, and breathable, while being somewhat waterproof. They cost just a bit more than wet suits, around $200 to $250. They consist of three layers: an outer shell, a waterproof barrier sheet in between, and fuzzy insulation material next to your skin.

They seem to be more of a viable option for folding kayakers than for rigid ones. The odds of going over in a folding kayak are much slimmer than in rigid kayaks. And, the quicker rescue possible in a foldable means less time hanging out in cold water risking hypothermia. Even the 2-millimeter versions of these specialty suits (i.e., sans vest) will give enough measure of protection for survival. Since so many paddlers are reluctant to put on confining wet suits, the specialty suits are a reasonable and practical answer to safety needs. If you go this route, opt for a looser fit than a dive shop is likely to specify. Such shops are thinking of divers, not kayakers who need to have freedom of upper-body movement while paddling. Even slightly loose, the suits will work in cold water to keep you alive until you can get back into your boat.

Other Considerations

Although pogies are great protection for your hands while paddling in cold weather, they'll be useless if you capsize. Neoprene gloves tend to be awkward and constrictive. If you're using neoprene gloves, get a larger size to compensate for this. Dishwashing gloves with liners are another possible solution.

To protect your feet, wear neoprene booties. Most people like to *(continued on next page)*

PROTECTIVE CLOTHING FOR WINTER PADDLING

(continued from previous page)
wear liner socks inside the booties. A synthetic liner with a wool middle layer would be a good idea. The nonzippered booties work best because they let in so little water. Zippered booties leak but are easier to put on, and they can be dried out more quickly.

Regarding headgear, wool hats and detachable non-down-insulated hoods from winter jackets are fine. Hardshell paddlers wear neoprene hoods because they plan to roll to self-rescue in a capsize. As a folding kayaker, you'll come out of your kayak, and, for the most part, your head will remain out of the water. But do wear a neoprene cap or its equivalent if the water temperatures are close to freezing.

Bring along a thermos full of hot tea, soup, or cocoa. Plan trips that cover smaller areas or that don't require too much time. Cut short your trip if there's any possibility of adverse weather. Stormy winter seas are more fierce than their summertime counterparts.

Numerous dry storage bags are common on the aftermarket, where they range in price, durability, and effectiveness. SealLine, Voyageur, Colorado Kayak Supply (CKS), and Northwest River Supplies are among the reliable brands. (You can find specific advice on using storage bags in chapter 13.)

Marine Handheld VHF Radios

At one point, such radios were not only inordinately expensive, they were also not up to the wet conditions experienced in a kayak. This has changed. You can get an excellent radio for around $200 that is capable of being submerged. In fact, any salt that accumulates on the radio can be washed off by placing it under a slow running faucet or, better yet, dipping it into a sink or pan of water. ICOM and Standard Horizon are two good brands. Both offer submersible radios powered by lithium-ion batteries like those used on cell phones. The advantage over NiCad battery–powered radios is in the ease in charging and topping off, which would ruin the battery life of a NiCad but have no ill effect on the lithium. Any marine-supply store or paddling shop will have an array of radios to choose from.

PFDs now generally come equipped with pockets that will hold a marine radio or have lash tabs for securing one. If you use a marine radio, have it on your person (i.e., in your PFD)—not in a deck bag or under your deck. And, please, tether it to your PFD or somewhere else so that you don't drop it overboard. The radios come in handy for weather reports and to communicate in emergencies, and they also let you contact commercial shipping and ferries in case you need to cross their channels or terminals. These commercial operators will appreciate this as kayakers make them nervous. A radio call by you will let them know you are responsible and aware of your surroundings.

Compass and Compass Mounts

You should have a compass with you, even if you don't plan to be far from the sight of land. A sudden fog or rain squall will quickly limit your sightlines. At such times your compass will be your only means of finding your way. Because you can't permanently mount a compass to a foldable as easily as you can to the deck of a rigid boat, the task is more complex. Luckily, foldable-kayak owners have a range of compasses and mounting methods to choose from.

Start your search by finding out what your folding-kayak manufacturer offers. Because its compass comes with its own device for mounting to your boat, choosing that brand will save you the hassle of improvising something. For example, the Silva 70UN is an excellent steering compass that you can also pull out of its holder to use as a hand-bearing compass. (You can also buy this excellent compass at marine supply stores.) Klepper sells various compass boards for using this compass on either single or double boats.

Some of the smaller marine compasses can be mounted to your deck with bungee cords. If you have D-rings around your cockpit area, attachment is a cinch. If not, you'll have to improvise. On some foldables with spraydecks, you may be able to permanently attach a light compass to the fabric by screwing it through to some backing material that will keep the compass in position and water out of the cockpit.

Anchors and Sea Anchors

Anchors and sea anchors are handy devices. In some situations, they become not only handy—but eminently necessary.

Don't get a heavy anchor, because you'll be lugging it around when traveling with your foldable. The type of light dinghy anchor found in marine shops will work well. Avoid any anchor with sharp ends that could poke at the fabric of your foldable. You could also improvise a utility anchor by filling a small stuff sack or mesh bag with rocks, but you'll have to remember to pick up the rocks before you shove off from shore.

Sea anchors have proved their worth in many circumstances by helping to maintain position when the wind is trying to push the boat back. During a rescue situation, deploying your sea anchor will help stabilize your boat by keeping it pointed into the wind, which is the least vulnerable position for reentry.

Many sea anchors are available, some quite cheaply at marine shops. Your best bet, however, is the more costly Drift Stopper made by Boulter of

Compass mount with a Silva 70UN compass.
(Michael Skott)

Earth. It works well in a kayak and has proved its durability. The Drift Stopper is easy to deploy and retrieve. Many hardshell kayakers use them to maintain their position in heavy winds. There are various ways to mount the Drift Stopper to your boat. With a large-cockpit foldable, the best way is to snake the sea anchor's holding line under your spraydeck and connect it to a rib. On Feathercrafts, loop the connecting line around the coaming.

Other Sail Rigs

Folding-kayak manufacturers usually list sails in their catalogs, as mentioned earlier. However, if you want a rig from the aftermarket that performs exceedingly well, look at what Balogh Sail Designs (BSD) has to offer.

BSD has become a supplier to hardshell manufacturers because of its reliable outrigger system. Known as BOSS, for Balogh Outrigger Stabilizing System, it allows the hardshells to be sailed upwind using the Balogh Batwing rig. Balogh also specializes in fitting the Batwing to foldable kayaks. It provides mounting hardware for all the major foldables that have open cockpits; i.e., Folbot, Klepper, and Nautiraid. BSD has also experimented with fitting the Batwing to Feathercrafts.

The Batwing is a very powerful sail that is

cambered like a windsurfer's sail using adjustable battens. The Batwing comes in various sizes to suit both single and double foldables. Its reefing zippers and snap-buckled straps allow you to decrease the sail area in a hurry if winds get too strong for the full sail.

Balogh also makes an excellent downwind sail called the Twins that is extremely stable because most of its power face lies low on the mast where it's least likely to unbalance your boat in a wayward gust. This sail rig looks like a child's kite, but upside down. You can double it over to make a triangular sail that can broad reach and almost beam reach.

Other Items

Every other sea-kayaking manual will tell you that you'll need a paddle float for your kayak. A paddle float is an inflatable bladder that you attach to one end of your paddle to use as an outrigger for getting back into your boat after a capsize. A paddle float is necessary with hardshells, which otherwise would be nearly impossible to reenter after a capsize, unless a second boat is positioned to stabilize the first. But because foldables are easier to reenter from the water, paddle floats are largely unnecessary for them. However, you may want to have one in case of extreme conditions.

You should have deck lines. This safety device allows you to grab onto your boat when you are in the water. A few foldables—some Feathercraft and Nautiraid models and the Klepper Quattro—come equipped with deck lines. If your boat doesn't, consider buying your own. While the decks of foldables give you more grabbing surface for hanging on than do sleek hardshells, you'll find that deck lines give you added insurance. Tie the line at one end or the other, loop it through the deck fitting at the opposite end, and then back to near your position in the cockpit area. This will give you something to hang onto while you disembark for landing.

Consider using a paddle leash. In a capsize, if you can hang onto either your boat or your paddle, you'll be able to retrieve the other. You can make your own or get one at a kayak shop, or you can even adapt something from the personal watercraft (PWC) world. PWCs have a leash with one end attaching to the driver's PFD and the other to the kill switch; if the driver falls off, the motor gets turned off. This type of leash is inexpensive and can be made to hold between your paddle and boat.

Other essential items are required by law. U.S. Coast Guard regulations (and those in many other countries as well) require that you have certain signaling devices such as flares, a horn or whistle, etc. Find out what is needed where you paddle.

In addition, it is smart to have some sort of light to make you visible if you paddle in the dark. At a minimum, you should have a just-in-case light with you at all times, even if your intention is to be back by noon. You never know if you may get ill or damage a paddle and then be stuck out on the water after nightfall. A number of companies, including ACR, Tektite, and Princeton Tec, make an assortment of flashlights that will work for this. What you are looking for is something that has a cone top that will provide a 360-degree light. If it is lightweight enough, you can put it on your hat or on the shoulder of your PFD. LED lights probably are the best since their bulbs will last nearly forever and are almost unbreakable. Plus, they will get fifty hours or more out of a set of batteries. For planned trips after dark, get a red and green light setup for your bow and a 360-degree light to place in back of you. Marine supply stores offer a split-lens red and green light for use in dinghies and rubber rafts; one company, Tektite, has an LED-system version with separate red- and green-lens flashlights.

Part Two

Handling Skills for Foldables

A folding kayak helps make you a better sea kayaker from the moment you step into one. Freed of worry about balance and stability, you are quickly on your way to becoming a proficient paddler. You can concentrate on developing the most important paddling technique of all—an efficient, sustainable forward stroke.

When the chips are down, a folding kayak enhances your efforts to weather rough conditions. Built-in seaworthiness magnifies the effectiveness of your repertoire of support and maneuvering strokes. If you're in situations over your head, these boats will often help see you through, as they have thousands of paddlers before you.

If catastrophe happens and you do capsize, folding kayaks greatly simplify the recovery process. They are exceptionally easy to reenter without the aid of other boats or the need for special devices.

This section of the book aims at making you a competent sea kayaker. It focuses not only on the single paddler but also a group generally overlooked in most manuals, those who venture forth in double kayaks. Paddling techniques, maneuvering strokes, and rescue routines are explained for both singles and doubles. This section will also help you in the lifelong process of becoming a savvy mariner, one who grasps that knowing how to avoid trouble is more important than knowing how to get out of it.

Paddling Techniques: The Forward Stroke and Other Essentials

Chapter Six

Learning to paddle a folding kayak involves goals and considerations that are very different from those needed to paddle a rigid boat. The gulf that exists between the two worlds is vast.

Other sea-kayaking manuals, which teach paddling skills exclusively for rigid kayaks, devote several chapters to the often-needed *defensive* paddling strokes for those boats. They go into elaborate descriptions of bracing strokes (high and low) that keep you from tipping, various ways of sculling to keep your rigid boat afloat on its side in severe conditions, and a number of variations of the Eskimo roll needed when you do capsize.

Although these instructions may be fascinating reading, they don't apply as much to a folding kayak because its first line of defense is its inherent stability and seaworthiness. You can't reliably roll a folding kayak as a real-life self-rescue method, or at least most people can't. The air sponsons along each side of a foldable tend to resist the action of an Eskimo roll, as does the basic width of these boats. (If you want to try to roll a foldable as an exercise, see the sidebar on page 135 for a couple of tips you might use.)

Because its wider beam positions you so far from the side of the boat, sculling is difficult beyond a certain angle. When you try to put a foldable on its side to scull, your body is higher than your paddle, which creates a precarious, plunging angle to the sculling motion. Bracing strokes, while useful to learn, are less applicable to a stable folding kayak. Besides, the bracing strokes you may want to use in a foldable are simpler.

It's too bad most manuals have you dedicate so much time to defensive strokes such as the Eskimo roll. While trying to perform these strokes correctly, you may get distracted from perfecting the most important stroke in sea kayaking, the forward stroke, the motion that gets you where you want to go. The forward stroke lies at the heart of sea kayaking and is one of its chief sources of pleasure. Being on the water in a foldable allows you to concentrate on the forward stroke without worrying about the arsenal of defensive moves required by a rigid kayak.

The forward stroke looks deceptively easy but has many subtleties that you'll also learn in this chapter. You'll learn the brace strokes you may find handy in a foldable, particularly a smaller one. And you'll learn how to use your paddle to make quick turns without a rudder. The strokes described below are meant to be used with single folding kayaks (that's a Feathercraft K1 in the photos in this chapter). Chapter 8 explains how to adjust them for doubles.

THE FORWARD STROKE

Anyone who looks at paddling as a chore, a necessary evil of venturing in a touring kayak, is missing one of sea kayaking's less obvious pleasures. The forward stroke is a form of enchantment. It involves fluid and powerful movements of the body that make you feel alive and that blend your landbound being smoothly with the watery element that makes up most of our planet. When you are proficient at the forward stroke, the miles and hours pass in an intoxicating trance of dancelike rhythm. A folding kayak is an especially good place to fall under this spell because you can concentrate on forward paddling with less concern for balancing your boat.

Not as Simple as It Seems

The forward stroke looks simple enough. You hold both hands out in front of you on the shaft of a two-bladed kayak paddle. Dip Blade A in the water and move it alongside you while swinging Blade B forward through the air. Then the process is repeated, only this time Blade B dips into the water and Blade A gets airborne.

Many novice paddlers do it just that way, without much thought or control of the process. After a short time on the water, they tire and are in pain. Though they may be getting a kick out of being afloat and communing with nature, they're not enjoying the paddling experience itself because they've failed to grasp the underlying complexity of the forward stroke.

Newcomers are not the only kayakers who, lured by the deceptively simple appearance of the forward stroke, overlook its intricacies. Many seasoned paddlers also miss the nuances, particularly those in folding kayaks. Since the boats are so simple to enter and take off in, it's easy to forget to develop basic skills, starting with the forward stroke. Paddlers may go along for years puttering through the motions but not really getting the power and enjoyment they might if they were to perfect the stroke.

A lot is happening in the forward stroke; it's not just muscling through the motions. Onlookers from the deck of a powerboat may laud what they think is your enormous upper-body strength making your boat move. Go ahead, bask in the macho image, but don't pump up those muscles. Relax them and put your mind into the stroke.

The description that follows dissects the forward stroke into its components and analyzes what is going on at each step of the movement. Even as you study the points, though, try to remember that the forward stroke takes place as much in your head as in your body. You have to be thinking it to get the most out of the technique.

Finding the Sweet Spot of Your Kayak and Paddle

"Sweet spot" is a term used in sports; for example, in discussing a baseball bat, golf club, or tennis racket. If you hit a ball with just the right spot on a bat, club, or racket, the ball will go farther or faster. The same is true when paddling. Every boat and paddle has a sweet spot that, if you can find it, will give you more glide and speed. Here are some ways of doing this.

Consider changing your paddle or trying different ones. There are some four elements in a kayaking sweet spot, the boat being just one of them. They are: the boat, you and your relative strength and finesse, your paddling skill technique, *and* your paddle. Nothing hurts finding and using a boat's sweet spot more than the wrong paddle.

Be extra careful in setting up your boat and seated position. With folding kayaks, there is a range of perfection in how you assemble them. If you want to find the sweet spot of your boat and paddle, then you have to make certain the boat is assembled with no flaws. It has to have the frame perfectly in the skin, the sponsons super-inflated and even, etc.

With some models, seats can wind up slightly off center in position; again, make certain your seat is perfectly aligned. Also think about the position of your foot pedals. You don't want the pedals too far forward; you need to have your knees bent some so you can push against the pedals to brace yourself in the boat in order to transfer power of your stroke to its forward motion. So make certain you are well fitted and well braced in the boat.

Always be conscious of what your boat is doing as you paddle, even when you're with other people. Sure, you are paddling for fun and may want to talk with fellow paddlers, but every so often you should take a few moments to think about your stroke. Observe how your stroke and stroke rate are in relation to what the other paddlers are doing.

Ask questions of yourself, such as: Am I getting more glide than they are with each stroke? How often are they placing their paddles in the water compared to me?

Plan to take some short paddling trips alone.

Do so specifically with the sole aim of concentrating on what is happening as you paddle stroke. You need an experimental mindset to observe your stroke and how it affects the boat's speed.

Find a place or conditions that may help you sense when you are hitting a sweet spot with your paddle and boat. A good start is to paddle with a favorable current. Its boost will give you a better sense of what is happening, at least when the boat is new, than if you are fighting wind or seas. Your stroke can be more relaxed and less choppy or strained. The current is taking you along, so you can concentrate on your stroke's form and how your boat is reacting to your paddling stroke.

Another criterion to consider in choosing a spot is to make certain you have some good reference points for judging what is happening with your boat. If you are out in the middle of a big bay, you won't necessarily know. But if you're paddling along a shoreline, say with lots of trees, you can start to see relative speed. A GPS also helps.

Exaggerate your stroke. Act almost like a melodramatic silent-screen actor emoting his or her role and perform the paddle stroke with a flourish. It isn't the way you normally would paddle, but by exaggerating you are emphasizing parts of the stroke, which leads to the next point.

Concentrate on each point of the paddle stroke. Think about such factors as how you are swinging the paddle, how the blade enters the water, your movement of the blade through the water, and its exit from the water. For a few strokes, think of just one of these aspects or other ones, such as how much pull or push you are making with the paddle shaft.

Constantly change the nature of your stroke. Do so, say, from fast cadence to slow, from more pull than push to more push than pull, more body rotation and less, and flexed elbows to locked elbows. Somewhere in such changes, you will be able to isolate the sweet spots.

One of the thoughts that should be going through your mind is that, during the forward stroke, your blade has very little longitudinal movement in the water. Instead, you are attempting to use your whole paddle to pry your boat forward through the water. The key to a good forward stroke is enhancing whatever leveraging force you can apply to that prying effort.

Your Physical Components

Many parts of your body come into play during the stroke. Here's what each part should be doing to get the most sustained and powerful output from paddling a foldable boat.

Torso or trunk. Most manuals start off by talking about your hands and arms, but the true center and most critical component is your trunk. Your torso should be relaxed, loose enough to rotate freely with each stroke.

You should be thrusting one shoulder ahead into the *push* part of the stroke, swinging from the hip. It's more like throwing a punch than a swimming motion. Your other shoulder should be moving back, leading through the *pull* part of the stroke. Your shoulders should never remain perpendicular to the line of travel of the kayak. They should be pivoting around an imaginary rod running down through the center of your head to your seat.

Always paddle from your trunk, because your biggest muscles—lower back, shoulders, hips, and stomach—are located here. These big muscles are less likely to fatigue than your arms and forearms. Arnold Schwarzenegger would give out before Woody Allen if he was using just his arms and Woody was putting his full body into each paddle stroke.

Since the deck of a foldable is usually higher than that of a rigid boat, more of the paddler's body resides below the cockpit rim. Therefore, foldable paddlers are less prone to using their full bodies, instead relying heavily on arm movement.

Don't forget body rotation in your paddling movements.

Legs. These too should figure decisively into the stroke. Your legs should be flexing and relaxing with each stroke. To use your legs properly you must brace or press your feet against some support.

You should be pushing or pressing on the foot *opposite* the shoulder that is pushing the airborne blade. This bracing action by the foot locks your body in position to deliver all the power of the stroke to the forward movement of the boat. Avoid thinking of this foot action as pressing on the same side as the blade being pulled through the water. That thought could make you focus too much on pulling the paddle and not enough on the upper-body push on the paddle shaft. Diagonal thinking is better than linear thinking in this case.

Feathercrafts have adjustable foot pedals to press against, even without using a rudder. Most other folding kayaks do not. It is important that your feet be pushing against some rib, and your knees should be bent or flexed, not straightened out fully. If, while your knees are bent, your feet don't rest on a rib, you should talk with your dealer. He or she may already have a device that fits the purpose or could help you improvise something. Or look at some of the suggestions in chapter 15, Modifying Your Foldable.

Hands. Keep your hands relaxed at all times, except possibly when heavy winds threaten to rip your paddle from your grip. Use a flat palm to push the shaft on the side cutting through the air, and keep your fingers open as if you wanted someone behind you to count them. Rest the shaft in the cupped fingers of the other hand to pull the blade that's going through the water. Don't have all your fingers of either hand tightly wrapped around the shaft. At most, let your thumb crook around the shaft.

A death-grip on the paddle tires the muscles

of the forearm and biceps. Hand relaxation is a bit easier in a folding kayak since you don't need to keep as tightly gripped for possible bracing as you would in a hardshell.

You should also keep your hand, wrist, and forearm in a fairly flat plane. Avoid cocking your wrist too far back at an acute angle. Look at it this way: a watch on that wrist should be more visible to God than to a paddler behind you.

Arms. Many people try to paddle with their arms bent throughout the paddling motion. That's a waste of your muscles and will lead to fatigue and possibly injury.

Your pulling arm should actually be fairly straight for moving the blade that is in the water. Pull the paddle by using your rotating shoulder and trunk to move the straight arm backward. By keeping the arm straight with the elbow almost locked, you make effective use of muscles in your stomach, back, and shoulder. The straightened arm acts like a lever to transmit the power of these strong muscles to the pulling motion. The straight arm also discourages heavy dependence on the weaker arm muscles for power. Rely on your arm's bone structure more than its muscles.

Your pushing arm obviously starts from a bent position, but you should straighten it out as you move the upper blade through the air. Then let the upper shoulder continue to push the extended, straightened-out arm as far as is comfortable. Again, as in the pulling process, the straightened arm transmits the power of your back and shoulder through bone structure while making only minimal use of arm muscles.

The Control Center

Your head is the control center, the computer that tells all the physical components what they should be doing at every moment. Your head should be making minute adjustments throughout your hours on the water, and it should be keeping some factors constant. You don't have to

be thinking about every step all the time, but do think them through enough so that you can put everything on automatic pilot.

You'll be adjusting the physical components in two ways. One, obviously, will be accounting for changing winds and sea conditions to keep your boat moving smoothly. You'll also be making small changes to shift the workload among all the muscles in your body. Sometimes, for example, you'll be using your legs strongly for a few minutes to reduce the load on your torso. Or you may let your arm muscles do the work for a two-minute burst in order to rest other parts of your body.

The factors to keep constant are elements of the stroke that give good prying grip in the water to move the boat ahead.

Here are some of the principal things your brain will be monitoring and fine-tuning.

The push and pull phases. You may have picked up from some instructor or manual the need to be doing both pushing and pulling at the same time. They usually suggest some fixed amount of effort for the push and so much for the pull, such as 35 percent push, 65 percent pull. Don't lock yourself into any static split of effort.

You should be making constant adjustment between pull and push. Sometimes the push will be 80 percent, other times the pull will be 80 percent. See what feels good, stick with that for a while, and then adjust the split so you don't fatigue any particular muscle group. Play with the tuning knobs feeding those push-pull instructions to your body, just as you might adjust the sound balance on your stereo tuner.

Even within each part of the stroke, do some monitoring and adjusting. For example, in the push phase, stretch out your arm a bit farther than normal for a few strokes. Or for a few moments don't rotate your torso quite as much as you've been doing.

You may gain some mastery by thinking solely of either the pushing or the pulling during your stroke. For example, concentrate for a few dozen strokes on just pushing the blade through the air and ignore the pull. You'll be pulling anyway to some degree. This focus will sharpen the powerful pushing phases. Then think for a few minutes of just the pull. Switching your tuner will help you get a feel for the right balance for prevailing conditions. If you're paddling into the wind, which is covered in greater detail in chapter 7, you may find that a greater proportion of push works better than a fifty-fifty balance. The ratio should never be constant for any length of time.

Fluid versus explosive movements. Some manuals tell you to be smooth and fluid in your motion. True, your motions should be fluid, but they also should be explosive. Both can exist in the same plane, and you should be training your body to do both.

Overall, you should have fluid movement in all parts of the forward stroke. Fluid motion is easy on the muscles, but explosive motion is easy on the muscles, too. It gives them rest during nonexplosive stages.

As your blade gets set in the water and your leverage is right, as explained below, you should move the paddle through with an explosive burst of power. Then relax all your muscles as you get set to place the other blade smoothly into the water. Meanwhile your muscles begin coiling up for their next burst of explosive power. You can vary how explosive you want these bursts to be. It's a good idea to keep power bursts short and to concentrate on staying relaxed between them. You can also go long periods without power bursts. But do make certain to put some bursts into your stroke.

Explosive power with rest periods as the muscles wind up is similar to what elite marathon runners and long-distance cross-country skiers do. The marathoner's foot hits the pavement with an explosive burst and takes off; the shoe seems hardly to touch the ground as the body floats relaxed to the next explosive foot plant. Cross-country skiers explode off each split-second planting of their skis with split-second rests in between.

Zone of power application. Some paddlers get confused about this topic probably because they are thinking of arm muscles instead of full trunk. The conventional wisdom says don't apply power right away as the blade enters water and don't continue power beyond the point where the blade is back parallel to your hip. However, torso rotation actually gives you a surprisingly wider zone than this.

If you have rotated your on-side shoulder forward with the blade, you have plenty of leverage to start applying considerable power as the blade dips into the water. If you were using just your arms to paddle, you couldn't.

The same is true for knowing when to let off the power. If your body has rotated back and the arm pushing the blade through the air is fully extending with the full force of your torso, then you can continue power to a point where the in-water blade is just going behind the line of your seat. At that point, your effort will be tapering off and your blade knifing out of the water. Your real cue to turning off power is not when the blade is parallel to you but rather when the pulling hand is coming almost parallel to your torso.

Think of this in degrees. As the blade hits the water, apply force at a rate equal to 80 or 90 percent of what you plan to be doing during that stroke. In the middle of the zone—say, from the point the paddle is catching well in the water—go to 100 percent of the effort you plan. Then as your hand gets in the vicinity of your seat, taper off to 50 or 75 percent of that effort as you bring the blade out of the water just behind your seat.

Obviously, these figures are too precise to monitor or control in real-life paddling. They're just intended to illustrate the varying levels of exertion during the stroke, starting with pretty close to full effort right away and tapering off later than usually prescribed.

Placement of blade in the water. The blade should be placed as far forward as you can comfortably rotate your torso and extend your arm out straight on that side. With the shaft parallel to the water's surface, dip the blade vertically down into the water. The blade should make little or no noise as it enters. This is one clue that you are placing it correctly.

Placement should also be as close to the boat as possible, but be careful not to bang the deck fabric or hull. Your best leverage is close to the boat where it takes full advantage of your torso rotation. You may, however, want to place the blade a bit farther out at times to work your muscles a little differently.

Hand placement on the paddle. Instruction manuals too often get hung up on precise measurements for where the hands should rest on the shaft. Their advice is that they should be shoulder-width apart. It's OK to start your first few strokes from that position, but be ready to change it often.

Hand placement is part of your throttle. Wider spacing between the hands can give you more power, but it leads to a slower cadence. Closer placement increases your paddle pace but is tiring. Play between the two extremes, even at the extremes, for a few minutes at a time. During the course of the day, your hands should be all over your paddle shaft.

Some paddles have special areas on the shaft designed for your hand grip, and some even include finger grooves. These paddles might serve for a short sprint, but if you're paddling a touring kayak, they wouldn't allow you to comfortably run your hands to other areas on the shaft whenever you need to adjust for speed and prevailing conditions.

Pivot point of the paddle. The pivot point should generally remain constant. To find this point, hang your arms at your sides and bend your elbows until your forearms are horizontal. Notice where this puts your hands. The point around which you should be rotating your paddle is about 8 to 10 inches in front of where your hands ended up. If you try to paddle with your hands and arms tucked too close to your body, your torso muscles will not wind and unwind fully into the stroke. If your hands are too far ahead of you, you'll waste energy and lose some of the leverage you need for a good forward stroke. Also, never let your hands cross over beyond the center line of your cockpit. This too wastes your energy and decreases your leverage.

Height of the airborne part of the paddle. Much of this control depends on the width of your boat, the height of the coaming, and the length of the paddle. Generally though, remind yourself to keep the airborne blade as low as you can, even if this means having the in-water blade farther from the side of the boat. You're definitely not going to get much power out of the pushing side of your body if its hand is thrusting out above the level of your nose.

Blade angle and depth. Your thinking should be sharp on these crucial considerations. The blade should be held as vertical as possible throughout the stroke. Be careful not to change the angle as you take the paddle out of the water. If you do, you'll scoop up water and tire your muscles.

The depth of the blade in the water should be shallow. None of the shaft should go under, just the blade. Digging the paddle in too deeply is hard on your body because it takes more effort. It also complicates knifing the blade out of the water at the end of the stroke.

There is an exception to this vertical angle and shallow depth of the blade. If you're feeling a bit unstable in beam seas or wind, you may want to skim the blade through the water at a different angle and to lead with the top edge. This semi-bracing stroke is more often performed

Forward stroke—
full extension.

Forward stroke—
straightened arms.

Forward stroke—
finishing up.

in hardshells and seldom needed in foldables. Bracing strokes are discussed in more detail later in this chapter.

Putting It Together

Let's go through a full forward-stroke cycle to see how you control the physical components so that they work together as a sustained, powerful lever for prying your boat forward. A good place to start is just where Blade A is about to enter the water.

Side B is coiled up to put power into pushing airborne Blade B as the torso completes its backward rotation on Side B. The foot on Side A begins to push on a crossrib or foot brace as Blade A enters the water to act as a levering point to diagonally support Side B's pushing effort and to directly counterbalance Side A's pulling effort.

Side B's shoulder begins to rotate forward with power as Side B's arm quickly straightens out ahead at a slightly lifting angle. Side B's open hand pushes the paddle, with the shaft resting on the fleshy part at the base of the fingers. The wrist stays fairly horizontal; i.e., barely bent. Side B's straight arm and uncoiling shoulder push ahead until its hand comes to the centerline of the boat.

While Side B is going through its push motions, Side A simultaneously pulls on Blade A with backward rotation of the torso and straight arm with little or no bend in the elbow. Side A's hand pulls the paddle with fingers loosely cupped over the shaft, wrist flat and horizontal. As this hand comes almost abreast of the torso, Side A's arm bends at the elbow to lift Blade A out of the water.

Side A is now coiled back for its turn to push on the airborne end of the paddle. The foot on Side B pushes on a crossrib or foot brace as Blade B enters the water, repeating the process.

This is a powerful forward stroke that you can keep up all day. Pay attention to torso and shoulder rotation, and keep arms straight and hands loose. Follow all the earlier suggestions on form such as blade angle and depth, height of paddle on the side away from the water, etc. Also make certain to fine-tune such variables as how much push and pull, and where your hands rest on the paddle.

TURNING STROKES

You'll have to turn your kayak from time to time, and you may need to apply the brakes hard every once in a while.

You could turn simply by paddling only on one side for a number of strokes, or you could just put twice as much effort on one side. But these are rather inappropriate methods of turning.

The strongest turns generally involve some boat lean and laying your body out to one side over your paddle. Your foldable's tremendous stability allows you to lean out more aggressively than you'd want to risk in a rigid boat. Many folding kayakers resist doing this, but once you've learned the turning strokes with sharp lean, you'll see how crazy it is to think folding kayaks lack performance.

Even if you have a rudder, you should learn to turn without it. Rudders depend on cables, yokes, pins, hooks, and other mechanical devices that have a way of giving out when you most need them.

The basic turns we'll look at are described as though you were using a single folding kayak, but they apply to doubles as well. (More details about how to turn a double folding kayak appear in chapter 8, along with variations for their specific needs.)

As you master these strokes, you'll also be developing confidence for learning the basic brace strokes that work well in a foldable. Braces and how to apply them are detailed later in this chapter.

Forward Sweep Turn

You'll use this turning stroke constantly. It works for turning while on the move and for coming

FEATHERING MAY HAVE THE EDGE IN A FOLDABLE

Early on, you'll have to make a choice between feathering your paddle or using it unfeathered. This decision is generally a toss-up, but feathering may actually have the edge when you're paddling a foldable.

A feathered paddle has its blades roughly at right angles to each other, and you use your control hand to turn each blade for proper entry into the water. The shaft rotates freely in the noncontrol hand. Whether you're right-handed or not, feathered paddles are generally right-hand controlled, only because you seldom can find paddles that make provision for feathering with left-hand control.

Unfeathered paddles have the blades in line with each other. You use each hand to turn the blades to the correct entry angle.

Supposedly, feathering is rough on the forearm and wrist on your control-hand side. That's why some people unfeather their paddles. However, the damage that comes with feathering is more the result of two different factors, not overuse of the control hand.

One, the feathering angle could be too great. You can avoid arm injury if the feather angle is less than 90 degrees. More paddles now come with feathering of 80 degrees or less. This reduces how much you have to cock back your control hand to get the opposite blade into the correct water-entry angle.

Two, incorrect paddling skills cause stress. If you learn good paddling technique as described in this chapter, you're not likely to hurt yourself, even when paddling long distances. Proper balance of the elements of the forward stroke and relaxing both hands will reduce stress on the control hand and forearm.

Feathering may be your best bet for paddling a folding kayak because a foldable heightens feathering's key advantage, and at the same time it reduces your need for the benefit of unfeathering. Even foes of feathering recognize that a feathered paddle gives an advantage to any kayak paddling into the wind. The feathered blade running through the air has its edge forward to slice through the wind's resistance. Feathering in these conditions is more efficient. Unfeathered paddling into the wind is harder because the broad side of the upper blade is being pushed through the wind. Because folding kayaks require longer paddles and wider and higher arcs, unfeathering is even tougher.

In hardshells, feathered blades increase the risk of a capsize in heavy crosswinds because the wind can catch the broad side of the blade as it swings through the air. Unfeathered paddles offer less surface area for crosswinds to bite on, but since foldables are inherently more stable than rigid boats, there is less risk of being upended by crosswinds if feathering.

about when you're standing still. (See discussion below.) Your turning radius will vary with how much you're willing to lean your boat and put your body over your paddle in the water.

If you're moving, here's how to get into the sweep turn from your normal forward stroke. As you prepare to dip the blade on the side opposite the direction you want to go, lean your boat slightly on that side. Instead of placing the blade close to the boat, dip it farther away and not so far forward as you normally would. Turn the blade so that the top edge leads the motion through the water in a slight skimming angle close to the surface.

Lean for a second on that skimming blade and sweep out to the side with your paddle rather than straight back as you would with the forward stroke. As the blade approaches a point in line with your seat, push off the blade as your hip and lower body level out the boat beneath you. As in the forward stroke, use your torso rotation and other key elements to power you around.

As you complete the sweep on one side, continue with your normal forward stroke on the other side. Then if you need to turn more, repeat the sweep stroke again. This will keep up your momentum and forward motion. The sweep stroke is part of the forward-stroke pattern, and you won't miss a beat.

Few folding kayaks offer a tight enough fit for you to put your boat on its side with just hip movement and raising the knee on the side you're turning toward, which is the way it's done in tight-fitting rigid kayaks.

But you can take advantage of the tremendous final stability a foldable offers to accomplish almost the same effect. What you wind up doing is not advisable for rigid boats but is perfectly safe in a foldable: Lean with your upper body so that its center of gravity is close to the side of the boat. Inherent stability in a folding kayak will keep you from capsizing so long as you don't hold that position for more than a second.

Before achieving the ideal sweep turn described above, you may want to begin by just sweeping the paddle out beyond the normal forward stroke arc, thus leaving the boat and your body upright and the blade vertical. This will turn you, but it takes strength. Next, sweep the blade out through the arc, but with the top of the blade as the leading edge. Also, lean a bit on the paddle shaft. You'll find that the skimming blade gives a good amount of support. Keep practicing, and eventually get the boat onto its sponson for a second or two as you sweep out with the angled blade.

You should be getting the feel for your boat, a sense of body lean, and a good idea how much support a shallow-angled blade gives you. Play with the angle between vertical (without leaning on the blade!) and 45 degrees off horizontal. You'll find an angle that suits your body size, your foldable, and your paddle's length and blade shape.

This turn works; by putting the boat slightly on its side, you raise the ends and change the effective keel line of the boat from the centerline to a point higher up on the curved side of the boat.

Forward sweep turn.

This temporarily gives you a "new" rockered keel line that helps the boat turn swiftly. Also, by leaning out on the paddle, you widen the sweeping arc and increase the power it gives the turning maneuver.

Stern Rudder Stroke

The sweep turn described above takes lots of room, so it's good for open water, and it won't cost you momentum. The stern rudder stroke described below will turn your foldable more quickly and securely, but you'll lose speed.

The stern rudder stroke turn is simple. You place your blade into the water behind you, toward the stern on the side you wish to turn toward. Have the blade perpendicular to the line of travel and fairly vertical. The power face should be toward the back or toward your kayak. Hold on hard to the shaft, and you'll turn quickly. Continue it long enough, and it'll stop your kayak.

Because the stern rudder stroke slows you down, you generally use it in moving water such as a following sea or wake from a passing vessel. If moving water is threatening to send you sideways, this stroke actually is your rudder to keep you going straight. In such conditions, the stern rudder stroke acts as a security blanket to settle you and

your boat down. (There's more on handling open-water conditions in chapter 7.)

Reverse Sweep Turn

The reverse sweep turn is like the sweep turn except that you sweep the blade from the rear forward. It will turn you in a hurry and with force, faster than the forward sweep can. But, unlike the forward sweep, the reverse sweep will tend to slow you down.

The reverse sweep looks very much like the stern rudder stroke at the start, but it has two differences. In the stern rudder stroke, the paddle is held fairly static with just some adjustments in the blade angle, and the reverse sweep starts farther out from the side of the boat.

The reverse sweep turn is also similar to the forward sweep in two aspects. In the reverse sweep, the blade sweeps forward, similar to the way the forward sweep stroke moves the blade back. And you also lean on the paddle shaft somewhat and rotate your torso.

When making the reverse sweep turn, keep the power face of the blade pointing back. Fine-tune the angle of the blade—somewhere between vertical in the water to sweeping at an angle—as the top edge of the blade leads the motion. This

Reverse sweep turn.

technique works well in a folding kayak to get you turned around fast.

Braking

To avoid hitting something ahead of you, you can use the turning strokes described above in some combination that will take you to one side, or you can apply the brakes. The best braking stroke requires severe reverse sweeps applied quickly on both sides.

Dig the paddle into the water about 45 degrees behind you with the blade out about 2 feet from the side of the boat. Slap its nonpower side down hard on the water and dig it in with a powerful reverse sweep, with the shaft pressing into your stomach for inboard support. Let up on the braking action immediately and quickly repeat the same forceful action on the other side. You should be able to do a full braking motion to two sides in less than a second and a half each. When you master this, you can come to an abrupt stop from full speed within about four strokes.

MANEUVERING WHEN NOT IN MOTION

Here are the best methods to get your single kayak moving from a complete standstill. These require some of the turning strokes described above.

Turning Completely About

To turn in the opposite direction from which you are facing, simply combine reverse and forward sweeps on opposite sides of the boat. For example, do a forward sweep on the right side once, then a reverse sweep on the left. Do that a few times and you'll turn 180 degrees, especially if you aggressively lean forward and out on the forward sweep strokes and stretch back and out for the reverse strokes.

Backing Up

In effect, you do reverse sweeps on both sides. It pays to twist around your torso, not only for power but also to take a glance at where you're going as you back up. Do not change the direction your blade is facing; keep it just as you would while paddling forward—its power face facing back. Some people turn their blades around on the mistaken notion that they can't paddle with the back of the blade. Actually, you get more than enough power from using the "wrong" side of the blade. More important, you'll be ready to move ahead quickly if you find yourself backing into any obstacle. If you had to stop to reverse the blade face, you might not be able to get out of the way fast enough.

Going Sideways

When coming alongside another boat or pulling up to a dock, you'll need to know how to make your foldable go sideways.

To maneuver sideways or broadside, you must use the draw stroke. First, turn your body toward the side you wish to move. Raise your paddle until the blade is out about 3 feet from amidships, with the power face toward you. Lean out a bit and have the blade enter at about 45 degrees.

Now, pry the blade toward you by pushing on the shaft with your upper hand and pulling with your lower hand. Don't let the blade come up to the side of the boat. Instead, about a foot from you, cut the blade out of the water, toward the stern, and then keep repeating this draw stroke until you get where you want to be.

BRACING

Bracing, sculling, and Eskimo rolling are required skills when venturing out in a rigid kayak, because these tricks of the trade counteract the underlying instability of most hardshell kayaks, especially when sea conditions worsen. Folding kayaks, while not untippable, are so stable and seaworthy that you may never have to use these defensive strokes. In fact, you'll find that when conditions have rigid-kayak paddlers low bracing and modifying their forward strokes into semibraces just to maintain their balance, you can confidently put down your paddle to eat lunch. Still, learning the basics of a few defensive strokes is worthwhile, just in case you ever need to add to the inherent stability of your foldable.

The problem is that it's a little difficult to put many folding kayaks on their sides in order to carry out high bracing strokes and sculling movements. Air sponsons resist the sideways motion, and the final stability is so strong that a folding kayak being tipped drastically to one side will often pop back up as if righted by some invisible hand. Even if you can get the boat on its side, the greater width of a foldable gets in the way of exercising some of the strokes.

Advanced high-brace sculling for extreme conditions depends on having your body stretched out at the water's surface with support from your paddle, which is sculling at a shallow angle to the water. In a wide, buoyant foldable, your body's position is significantly higher than your sculling blade, so the resulting angle lends little or no support to your body—and may plunge you in.

The Low Brace and Folding Kayaks

The low brace is a paddle stroke that uses the back of the blade, the nonpower side, to give you support to recover from a potential capsize.

Here's the basic movement. Hold the paddle shaft low, your hands positioned at the normal forward-stroke rest position, and then push down on the nonpower face directly out to your side. Water is dense enough for you to lean strongly on the blade at least momentarily and, with some variations, have sustained support.

The low brace differs from the more advanced high brace in its hand and arm positions and in which side of the blade provides the support. In the low brace, your arms are in front of you (or to one side as you lean on the shaft) and generally held low. Your wrists are horizontal and facing down. In the high brace your arms are held closer to your body, generally up about chest height or slightly higher. Your wrists are turned back to vertical or near vertical. For the high brace, the power face is down, unlike the low brace, in which it is up.

The high brace is preferred by rigid kayakers in extreme situations. It gives greater support than the low brace and allows more radical lean, even to the point of lying prone in the water on your moving paddle, if you are one of the few who get to that expert level.

The low brace is almost as effective in a folding kayak as a high one for rigid boats, thanks to the foldable's greater stability and resistance to capsizing. Those characteristics also allow you to push low bracing beyond the limits it has in rigid boats. Looked at another way, a folding kayak already comes equipped with the stability that you can only achieve in a rigid boat through low bracing strokes without you doing a thing. Add low bracing to a foldable, and you achieve a level of stability that you can only get in a rigid boat through high bracing techniques.

The only place you may need—and can work—a high brace effectively in a folding kayak is in surfing conditions with waves higher than 3 feet. And that brace would be such a modified version that, in effect, it would be a low-high brace. It's used so rarely in folding kayaks that it will be covered in chapter 7, which covers operating skills.

Practical Low Bracing Techniques

Below, in ascending order of difficulty and support, are the low bracing techniques that work well in foldables and take advantage of their inherent stability. The strokes include a turn stroke you may find handy that relies on a low brace for support.

Slap brace. The low slap brace is a quick-recovery technique that is often used to steady rigid boats. Since a foldable is steadier to begin with, you'll seldom need it. But if you do resort to a slap brace, it'll be doubly effective, reinforcing the boat's natural tendency to pop back up from extreme tipping angles. This pop-back tendency acts almost like the hip snap used as part of any brace in a rigid kayak.

You could use the slap brace if you were suddenly jarred over to one side. To begin it, you reach out in a lean with the paddle, then slap the nonpower side down hard on the water and push off from the rebound created by the water's resistance to the impact of the blade. To gain the most effect, your outer arm is held straight and your inboard hand is kept low. This angle assures a flat slap on the water, so there's very little danger that the blade will plunge in. The slap brace gives you, at most, about a second of support before the blade sinks, unless your boat is on the move.

To use it effectively, the slap brace should become second nature to you. Practice it on every outing, even in calm conditions, and on both sides of your foldable. It will help you develop the instinct to use paddle support to bring your foldable back from extreme tipping angles. The normal instinct for folding kayakers is just to right their boats by throwing their weight to the side opposite the potential capsize, something you can usually get away with only in a foldable. The slap brace is much more effective and almost guaranteed to get you back from extreme heeled-over angles.

Sweep low brace. Rigid kayak paddlers normally need more than the second of support afforded by the slap brace described above, so they depend on the following technique.

Low slap brace.

Sweep the flat blade along the water's surface in a small arc, starting with the blade out to one side at a point a few feet behind you. Then sweep the flat blade forward with the leading edge slightly up. The moving blade planes on the surface, giving enough support that you can lean on it without capsizing. When you have the blade about parallel to the seat, push up on it the way you would in a slap brace.

Since your foldable kayak gives you a far more stable platform from which to work the sweep, you can do the same sweep low brace with less of an arc and with greater lean, if you wish. Make certain to keep the paddle shaft as flat as you can, because, with the greater width and buoyancy of the air sponsons, your leaning position in your cockpit is higher than it would be in a rigid kayak. Your paddle blade may tend to plunge in if the shaft is at an acute angle to the water.

Sculling low brace. This is a hybrid brace. Sculling is generally considered something you do off the high brace, not the low brace. But sculling in folding kayaks is best done from the low-brace position because a high brace might tend to dig the blade into the water.

Low sculling brace.

direction, the leading edge of the paddle should be slightly raised. Do not run it absolutely flat.

Bear down on the paddle shaft as you go through the sweeping or sculling arc. The moving paddle will support your weight. Keep your body as low as you can and your arms as far down as possible.

Telemark low brace turn. This low brace produces an elegant, fast turn when you're on the move, and it has all the grace of the ski turn after which it is named. You can turn to point almost directly back in the direction you came from. It looks very impressive and gives you a nice way to come up sideways to a landing spot. It works very well in a folding kayak because the sponsons lend stability throughout the turn and their round sides slip around smoothly with little drag.

Start by holding your paddle in the normal low-brace position. Reach out alongside you with your outstretched arm straight and the paddle low in the other hand. With the power side up, sweep the paddle back through a 3- to 4-foot arc that starts slightly in front of your body. Then, in a continuous motion, sweep the blade forward again to the start position. Keep doing this at a steady, unhurried pace. As you sweep in either

To begin executing the telemark low brace turn, you should already be moving with a current or paddling hard to build up some steam. Lay out a low brace on the side you wish to turn toward, and have the blade about 45 degrees behind you, with its leading edge raised as in the sculling sweep motion. Water pressure under the back of the slightly angled blade will give you enormous support. The more aggressively you

Telemark turn.

lean on the skimming paddle, the faster and sharper you will turn. You should also be placing the boat on its air sponson on that side to get more rocker in the hull for the turn.

As you come around, your boat will slow down. You can continue the turn by finishing with a sweep of your paddle toward the bow as you level out the boat.

Practicing Braces

To get a feel for the fundamental movement, first practice the low brace in shallow water, about a foot or so deep; i.e., enough to float the boat. If you're not doing it right, you can at least push yourself back up when your paddle touches the bottom. This practical experience will teach you just how far on its side your foldable can go before it finally goes completely over.

The slap brace should be firm, but it shouldn't sound as if someone has belly-flopped off a high diving board. Keep leaning the boat farther over each time before you slap brace.

You'll notice that it's harder to push off the paddle brace if you're keeping your body erect or trying to lead the recovery with your upper body and head. Lead with your lower body, and keep your head down and trailing your body as you right. This way, you're letting the boat level off and bring you up with it.

Doing the exercises first in shallow water will encourage you to be more daring in leaning your body out and in stretching farther to your side with the outbound blade. After you gain confidence in how far you can get the boat over and still pop back, you'll be ready to do this maneuver in deeper water.

Operating Skills: From Launch Site to Open Water and Back

Chapter Seven

Some people think folding kayaks come with "Handle with Care" stickers plastered all over them and that they'll self-destruct on the first rocky beach or splintery dock. They think folding kayaks are fair-weather friends, not up to the performance required in heavy seas and winds. Both these impressions are so false that they'd be laughable—if it weren't for the fact that many paddlers believe them and, therefore, miss getting into a breed of vessel that's innately one with the open sea, that could give them decades of hardy service without kid-glove care.

Landing or launching a folding sea kayak is pretty much the same process you'd use for a rigid sea kayak, but with a big exception—you can get in and out of a foldable much more easily. You'll appreciate that characteristic difference when you try to land alongside a high dock or on a beach that's being slapped by the massive wake of a passing tugboat-barge combo. If you treat your foldable's skin as you would the hull of a fiberglass kayak, with perhaps a bit more care, you'll be able to enjoy all of its thirty-year life expectancy.

Here's some sound advice for handling your foldable in launching and landing and for dealing with most conditions you're likely to meet in open water and coastal areas. These techniques are aimed at single folding kayaks, but they basically apply to doubles as well. Chapter 8 describes the specific ways you use these techniques when paddling a double folding kayak.

LAUNCHING AND LANDING

One of the first things you'll notice about launching a folding kayak is just how easy it is—you just step in. There's nothing precarious about landing, either: You just step out. Here's exactly how it works under launching and landing conditions that range from the easiest to the toughest.

Calm Beaches and Shorelines

If you were using a rigid kayak even under such benign conditions, you'd first have to learn how to use your paddle to stabilize your boat to avoid an embarrassing spill a foot offshore. Fortunately, you don't have to use this technique for a foldable, except under certain circumstances.

This method, you'll note, is hard on paddles and occasionally leads to a chipped blade, broken shaft, or both. Place the shaft behind your seat at a right angle to the boat and rest one blade on shore or in shallow water. Grab the braced shaft and, with your weight on it, use the paddle to support you as you climb into your tippy rigid kayak.

To launch a foldable from a shore or beach, you don't need to do anything with your paddle, as you see rigid kayakers doing. Simply place your foldable in water that's deep enough for it to float with your body weight aboard and step in. The boat can be parallel to shore or pointing out, whichever is easier at the time.

Landing is the same process, but reversed. Step out with the boat just at the water's edge. You don't ram the bow on shore, as in a fiberglass boat.

There are exceptions. When you first get one of the narrower mini-foldables, you may want to use the braced-paddle entry method described below. This is what rigid kayakers must do every time they climb in, even in calm conditions.

PUSH-OFF START

The push-off start in a foldable isn't hard to learn. In effect, it looks like you just push your boat alongside of you and, while it's still moving, jump in. You could never do this in a rigid boat, but it's handy for launching a folding kayak in anything from a dead calm to foamy water stirred up by light waves. Learn it and practice it in calm conditions.

Here's how you do it. Start by leaning over your boat in shallow water with one hand on each side of the coaming just about a foot ahead of the backrest of your seat. You'll be balancing yourself on your hands and arms, so make certain you have a good grip and the position feels secure. The far-side hand should also be grasping your paddle, which is laid along the opposite side of the boat. Push your boat forward and, while it's moving, throw your weight onto your hands and—suspending yourself over the cockpit opening—swing both legs in. Pivot your body in. You may first want to just see if you can vault into your boat from this position while it's standing still.

The movement is similar to the way you push a bike ahead with two hands on the handlebars and throw one leg over the bike as you get on. The secret is to hunch over your boat and keep your body as low as you can, allowing just enough clearance to swing your legs into your moving boat.

As you practice this moving start, you'll find that entering from one side may feel better than the other. It's all right to develop such a "sweet side" for this maneuver; calm or foamy-water conditions aren't likely to dictate that you be able to perform it equally well from either side.

Lay the paddle's shaft behind your seat at a right angle to the boat and rest one blade down in the shallow water. Grab the shaft, put your weight on it, and use the shaft to support you as you climb in.

But the odds are that once you get used to the balance of your new boat, you'll hardly ever need to use a braced paddle for launching or landing. In any of the foldables, you might want to use a bracing if a choppy wake is slapping the shoreline. Even if you do, you don't have to put potentially damaging weight on the paddle while using it as an entry support. Just having the paddle resting in the braced position will suffice for entering your foldable.

High and Low Docks

Docks keep your feet dry but are trickier to handle because any kayak tends to move out and away from the dock as you enter and lower your feet into it.

The open cockpits of Folbots, Kleppers, and Nautiraids are easier to get into than Feathercrafts, but if you have your spraydeck attached to any open-cockpit foldables, they'll be a little harder to enter as well.

Lower your boat into the water carefully so it won't drift away, and hang on to the coaming or a line. Then, here's what you do, depending on dock height.

Low docks. If the top of the dock is less than about 2 feet above the water's surface, first sit down on the edge of the dock, then place your feet in the boat forward of your kayak seat. Twist your body onto one buttock on the dock with your weight on your arms and lower yourself in. Keep your weight off your feet as much as you can during the process so you don't push the boat out from under you by your entry movement.

When landing at a low dock, reverse the process. Get a grip on the dock's edge first. Once your arms are on the dock and supporting your weight, lift yourself out of your seat and get up into a seated position on the dock. Your feet are in the boat, keeping it from drifting away. Lean over to get a grip on the boat and take your feet out.

High docks. The process is similar to that for low docks—only harder. It requires agility, upper-arm strength, confidence, *and* commitment.

Here are several things to remember before starting. If you have the boat tied off, make sure you can loosen your tie line from your seat in the kayak after you're sitting in it. Set your paddle near the edge of the dock so that you'll be able to reach it. If the dock is very high, you may want to secure your paddle onto one of your boat's deck lines before lowering the boat.

Sit at the dock's edge with your feet suspended over your kayak's cockpit. Then, twist around to one side, facing the dock. With your weight totally on your forearms, begin to lower yourself until your feet are touching the floor of your foldable. Continue to lower yourself in with your arms stretched up, if the dock height requires this. Your foldable isn't likely to tip on you,

Even unorthodox methods work in a foldable!
(Wolfgang Fischer)

but it might want to push away as you move your feet forward into a seated position.

Landing at a high dock can be complex. A deck line tied to the bow will be handy for hanging on to your boat after you get onto the dock. If you have to pull the boat up, you may have quite a reach down to retrieve it, so a line becomes even more necessary. What about your paddle? Throwing it up on the dock might backfire if you find that you can't manage to get up onto the dock right away. You may want to leave your paddle tied off on the boat.

Let your foldable's stability enhance your exit. You can stand in most folding kayaks even without the support of a dock. (It's one of the confidence builders covered in chapter 10.) Stand up slowly while holding firmly on to anything on the dock; if you merely hold an open hand against some vertical surface, you might push your boat away as you stand. Raise yourself with your arms to a point where you can either sit on the dock or throw yourself up there in a prone position.

Paddling Out Through Surf

Surf conditions can be hard on any boat. Much depends on the nature of the rough water you're encountering. If conditions are fairly calm, merely foam or low lapping waves near shore and larger ones breaking farther out, you'll have at least enough of a paddling start to build up momentum to deal with the larger waves. If big waves are breaking right at the shoreline or close to it, then think seriously about picking a better launch site or waiting for better conditions.

If you study the general shoreline from which you're hoping to launch, you'll probably find a less vulnerable stretch that's free of large breaking waves. Exactly where depends on the depth of the water, the width of the beach, the proximity to offshore obstacles, which direction the beach faces—a host of variables. As a general rule, you're most likely to find the more hospitable spots away from the dead-on center of a beach, toward the sides of a cove or bay—but not too far to the sides. As you go farther out toward the points of land that define a cove or crescent beach, conditions can be even rougher than at the center.

When you find a better spot, study what's happening out to sea. You may be able to detect the wave pattern. Some people believe they can count the sets or groups of waves so they can make their entry or exit during the break between groups of waves. Even if you can't get a fix on sets, however, you'll get a clue as to when big waves are building up. Note the height and shape of big waves when you first spot them offshore. While you're watching, you're almost guaranteed to see calmer areas, perhaps where the water is deeper or where waves are being deflected away. Also, notice how the water pulls out from the beach.

If you have time, it may be better to wait until another part of the day when the surf is less formidable, at either a lower or higher tide, for instance. If you're on a camping trip and have the equipment to stick around comfortably, you should wait. What's more, handling a gear-laden boat through surf is a daunting experience.

Getting into your boat. If you must launch in surf, the stability of your foldable will come in very handy here because you won't have to lose time bracing your paddle behind you to get in. But if all you're dealing with is foam from waves washing ashore, you can take a running push-off start.

Moving out. Don't bother to attach your spray skirt at this point, because you don't want to lose the momentum built up by your push-off start. Paddle hard at a sprint pace. Don't let up even as you confront the first wave, but keep your paddle low. Pry the blade into the face of the wave to give it purchase and pull yourself through or over the wave. Keep this up until you're clear of the surf zone.

Several tricks: keep your body low and lean

Coming through the surf in a K1. *(Feathercraft)*

forward if possible; be conscious of meeting the wave with the blade's edge, not its flat back; and don't raise your arms in triumph as you go over that first terrifying wave, because there are probably others on their way.

You have at least these two things going for you. While you're paddling out, you can see the waves coming toward you, so you're not dealing with anything unseen. Also, pushing into waves is a very stable position for any kayak, even more so in a buoyant foldable.

Landing Through Surf

This is the toughest condition you're ever likely to encounter. Any boat is at its least stable when running in the same direction the waves are moving because it tends to want to broach, to be moved sideways to the face of the wave. From seaward, it's difficult to judge the height of waves or how and where they're breaking. Some of the pointers for launching your foldable into the least problematic surf area also apply for landing it in the surf.

If you can wait to land, it may pay to do so, especially if you're only marginally confident about handling the challenge at that moment. A folding kayak permits you to wait for the better moment because you can lay out a sea anchor while you're

still well offshore and just hang out. You can even take a rest in your foldable by kicking any gear out of the way and stretching out.

Even if you can't see enough of what's happening with the waves, you have some judgment options. Remember how waves generally tend to hit strongest at the center of a beach and weaker toward the sides? Is this true where you are? Since you're already out on the water, you're probably able to paddle on to another stretch of beach where there's a more sheltered landing spot, perhaps caused by an island, a headland, or bottom contours. Try to remember what the coastline looked like a few miles back. Were there some better landing sites?

Once you've determined that you're about to paddle in through the surf, these pointers should see you through in one piece.

Paddling in. Unless you're very skilled, you are always better off with a cautious approach rather than coming in hell-bent-for-leather on the crest of a wave. Begin by trying to stay on the back of waves, not ahead of them or surfing them, at least not when you're getting closer to the zone where they may start their curl and break. If you're riding a wave, leaning back in your seat will help keep your bow up, thus counteracting any tendency for the bow to plunge under.

Use the stern rudder stroke to help keep your boat moving straight and to avoid broaching. Back paddle to keep from being pushed faster than you're comfortable going. You can back paddle to keep off the front of a wave, even one that seems about to break. It's amazing how well this works for controlling your kayak.

If you do broach, you may be forced to ride the wave in sideways, because there's little chance of getting straightened out again. When broached on a low wave (less than 2 feet tall), lean your foldable toward the wave and use a low brace to support you by placing the blade onto the top of the wave. Your foldable's buoyant sides will help you with this. If the wave is higher, you'll need to do a low-high brace (see sidebar next page). It could be a long ride.

Although you won't be able to get yourself straightened out so that you again are facing shore, you may have a chance of getting yourself pointed seaward, depending on the wave. Being turned to seaward is not a bad position to be in, as discussed below.

About face. At some point though, you may have to commit yourself to paddling hard to get out of the near-shore part of the surf zone and onto the beach. Make certain you have the room and time to do so. And, remember that water washing out from shore will slow your progress.

Here's an alternative landing approach that works especially well when your boat is so laden with camping gear that it's hard to maneuver and build up speed. Go in backward. It's not a sissy thing to do—actually, it's pretty smart. You can see the waves coming because you're facing seaward, just as you are when launching. No monster wave is likely to sneak up without your seeing it, and you're in no danger of broaching if you're paddling into the waves. Your forward stroke is more powerful than your "rear-ward" stroke, so you can keep from being propelled too quickly toward the beach.

The hard part is seeing where you're going.

But turning around to take a peek toward the beach is much easier and safer in a stable folding kayak than it would be in a rigid boat, where you'd have to brace to one side for that important peek. A rigid kayaker rarely considers backing in, but for a folding kayaker, backing in is quite a viable, if undramatic, way to come in through surf.

Getting out of your boat. You'll want to do this in a hurry so the next wave doesn't hit you. Once you're in the backwash foam near shore, jump out quickly, taking advantage of the stability of your foldable. Get your hands on your coaming on either side and arm-press yourself out of the cockpit—to the seaward side of your boat if it's being turned parallel to shore. This will keep the boat from being pushed against you by the end of the next wave and knocking you over. Hang on to your boat and drag it on shore. Over time, dragging it very far can be rough on the hull, so do it only if wave action at the water's edge is likely to bang it up worse.

OUT ON THE WATER

On open water, folding kayaks have good sea manners. And they have some special tricks up their sleeves that you'll find handy on a storm-tossed sea.

Open-water conditions present many challenges. You'll encounter a wide variety of winds, waves, swells, boat wakes, and currents, especially as you paddle in and out of close coastal quarters.

Wind

Wind is an ever-present companion for the sea kayaker, part of being out on the water. It affects the way you paddle and what you're able to do on any given day.

Wind quite often is predictable. Monitor your weather radio forecast of wind conditions.

LOW-HIGH BRACE

If a wave is taller than 2 feet or so and is too high for you to place your paddle on, you'll need to do a low-high brace. This is a form of high brace that uses the power face of the blade, but you use a radically different arm position than rigid kayakers use in their high brace. You'll use the low-high brace only when broached on a high wave.

If broached, put your paddle into the face of the wave with its power face down. Your hands are hanging on to the shaft for support, your wrists are cocked back and not flat as in a low brace, and your elbows should be kept down, tucked in close to your body. The shaft should be held low near your chest, about nipple high. All your weight should be on the shaft and pushing down on the power face of the blade, which is planted in the face of the wave. The power of the wave will keep you upright as long as you lean into it on the blade.

Do not raise your elbows. If you do, you risk damaging your shoulder blades as the force of the wave pushes on the blade.

The low-high brace allows you to have your wrists in a better support position than can be maintained with a low brace. If you tried using a low brace on a high wave, you wouldn't be able to hold your paddle against the force of the wave. By keeping your elbows low and almost locked to your sides, you have your whole body counteracting the wave's force.

Two conditions to be wary of are heavy winds and winds blowing against the tide or current. When a wind is blowing at more than 15 or 20 knots, it can present a problem no matter which direction it's coming from. If the wind is coming from the direction you want to head, you're in for a physically demanding time. Coming from your beam, the wind will force you to alter your paddling style. From behind you, it could be unsettling. If a heavy wind is predicted to be coming from behind you, avoid the temptation to take a free ride in the morning because your return trip in the afternoon will probably be against that same wind.

Wind in opposition to the tide and current always results in one thing—heavy seas and breaking waves. This is especially true in coastal areas such as bays, estuaries, and rivers. Since the direction of most tides and currents changes every six hours or so, what was a calm sea with an annoying little breeze in the morning can become a washing machine later in the day, due solely to the tide changing into opposition with that breeze.

Here's how to deal with wind and its consequences.

Head winds. Wind coming straight at your bow is the easiest to contend with because it has no effect on your boat's tracking. Every boat will go straight when paddled into the wind; however, it does require a certain mind-set to conquer a head wind.

As a rule of thumb, when the wind exceeds 10 knots or so, it will cost you 1 knot of speed for every increase of 10 knots. So 20 knots of wind will slow you down 2 to 3 knots. In effect, you may find yourself paddling in place.

Your only solution is to paddle harder. An interesting phenomenon seems to occur. If you're paddling only at a moderate level, you don't move. If you increase your effort 25 percent, you start moving not just a little, but a lot. Your progress will be significantly more than that 25 percent increase would normally get you in calm

What you learn from the forecast may help you decide to paddle a northerly course that day instead of a southerly course, or vice versa. You may even want to postpone your trip until the winds die down.

conditions. It's as if you have broken through some barrier and are once again free.

How do you get that extra burst to buck the wind? Try leaning forward more than you would for your normal paddling stroke. Leaning does three things. One, it cuts down your surface area that is resisting the wind. Two, it reduces the resistance of your paddle blades, since leaning also gets them lower to the water's surface. Three, you're able to reach even farther with each paddle placement, which will elongate the zone of power application of your stroke.

Another strategy is all in your head. Get angry at the wind, consider it a challenge, and do something to work yourself up mentally to fight the wind. A few ounces of sheer determination equal many pounds of muscle when you need to slug it out for long hours against heavy wind.

Beam winds. These seem to present less of a challenge to folding kayaks than to rigid ones. Unless beam winds are very severe, they won't unsettle your foldable. Even if you're paddling with feathered blades, side winds catching their flat surface will not threaten to tip your boat, although they may rip your paddle out of your grip. Beam winds are one of the many reasons to either carry a spare paddle or use a paddle leash.

Beam winds can throw any kayak off track. Most kayaks tend to turn into the wind like a weather vane, so many people respond by paddling extra strokes on the upwind side to keep their boats running straight. A rudder can be handy at such moments, but good paddling technique is a better solution. Try the following:

Lean your boat a bit toward the upwind side. This is very easy to do and maintain in a foldable with no risk of a capsize. Leaning reduces your windage a bit and, if maintained over a distance, will help most kayaks track better. Or you can lean it only momentarily to windward when pulling the windward blade through the water. In effect, this becomes a quick turn toward the downwind direction that compensates for the boat's tendency to point upwind.

Choke up on the downwind side of your paddle. This extends its effective length on the upwind side. It allows you to paddle at a normal pace while the slightly extended paddle adds force on the upwind side, thus keeping the boat from turning into the wind.

Following winds. Your boat might want to turn into the wind coming from behind, but only if you slow down or stop. In that case you may find your boat turned upwind within a few seconds. If you're paddling at a normal pace, you'll enjoy a nice boost from the wind and will need to make, at most, minute steering corrections. The problem with a following wind is that it often creates a following sea. More on that below.

Waves

The word *waves* has a dangerous sound to it, but waves needn't be scary. Many of the waves you'll encounter in open-water paddling in large bays and offshore are ocean or current *swells*. These elongated bumps seem to pass along the water's surface, and any rigid or foldable kayak will ride over them gently. As the big ones pass under your boat and you can see down into the chasm between them from high up, you may feel a little apprehensive—but they present no danger.

Where they can present a problem is in closer quarters near land and in estuaries. As the swells move into shallower water, they start developing *crests*, and they eventually break. In narrow confines at the mouth of smaller bays, they can start stacking up to create either turbulent seas or *breaking waves*.

A *boat wake*, that V-shaped trail of disturbed water that streams out behind bigger vessels, is another type of wave you'll encounter. Ferries can send off wakes as high as 5 feet, particularly near shore, and these may tend to break. Throw in the wake of other vessels passing by, and you get a confused sea situation in which waves collide, crisscross, and come at you from different directions.

Here are some common wave conditions and how to operate in them with your folding kayak.

Straight-on waves. Just like when you paddle out through surf, this is one of your least worrisome wave situations. You can see what is happening, you're not likely to be thrown off course, and your kayak is in its steadiest position. As when paddling into a head wind, you have to tough it out by putting some determination into your stroke.

Beam waves. These can be very unsettling in rigid kayaks, so their paddlers flatten out their paddle blades for stability on the wave side of the boat to be ready to brace into beam waves. But in a foldable, you can relax in all but the largest of beam waves, taking them broadside and just riding over them. The sides of a foldable have considerable buoyancy that resists the tendency to sink sideways, a trait that requires a hardshell kayaker to low brace. In a sense, the folding kayak's buoyant sides provide you with an automatic form of low brace. The same principle holds true in boat wakes. But do be careful if you're caught in shallow water without a spray skirt, because beam waves or boat wakes from the side could break and give you a lapful of water.

If beam waves are large, however, you may want to change course slightly to take them at a different angle, just to avoid getting knocked around or getting water splashed into your boat. You don't need to change course so much that you're heading straight into them; a shallow angle will usually suffice.

Waves from behind. Following seas are not a problem unless they develop powerful waves. As in surf, such following seas can throw off your tracking, and your boat will try to turn in the direction from which the waves are coming. To counteract heavy following seas, use correction strokes such as the stern rudder stroke and forward sweep. Also, at the top of each large wave, you can straighten out your boat quite well because its ends will momentarily be out of the water. This allows you to turn your boat by pivoting on its center.

Confused wave patterns and stacked-up water. Here's probably the worst position to be in: Fresh waves and wakes are coming at you from one side, and on your other side, earlier waves are coming back at you after having bounced off of bulkheads and rocks on shore. On top of that, you're in a narrow estuary that is feeding water from a large sound into a small bay, and it is stacking up.

Your problem may have been avoided if you had read your charts and tide tables (see chapter 9). They would have suggested that you avoid being in that location at specific times. But you do have some outs.

Paddle out from shore a few hundred feet if you can, because reflected waves usually have less force the farther you are from the shoreline. Also, if you just keep paddling hard and keep up your momentum, you won't be tossed around so badly by the confused seas. Relax your mind. The odds are minuscule that such conditions will capsize a folding kayak. Its flexible skin will absorb much of the force of the confused water, and your boat will remain steady with minimal banging around.

Current

At some point in your kayaking life, you will find yourself paddling against a current. It might be on a river, strait, or estuary. The secret to success in upcurrent paddling is to be both strong and smart: *strong* in the sense that you maximize to your advantage every physical aspect of you and your boat, and *smart* in that you fully think through the hydraulics involved and search out paths of least resistance to your paddling effort. Here are some tips.

Stay close to shore. This is quite obvious to most paddlers, but it is surprising how many newcomers don't know this. Near shore, the water is usually shallower. Moving water, when going over shallow depths, tends to slow down because of friction against the subsurface.

The along-shore doctrine is a good basis for an upcurrent strategy, but you need to be smarter than that. Even paddlers who know the along-shore advice may not understand other factors at play. For example, which shore? There are usually at least two, but if there's an island in the vicinity, you'll have more shores and more routes.

Also, there's the matter of you and your boat. A force is restraining your progress. How can you operate more strongly to overcome that restraint? The points below are meant to help you be stronger and smarter in your approach.

Be well braced in your kayak. You need to be firmly locked in your boat in order for the forward force created by your paddle to be transformed efficiently into forward movement of the boat.

Lift your rudder. When going into a current, you absolutely do not need a rudder to go straight; a head-on current will tend to keep any kayak on course. If you use a rudder, this will create considerable drag. Make certain the sponsons are inflated Goodyear-blimp tight to make you more streamlined in the water.

Be determined. As in many sports, a good percentage of any effort is mental. You need the right attitude and determination to beat a current. Get mad. Don't let it beat you.

Study the body of water prior to your trip. Look at the chart for the area to determine relative depths of water at various places along your intended route. Make a mental note of this as it will tell you where in the river, strait, or estuary you should be at various points. Obviously, you are aiming for shallows, but that is not the only consideration (see points below).

Don't overlook current tables. You may not have to fight a current at all. Sometimes it is better to wait for a tide cycle turn to favor you.

Get a handle on fundamental hydraulics to see which side of the river or strait you should be on. When water goes around a point, on the inside of the turn the water moves slower. On the outside, the water, rushing to catch up to water running on the inside of the turn, moves faster.

There are several provisos on this phenomenon. It holds only or mostly when water is all of the same depth. If the outside of the turn is into shallow water, the current will be weaker there. If the inside of the turn is quite deep, the current will be quite strong.

You should generally start off by being on the side of the river or strait that's on the inside of a turn. If the current seems too strong, then get over to the other side of the river.

Take advantage of eddies and back eddies. As the current flows around a point or obstruction into the river or strait, it offers you some advantages. That point will leave relatively still waters in its shadow, or eddies. Also, some of the current's flow will wrap around and move along shore in the opposite direction; i.e., create back eddies that run counter to the mainstream of the current. That counter-flow may be several hundred yards long. Take advantage of it. The eddy line is fairly easy to spot—usually there's foam or flotsam in a straight line.

Chapter Eight

Paddling and Operating a Double

Paul Theroux, who was kind enough to write the foreword to this book, once wrote in a magazine article that those who paddle a double should be nominated for sainthood. It may seem that way at times, but if you have the right mind-set and do a bit of adjustment and compromise, the experience of paddling a double can be very rewarding . . . in *this* life.

Double folding kayaks are definitely a world unto themselves. Not only is the experience different from that of the singles, but so is the way you operate a double. The pleasures and benefits a double bestows on its two crew members often exceed what they'd receive from paddling two single kayaks.

Within a double's close proximity, you and your fellow adventurer will be experiencing this new world at the same time, intimately. When either of you spots interesting and unusual things, it's easy to point out. You're in the perfect position to talk about the discoveries you're making. Since your partner is within normal conversational range, you can even whisper to each other so you won't startle the wildlife you're observing. A double can even give you two different views of the world around you just by switching seats. The change in perspective is uncanny.

A double also lets you share the paddling load. One partner can slack off for a spell while the other continues to paddle. Often a double allows two people to go farther than either one could individually.

Doubles do involve compromise. In a double you and your partner are literally "in the same boat," so you both lose some of your independence. You have to agree whether to dawdle or move fast. One person can't go ahead and wait for the other to catch up, as you can in two singles. You must adjust your paddling pace and style to those of your partner.

But, even as you lose some independence, you gain something of immense value: a sense of satisfactory social intercourse that comes with the teamwork needed to power forward, make turns, and deal with the natural elements. As you learn the techniques that make moving as one possible, you'll find yourself bonding closer to the friend or loved one in the other seat. This feeling of wellness that comes with teamwork is foreign to the solitary world of the single kayaker, even one who's operating in a group.

Safety is another consideration. You'll never get separated from your paddling buddy by wind, waves, or fog, wondering where the other person is. A double foldable is inherently more stable than even a foldable single, and if capsized, a double is much easier to reenter than a single.

Doubles often require such distinctly different techniques than you would use for single kayaks that they warrant separate consideration. Below are pointers about how to paddle doubles and about handling them in certain launching and landing situations.

PADDLING, TURNING, AND BRACING BASICS

To gain the benefits, camaraderie, and safety of a double, you and your partner must become proficient in coordinated paddling and teamwork. For starters, make certain that you have absorbed the driving lessons covered in chapter 6. These are also the fundamental building blocks for paddling and maneuvering a double. Then, consider the following suggestions to help you and your partner become a more effective crew.

The Forward Stroke

All the principles needed to develop a good forward stroke in a single apply equally in a double. You use your body components in the same way. You should be rotating your torso, using your legs, adhering to the suggestions for hand position and looseness, and keeping your arm straight in various parts of the stroke.

But, clearly, paddling in tandem can put some restrictions on your movement. For example, if seated in the back, you're limited in just how far forward you can swing your paddle. Doubles

Forward stroke in a double. *(Walther/Klepper)*

generally seat the two crew members close enough that they have to avoid clanking paddles. The exceptions are the Feathercraft K2 and Klondike, both of which have more than enough room between the paddling positions to permit less coordinated paddling strokes.

In other boats, you'll want to synchronize your paddle strokes for at least three reasons: clanking paddles together can be hard on the blades, jerky movement through the water causes drag and wastes the energy of both paddlers, and paddling in unison is aesthetically pleasing—it certainly looks better than two individuals flailing about.

Here are some suggestions for getting the most out of your forward stroke in a double.

Put the more powerful paddler in front. Your double will move better if the stronger team member is in front because this position offers greater clearance for a powerful forward stroke. Double kayaks narrow toward the bow, beginning at the front cockpit area. This gives the front paddler a chance to place the blade in the water closer to the boat, where it can deliver greater straight-back power. Less deck interference also means the front paddler can reach farther forward for a longer zone of power application.

Very few teams follow this advice, however. In many couples, the man wants to be in the back seat, where he can be in charge of turns and course. The rear position controls the rudder and usually does more in rudderless turns.

When you paddle in the rear position, you're responsible for coordinating your stroke with that of your partner up front. Paddling in tandem is like dancing. One partner leads and the other follows—or you risk stepping on some toes.

Only the person in back can see what the other person is doing, so it naturally becomes that person's job to follow any change of pace set by the person in front and also to avoid hitting paddles. Whenever paddles clank, it's probably the fault of the person in back.

If you're in back, try to anticipate what the front paddler is doing. Play these games with yourself: try to match the exact angle your partner's blade is slicing through the air, or try to place your paddle in the water at the same moment. Think of tandem paddling as a contest in which you are being judged on synchronization.

If you're in front, recognize the limited range of motion your rear partner has. When you set a paddling pace, be aware that your partner may not be able to match it. You're in the better position to paddle at a faster beat because of the extra room you have. Your partner cannot extend forward as fully as you can and is also concentrating on not hitting your paddle.

Signal any major paddling changes you are about to make. If you're in back and want to stretch farther forward into your stroke, let the front person know so he or she can give you a bit more room. If you're in front and intend to pick up the pace, warn your partner.

If you're the front paddler and you need to put down your paddle, place it far enough forward that your partner still has clearance to continue paddling unimpeded. This occurs when you stop paddling to check a chart or take a drink. If your rear partner has to quit paddling just because you didn't leave clearance, your kayak will lose momentum.

Turning a Double

Doubles differ radically from singles in the way you turn them. Tandems generally are longer than singles and track better—i.e., they run straighter—so they often don't respond as well to the turning tricks. But when you develop the skills and good teamwork, you'll be surprised how maneuverable a double can become.

Teamwork is the big key at all times. The person behind doesn't get the undisturbed panoramic view, but he or she does control the rudder. The front person can see obstacles better, but he or she shouldn't be initiating turns. So the two paddlers must constantly be in communication to decide on turns.

Your position in the tandem determines what you can and cannot do in turning strokes. For example, if both partners tried to do the forward sweep the way they would in a single, that turn could be largely ineffectual in a double. Leaned turns are also harder unless each team member makes the same adjustment for relative position in the boat.

Rudders are practically a must in double kayaks. They help keep a double going straight when partners are mismatched in their paddling styles and strength, and they're very useful for making turns. Even though you may never use a rudder to turn a single boat, you'll find it very handy almost all the time in a double.

Even so, you and your partner should learn to turn by paddling technique, without a rudder. That way, if your rudder cables get disconnected or the rudder is damaged, you'll already have the team coordination to maintain control of your boat. Good turning technique is useful in conjunction with your mechanical rudder to shorten the radius of your turn, complete turns more quickly, and even avoid obstacles.

We've looked at some of these standard turning techniques when talking about singles, but let's see how they should be applied specifically in doubles.

Forward sweep turn. Several differences apply to doubles. First, you may want to be more careful about how much you lean out. Doubles are more stable than singles, but you don't want to push your luck. Two people leaning in one direction can throw each other off. Second, if you're both doing a forward sweep on the same side, you should adjust the zone in which you are applying the sweep, depending on your position in the tandem.

In leaning out on your paddle, start by doing so only about half as much as you would in a single boat until you and your partner get a feel for how far over your combined lean takes the boat. To be on the safe side, angle the blade a bit to work a form of brace into the sweep. Remember, the top edge of the blade should be leading the blade's movement through the water.

If both partners are forward sweeping on one side, you should do the following: If in front, do your sweep stroke mainly ahead of you. Reach forward close to the bow with your paddle and sweep back no farther than your seat. This assures that you are, in effect, moving the bow away sharply from the side on which you are doing the sweep turn stoke. If you're in the rear, start your sweep at a point level with your seat and continue the sweep stroke as far back as is comfortable. If you try to sweep in the zone forward of your seat, you'll be attempting to move the broad side of your boat around, which is largely a wasted effort.

Working plenty of torso rotation into the sweep will make the stroke doubly effective in a double, no matter which position you're in.

Stern rudder stroke. Since you're not alone in a tandem, you can actually improve on the stern rudder stroke. While the rear person is doing a stern rudder move, the front person has two choices: do a forward sweep on the opposite side (not a reverse sweep) or continue normal paddling. A sweep will turn the boat sharply toward the side of the stern rudder stroke. Continued paddling will reduce the loss of momentum that ordinarily results from stern ruddering.

Some instructors suggest using what's called a bow rudder stroke in conjunction with either a stern rudder stroke or a sweep by the rear paddler. The bow rudder, however, is a difficult turn stroke to get right; it depends on a certain angle of the blade, its exact placement, the distance from the side of the boat, and other factors. Many people find it too strenuous to hold for long against the water pressure that builds up, especially since the bow rudder takes place in front,

Stern rudder turn in a double.

where they have the least leverage. So, the best advice may be to avoid it.

Telemark turn. Though this is a bracing stroke, it is probably best thought of as a maneuvering one. As in any lean out for bracing in a double (see below), you should exercise caution not to let two overzealous partners go too far over to one side.

The telemark turn done in tandem looks stunning, but to be on the safe side in the beginning, the telemark should be performed by the rear paddler only. The front person should let up on paddling and enjoy the feel of the turn.

Once you have gained confidence, you both can participate. The rear person can be quite aggressive in leaning out, and the front person can do some leaning on the paddle to help see the telemark through. The rear person should call out the direction of the telemark, the side he or she wishes to turn sharply toward. Paddle once on the off side and then start the telemark. Try to keep the paddles wide apart for greater effectiveness.

Maneuvering a motionless double. To get turned around 180 degrees, you can take advantage of the fact that there are two of you. One does a reverse sweep, the other a forward sweep. Who does what? Let the front person do whichever is thought of first. The rear person, like any good dance partner, follows the lead and does the opposite turn stroke on the *opposite* side of the boat.

Backing up is done as in a single. Both of you back stroke and look around. The back person gives directions.

The draw stroke is performed pretty much the same as in a single. Again, be careful how much you're leaning out in placing the paddle for the draw stroke so you don't find yourselves in a precarious position.

Bracing in a Double

The low brace is definitely the only type of brace you should be doing in a double, even a hardshell. It's tough for two people to coordinate the degree and timing of their body lean to the point necessary for proper high bracing.

Even the more limited range of lean in the low brace bears watching. In a single boat, you are the only force doing the leaning. In a double, two of you are leaning. How do you coordinate how far you go to one side? How do you determine exactly when to push off the support of the brace to bring the boat upright again? The timing is so acute that you could easily screw things up. Here's some advice.

Slap brace. If either one of you senses that the boat is tipping over, do a slap brace. Don't wait for the reflex action of your partner to kick in—or to discuss it. He or she will be thankful you did the brace.

Practicing the slap brace carefully can also be something of a game. To start, you agree that at the count of three you will lean the boat over as if it were being tipped by a wave. One partner counts out loud, one does the tipping action, and both of you slap brace.

Sweep low brace. If you feel you need to do a sweep brace to gain some support, don't wait for your partner to react—just do it. But do have a prior agreement on which direction you will sweep. Avoid getting tangled up. If you're in front, sweep mainly parallel to your seat and slightly forward, even if this isn't the most powerful spot for low bracing. If you're in the back, you do have room to perform the sweep from behind you up into an area parallel to your seat.

Sculling low brace. As in the telemark turn in a double, you may want one person to do the sculling motion at first. You can both try the sculling motion after you're confident you can coordinate the push-off motion for recovery.

Care should be taken with the surface area each is sculling through. You would not want to collide or crisscross paddles during this sensitive stroke. If you keep the sculling arc small, say about 2 feet, and directly out from your seats, you shouldn't clash. Again, you should agree beforehand on a signal for when to push off in recovery from the sculling motion. Then, start the push-off as the blade is moving rearward in its arc. Don't forget to keep your heads down, letting the boat come up first, followed by your bodies and then your lowered heads.

LAUNCHING AND LANDING DOUBLES

Double folding kayaks launch and land even more easily than single foldables. Two paddlers are better than one for steadying the boat: One can hold on to the boat while the other gets in. Having two paddlers simplifies other tasks as well. For example, one partner can hold both paddles while the other gets in.

Below are some tips on launching and landing doubles, starting with the easiest situations and progressing to the real challenges. You may want

Learning how to brace in a double.

Beach launch.

to reread chapter 7, which covers how to handle these situations in a single boat.

Calm Beaches and Shorelines

As with single folding kayaks, doubles do not require that you use your paddle as a brace when getting in. You and your partner both step directly into the boat.

Usually the rear paddler holds the kayak steady while the front paddler climbs aboard. Then the rear partner steps in. Only under unusual circumstances would the front paddler need to steady the boat in any way, since his or her weight is already steadying it quite sufficiently. It's best to keep the double parallel to shore so the front paddler won't have to get in from deep water, which would require a higher step-in.

High and Low Docks

Doubles really simplify this process. Here are several methods to mount from a low dock. In one, both paddlers sit on the edge of the dock with their feet planted in the boat in the vicinity of their seats. The front paddler slides in and gets situated in the front seat, while the rear paddler continues to steady the double with his or her feet, which are still in the boat. The front paddler, seated, grabs hold of the dock with hands or forearms resting on the edge. The other paddler drops down into the rear seat.

Docks that are 2 feet or higher require a slightly different technique. If you can reach the boat's coaming with your outstretched arms while lying prone on the dock, it's fairly easy for either one of you to steady the double while the other boards the kayak. Follow the boarding procedure for singles: sit on the edge of the dock, turn your torso around so you're facing the dock with your weight on your arms, lower your feet into the boat, and then drop into your seat. The paddler already in the boat holds on to the dock while the other paddler enters in a similar way.

Landing a double at either low or high docks is similar to landing a single, except that you've each got the other person to keep the boat steady. One person gets out and then steadies the boat from the dock's edge while the other person exits. With particularly high docks, the first person to exit can secure taut lines from both ends of the boat to the dock, which helps steady the boat enough for the second person to stand up and pass gear to the first partner.

PADDLING OUT THROUGH SURF

Pick a launch spot that offers the calmest conditions for getting onto the water, just as you would in a single. Remember, on almost every beach you can find calm areas toward the sides of the cove, where wave action is refracted. Not so at its center.

Get your double into a bit of water. The rear person remains outside of the kayak, holding the bow steady and pointing into the direction of incoming water. The front paddler gets in and quickly attaches the spray skirt so any lingering waves and foamed-up water can't lap in.

The rear paddler stands alongside the rear cockpit area and waits for a break in the wave action. When backwater starts washing out, or during a lull, the rear paddler jumps in with the push-off running start described in the sidebar on page 107. The rear paddler makes no attempt to attach the spray skirt since little water should get in; it's more important to keep moving before the next wave hits. Besides, the front paddler's body acts as a shield, protecting the open rear cockpit.

Both of you should now paddle hard into the waves. Keep low so you don't create too much surface for waves to crash against and slow down your progress. When the boat's moving into a wave, keep your paddles low and pointed into the wave. This will prevent losing a paddle or getting banged by its shaft. As you enter a wave, use your paddles as prying bars to get through it. You should soon clear the immediate breaking-wave zone.

COMING IN THROUGH SURF

Your best bet in a double folding kayak that is carrying a full load is to avoid surfing in the first place. If you've done your homework with charts and have a good estimate of your traveling range, you should be able to avoid getting into a situation beyond your skill level. (See chapter 9 on commonsense sea kayaking.)

Winds and waves change, however, and a place that normally is benign can suddenly gather more wave action than you bargained for. When that happens, what do you do? First, study the situation closely. It's not unusual for paddlers, even those with lots of experience, to spend thirty minutes or more looking things over. Being in a double helps this reconnaissance since you have two sets of eyes to watch and two sets of paddles to keep you from being drawn in by the power of the outer waves. Come in as close as you can under control, because it's harder to read waves from seaward than it is from land. Is any part of the beach not being hit hard or maybe getting only small-wave action?

When you do decide to attempt landing, you have the same choices you would in a single: to come straight in or go in backward—facing the oncoming waves. Coming in backward allows you to see the surf as it builds up and comes toward you, so you can position yourself much better in respect to each wave. Also, since you won't want to use a rudder while coming in anyway, you'll have an easier time steering while facing the waves than if you were running with them.

If your double is loaded with gear and you're not confident you have the waves figured out, landing backward may be your safest choice. When going in backward, allow yourself to be pushed in a bit toward shore, paddle hard against the next big wave, get pushed in a bit more, paddle hard again, and so forth. This routine can be tiring, but it gives you terrific control.

If you decide to come in facing the beach, get your rudder out of the way, if possible. Plan to make most of your movement toward shore on the backs of the waves rather than in front of them; the front side is where they may move you in so fast that you lose control or where they might break right on you. The front paddler should be alternating between two types of strokes under command of the rear paddler: quick forward strokes to move into good position on the backs of the waves, and sweep strokes to keep the boat perpendicular to the wave's direction of movement. The rear paddler should be paddling and applying rudder strokes.

Paddle hard enough to keep up with the speed of the wave. It helps to throw your body weight forward a bit. If you find that the nose of your double is starting to dip into the water, both of you should lean back hard to counterbalance this. If the nose continues to dive, then let the boat broach or go sideways to the wave rather than pitchpole down.

When your double is sideways to a wave, go into a brace, leaning into the face of the wave. If the wave is less than 2 feet high, use a low brace. If higher, use the modified low-high brace cov-ered in the sidebar on page 112. Either way, both of you should lean the boat into the wave, supporting yourselves on the blade that in turn is being pressed up by the wave's force. While there's no logical reason for this, whenever you go into a brace on a wave, your boat will seem to slow down, and this in itself can help you regain your composure.

No matter which way you go in through the surf—backward, forward, or on a broach—when you near the beach get ready to jump out fast. If possible, both paddlers should jump out on the seaward side of the boat and move it quickly ashore. In a double foldable, it may be easier for the rear paddler to jump out first. The reason is that the front cockpit area is generally higher and more restricted, making it a bit harder to exit than the back. Your objective is to move fast to get the double out of the way of incoming waves and away from the sucking-out action of water as it returns to sea.

Sea Savvy: A Guide to Commonsense Sea Kayaking

Becoming a competent sea kayaker requires more than just paddling and operating skills, and it goes beyond proficiency at self-rescue in the event of a capsize (see chapter 10). To be truly adept in the watery environment upon which your kayak is afloat, you need to have the whole package, which we call *sea savvy*.

The ability to navigate is part of that package. Navigation is a complex and technical subject that can only be covered adequately in a book dedicated to that subject. One good navigation manual, *Fundamentals of Kayak Navigation* by David Burch, is a seminal work specifically devoted to kayak navigation (see Suggested Reading in the appendix). Your study of such books should be the cornerstone of your kayaking endeavors.

Taking a formal course in coastal navigation is another component of your sea-savvy package. Many excellent classes are offered by hundreds of U.S. Coast Guard Auxiliary groups, U.S. Power Squadrons, and private sailing schools. Look for similar courses at science museums, planetariums, and universities. Most navigation courses are tailored for the skippers of vessels that are much larger than yours. But, as a mariner, you too need to know how to use a marine compass, read nautical charts, understand the various aids to navigation, take a fix to establish your position, do dead reckoning, and so forth.

Even with the best navigation skills, you still need another component to steer clear of trouble while under way: common sense. Below are a dozen guidelines to help you develop the necessary smarts. Of course, these guidelines are not all you'll need to know, but they'll start you thinking. They cover three important activities: keeping tabs on your environment, understanding the rules of the road, and making your way.

KEEPING TABS ON YOUR ENVIRONMENT

Unlike the ancient kayakers, you have all the advantages of modern technology at your disposal for keeping track of the natural elements. These modern gauges will let you know what to expect, what to avoid, and how to get where you want to go. Sometimes, they'll even advise you not to sally forth that day. Heed the advice.

Listen to Your Weather Radio

The U.S. government's oceanographic and atmospheric administration, NOAA, broadcasts its local weather forecasts over National Weather Service radio stations throughout the country, and you can pick up the broadcast that's specific to your location on an inexpensive VHF weather radio, which you can purchase at RadioShack (it sells the cheapest) or in marine supply stores. You can also find marine weather on the Internet at most weather-report Web sites (see the appendix for some suggestions). You should always consult these marine forecasts before you make your plans to set out, because they'll tell you exactly what to expect for large regions of the sea coast or inland bodies of water. Notice their relationship to where you plan to paddle.

It's a good habit to follow marine forecasts even when you're not planning to paddle. By tracking this regularly you learn to recognize the normal weather patterns for your local marine environment and also the conditions you should be wary of. Forecasts of 5-foot seas may be normal for one location, and abnormal for another. The only way to know is to monitor the local marine forecasts.

No weather forecast can substitute for common sense. You have to provide it yourself. If your abilities are no match for the local weather conditions on the day you plan to paddle, have enough humility to back off. Or use the weather information to select a better stretch of coast or bay for paddling that day.

Whenever conditions are changeable, bring the radio along (in a waterproof bag) or use the marine weather channel on a marine handheld VHF radio. Listen again at midday; it may be time to beat a hasty retreat before weather worsens. A weather radio is a must on any camping trip.

Consult Your Charts

Marine charts are your road maps. Study them before you start off to identify all available routes and to determine which routes favor you. Consult your charts regularly while under way.

Marine charts are not hard to read. You'll find a guide to the meaning of symbols in what NOAA calls *Chart No. 1*, really a small manual. A navigation book or course will help you understand the specific information you'll need to draw from your charts.

As you lay out your chart before a trip, take note of the general lay of the land in relation to the water along your intended course. Look out for ship channels. See if any large bodies of water feed through narrow passages. Look out for those little wiggly marks in the water areas that designate tide rips, whirlpools, etc. Note any land masses that could block the prevailing wind and provide you with shelter, or, conversely, expose you even more to its blast that day.

You should also be looking on your charts for landmarks such as towers, smokestacks, sea buoys, and so forth that will help you identify where you are as you paddle. You should be gauging distances and determining whether you are up to the rigors they will require of you.

Look Up Tide and Current Information

This information can make the difference between an enjoyable trip and a miserable one. The U.S. government publishes data about tides and currents, and you can find the information in some newspapers and special manuals put out privately. For example, *Eldridge Tide and Pilot Book* is a classic text that covers the U.S. East Coast, complete with a folksiness reminiscent of the *Farmer's Almanac*. Most marine stores have handy, pocket-size tide booklets that list the heights of the tides for each day of the year. And there are Web sites that contain this information as well (see the appendix).

However, the directions currents take and their timing are generally more meaningful for sea kayakers than the differing heights of tides. And that's why, as a paddler—unlike skippers of bigger boats—you need to know what the currents are doing.

Currents are caused by the movement of water. Along continental coastlines, there's generally a *longshore* current moving slowly in one direction. Another kind, *tidal* currents, are caused by the tides of the oceans and Great Lakes. *Freshwater* currents are a third kind, caused by fresh water flowing from one place to another. Tidal currents reverse their direction once or twice a day, but river currents flow in one direction only. But wherever tidal water mingles with a freshwater flow, such as near coastal river mouths or in brackish estuaries, their currents affect each other. It is not unusual for an ocean current to overcome a river current for part of the day and flow against it, even 100 miles upriver from the mouth. Moreover, wherever a freshwater current gets restricted, such as in a narrow river gorge, the velocity of the current increases. Tidal currents get stronger or weaker not only where they're restricted, such as over an undersea shelf, but also due to the changing height of the tide.

Coastal paddling is greatly affected by the patterns of movement of water in and out of bays, estuaries, and rivers. In many places, you can take advantage of the local tidal currents by timing your trip to flow with them in one direction for part of the day and then be boosted homeward when they reverse. If your favorite coastal passage normally has a southbound longshore current, and if a storm brings winds up from the south, be prepared for the stiff chop that forms wherever wind direction opposes the current direction. Tides also can affect your plans. For example, high tide may let you take shortcuts over sandbars that, when exposed at low tide, would force you several miles out of your way.

The highest and lowest tides intensify during the full and new moons and when the moon is in perigee, the closest to us in its orbit around the earth. Pristine beaches can become foul-smelling mud flats at those low tides and leave you and your laden boat far from the water.

Check Your Compass

Learning how to use a magnetic compass is essential. You'll need a hand-bearing compass or a steering compass, or both. In determining the line of position of two or more charted objects, you hold the hand-bearing compass in one hand and point it at the objects. The steering compass tells you what direction the boat is pointing because it fits into a mounting bracket that has been lined up with the boat's centerline. You may prefer a steering compass that also serves as a hand-bearing compass, so that you just lift it from its bracket whenever you need to take a hand bearing. Other aids, such as data scopes, can also help you take bearings, but they're costly.

Before you even get started, you'll use a compass to mark your various *course headings* (travel directions) for your trip in conjunction with your chart. Do so even if you know you'll be able to see where you're going, because if fog or a rain squall rolls in, your sightlines will be shortened or blocked out entirely. Your compass heading will be the only guide for which direction to turn to go on or turn back.

Check your compass regularly, even when you think you know exactly where you are and where you're headed. You may gradually be drifting off course without realizing it. The more you use your compass, the more confidence you'll gain. Whenever in doubt about your position or course, trust your compass—not your internal sense of direction.

RULES OF THE ROAD

Going out on the water is like going out on a highway where separate rules apply to trucks, cars, bikes, farm vehicles, and pedestrians. In the nautical world, each different type of vessel has its own rights and responsibilities. As a kayaker, you need to understand the limits of your rights, the enormity of your responsibilities, and what to expect from all the other types of boats sharing your environment.

Understand Who Has the "Right of Way"

The complex rules for navigating on inland and international waters are set down in the Navigation Rules, International–Inland. The rules cover the rights of vessels that are encumbered by commercial fishing gear or limited in their ability to maneuver within a marked channel, about who is responsible to yield to whom in a crossing or overtaking situation, and much more. Some kayakers believe that they're the most encumbered vessels on the water since they don't have motors or sails, and that they therefore should have the right of way. Theoretically, yes; in practical terms, no.

What applies to kayakers is the unwritten rule of gross tonnage: If they're bigger than you, get out of their way. Since even the heaviest sea kayak is lighter than the average dinghy, it weighs in at the bottom of the pecking order. You may have a right to be in a certain spot, but you risk being "dead" right if you get run over by a barge operating out of channel. Besides, even though your vessel is merely muscle powered, you have a surprising range of movement and number of ways to dodge around. Use these advantages to stay out of the way of others.

Learn to Judge What Traffic Is Doing

At all times, as in any traffic situation, you should swivel your head to spot potential danger. In the words of one baseball philosopher, "you can see a lot by watching." The waters and moving boats have clues written all over them about what they will be doing next.

Channel buoys tell you where big ships and barges will be running if they don't want to run aground. Learn how to read buoys so you'll know if you're inside or outside the channel and, if you're inside, which lane you're in. Look out for sailing regattas and races; often they set triangular orange markers that should warn you off. Keep tabs on the locations of sandbars and shallow water; you can be pretty sure the larger craft won't come near them.

Take a look at any boat coming into your vicinity. You can generally determine if it's on a collision course with you by looking at the centerline of its bow. If you see equal amounts of boat on both sides of the centerline, it may be a hit. If more boat appears on one side than the other, it's a miss. Unless the current is pushing one of you sideways, of course.

Similar hints are apparent from the water cutting off the boat's bow or at night from its red and green running lights. Study vessels as they pass safely by you to learn the tricks of reasonable expectations.

Work on Being Seen and Signal Your Intentions

Bikes on roadways carry neon-orange pennants on tall rods, and their riders wear reflective clothing. You should be doing something similar to make certain you and your tiny craft are visible to the helmsmen of powerboats, sailboats, and merchant ships. Opt for brightly colored PFDs. (It's not by accident that Canada sanctions only the colors yellow and international-rescue-orange for life jackets used in its waters.) You can help other boaters see you by using colorful paddle blades; yellow is a top choice.

If you carry a marine radio, contact to larger craft, telling them of your intentions to cross busy channels or to move into docking areas. The worst way to signal your intentions to other boat traffic is to act erratically, turning here and there.

If you're with other kayaks, stay close enough together so that you can operate like one larger vessel made of numerous kayaks. This grouping will help other boats spot you and avoid you. If a larger boat seems hesitant about your movements when on a potential collision course, you should stop moving. Signal to the other skipper that your "motor" is shut off—that you don't plan to move forward—by putting down your paddle and crossing your arms. Once assured that you won't dart out in front, the other boat can proceed safely by you. (For more, see the Ten Commandments of Dealing with Traffic at the end of this chapter.)

MAKING YOUR WAY

These remaining sea-savvy pointers will help you know where you are at all times so you'll be able to control your situation—as much as anything can be controlled on open water.

When You Start Off, Make Certain to Look Back

This seems like such common sense, but an amazing number of paddlers fail to take visual bearings on their launching site. Later, they don't recognize where they put in and can't land. Looking back starts you off on the right foot for the rest of your trip. As you make a habit of seeing how the world will appear on your return trip, you'll also be spotting any boat traffic that may be sneaking up on you from behind.

Take your first back-sighting about a hundred yards offshore. Take note of landmarks that should help you distinguish the spot from its surroundings, such as a prominent house, a flagpole, and so forth. Turn around again after another few hundred yards and you'll start seeing other reference points on the horizon, such as a large water tank or radio tower. Etch these mental images in your head.

Read the "Road Signs" You See Along the Way

There are many road signs on land and water that can help you gauge how far you've come, and how much farther you need to paddle. They'll also let you know how weather changes might affect you later as you retrace your route.

Have a clear idea of which buoys you should expect to see on your trip. They are numbered, so you can count them off on your chart as you pass and get a broad idea of your location. Buoys move around in the current and wind because they're anchored to the bottom of the waterway with flexible chains or cables, so you should use these floating navigational aids only to indicate your general location.

Look for shallows and sandbars that relate to your chart. On your return trip, will they be covered or exposed? Will an incoming tide make the area treacherous as you return?

Keep looking for reference points such as smokestacks, church steeples, and towns on the shoreline and in the distance behind. All of these feed you useful information on keeping your bearings. You don't necessarily have to use your compass for an exact position; just take note of your general position in relation to these road signs.

Keep Track of Wind and Compensate for Its Effect on Your Course

Wind will almost always shape your paddling day. Strong head winds could change your destination since they slow you down and limit the distance you cover. Be wary of tail winds. The free ride they give you in the morning will be against you in the afternoon, possibly forcing you to paddle until nightfall. And if you were planning to ride a favorable current on the way back, that wind would create strong wave action against you.

Beam winds will toss you off course. If you must make a specific landfall on the far side of an open crossing, you should compensate for the effect of beam winds. There are complex formulas for compensating for the side drift. You'll be reasonably accurate, however, if you adjust your course 20 to 25 degrees to windward.

Be Careful in Judging Distances

On the water, distances can look deceptively shorter than they really are. What might look like a point of land 3 miles ahead may be 6 miles or more in the distance. You could easily overcommit yourself on what seemed like a short crossing to an island. The better way to judge distance is to use your chart, not your eye, until you develop a better sense of distance.

Always Leave Yourself an Out

Have an escape route or bailout option. It's very easy to get into situations that are over your head.

Unless you work out some alternate routes or find places along the route where you can cut short a difficult trip, you could condemn yourself to a hard and possibly dangerous trip. When disaster befalls paddlers, it's usually because they saw no choice but to press on with their original plan, which led them into deeper trouble.

Look at your chart. Note places where you could easily pull out if you had to. Use the chart to plot out alternate routes that can help you escape from bad weather or unusual winds, just in case you deem such action necessary. If you give yourself an out, you can always come back to paddle another day.

THE TEN COMMANDMENTS OF DEALING WITH TRAFFIC

Folding kayaks tend to be the boats of choice for city dwellers because they are easy to store in small spaces. This means folding kayakers are often more likely to be paddling in traffic than their rigid-kayak brethren.

Here are the ten commandments of dealing with traffic. Like the Ten Commandments of the Old Testament, the Traffic Ten are a key to your "salvation." And like the original commandments, the Traffic Ten can be grouped into categories that will help you remember them whenever you're tempted to let your guard down.

The first three commandments stress the attitude you should have when on busy waters; the next three focus on the intelligence you should be gathering; the next three alert you to some potentially deadly optical illusions; and the last points to a lifetime calling to help you survive.

1. Be Like an Owl

Owls not only have big, wide-open eyes that take in everything—they can swivel their heads to face backward. An owl would make a great traffic survivalist paddler.

Folding kayaks—most of them anyway—make it fairly easy for you to turn around because of their stability. Take advantage of this feature to look behind you regularly when in traffic. Develop a pattern of, for example, looking back when making every fourth or fifth stroke. Have a chant in your head such as "pad-dle, pad-dle, pad-dle, pad-look." Most of us find it easier to turn our head around toward one side than the other, our so-called "sweet" direction. Find out what yours is and turn that way as part of your ordinary paddling routine.

Don't let anything—such as reaching for your lunch bag or canteen—disrupt your vigilance. It's when you least expect it that something is bound to overtake you.

If you are in one of the tippier foldables or in a borrowed hardshell, make certain you can turn to look behind you. If you're having trouble doing this, learn how to do a sculling motion with your paddle that will allow you to get enough support to look back. If you can't do this comfortably, don't use that boat in busy waters. No amount of sleekness is worth your life.

2. Work on Being Seen

The windmilling motion of your paddle stroke can catch the eye of even the most dazed motorboat operator. Brightly colored blades like white and yellow work especially well to attract attention when they are being swung around. Of the two, yellow is better; it doesn't blend in with anything. White is OK, but sometimes it can be lost against a backdrop of whitecaps in choppy waters.

Avoid stylish colors for your paddle blade, such as purple. If your favorite paddle is black or some other hard-to-see color, you should add strips of retroreflective tape to the blade, both on the power and nonpower face. The tape available at marine stores for putting on PFDs is pretty waterproof and won't come off.

Working on being seen starts early in the game. If the precise color of your boat's deck is of no particular importance to you and red is available, choose it since red is the color that can be seen from the farthest distance. In a widespread group of kayaks, the red boats are the last to disappear from sight. There are more square feet of visibility in your deck than in anything else you have out there: use it to your advantage.

There are only three colors you should be considering in your choice of PFD—yellow, orange, or red, in that order. Other colors may look nice but aren't very visible. Your vest and your hat are the highest points on you while paddling and thus most likely to be seen; pick standout colors for both.

3. Always Act as If You Cannot Be Seen

Face it: your boat is tiny, and you are tiny in the spectrum of things that are moving about on the open water. Following the second commandment gives you an edge, but don't stake your life on it.

Assume that, as far as traffic is concerned, you are dressed in commando camouflage in an olive-drab boat and moving stealthily around. The less you rely on the vigilance of others to spot you, the better off you will be.

4. Know Where Boat Traffic Is Coming from and Going To

Even though you're in a *sea* kayak, most of your paddling will be done along *shore*. Surprisingly, this is where you can be more vulnerable, since you may be tempted to feel secure, but large boats can come out of wharves and into you as you pass in front, or run over you as they enter a dock.

As with the fifth and sixth commandments,

intelligence processing begins on shore. In the case of this commandment, consult a chart before you start off to determine shore facilities that may put traffic into your path. Make a note of ferry slips, oil depots, commercial areas, marinas, etc. When under way, be extra alert as you approach these danger zones.

5. Know Where Channels Are

As in the previous commandment, check over a chart beforehand to note channels in the area where you're planning to paddle. Look out for trouble spots such as where channels come close to shore. Some channel markers are on land; i.e., you can't escape traffic by going to that side of the channel. Also, determine where channels split into offshoots; it is easy to get confused in these areas on whether you are in a channel or not.

When under way, take constant notice of the channels. Keep out of them as much as possible. When crossing one, look both ways before proceeding. You want to make certain you have enough room to make it across without getting hit or causing a problem for larger ships that are confined to the channel because of their draft. It is a judgment call on how much time and distance you need; until you have lots of experience at determining the speed of various types of vessels under varying conditions, err on the side of caution. Don't be impatient.

6. Know Your Currents Cold

Again, this is an exercise that begins at home. The speed and direction of currents obviously dictate the direction you may want to head in as you set out, but this information is also absolutely vital for dealing with traffic. For example, currents will either boost or hinder a vessel's movement under certain conditions, something you need to know if you plan to cross ahead of the vessel.

On the water, see how the currents are really acting compared to the predictions in currents and tide tables. Many factors can change the predictions, such as heavy winds can increase the effective speed of currents and, if in opposition to the current, will result in higher seas that will affect your own ability to maneuver.

7. Recognize That Large Vessels Appear to Be Moving Slower than They Really Are

This is the first of the three optical illusions you must take into account when judging vessel traffic.

Check this deadly illusion out for yourself. Stand on a dock in a no-wake zone and focus your attention on a set point in the water as boats go by. Watch as a small motorboat and then a larger vessel go by at what should be the same speed because of the zone. The larger vessel seems to be going slower. Why? The smaller boat passes your sighting point in its entirety right away, while the larger one still hasn't completely passed, even after its bow crosses your sighting point. The effect is that it seems slower.

In practical terms, this means a paddler often underestimates the speed of large vessels, which can't stop quickly or make quick turns for the most part. Don't fall into this trap.

8. Be Aware That Vessels Seem to Be Farther Away When Viewed from a Low Vantage Point

There is hardly a thing afloat that is lower than a seated kayaker. This low position already makes your situation quite tough by limiting your horizon and how far you can see. Your problem becomes even graver because vessels appear farther away than they really are.

9. At Night, Take into Consideration the Effect That Lights on a Vessel Have on Your Depth Perception

Whether a vessel is all lit up like a dinner-cruise ship or just carries the minimum amount of lights required by law, such as barges, their distances from you are deceiving. They almost always seem much farther away than they really are.

If you are caught out at night, or choose to paddle in darkness, be careful of this phenomenon. Take no chances at all regarding necessary crossing times to get out of the way of vessels at night.

10. Make a Lifelong Practice of Studying Vessels When Out on the Water

There is no such thing as generic traffic. For example, a ferry differs from a freighter in speed and turning ability. The ferry can go anywhere and stop in a few seconds; the freighter is limited in stopping distances and where it can go. A vessel's abilities change with prevailing conditions. For example, a lightly loaded barge on an outgoing tide and with a following wind will move much faster than a heavily loaded barge that is bucking currents and wind.

Study such differences every time you paddle in traffic. The knowledge will make you a more savvy and safer paddler.

Developing Confidence, Learning Rescue Skills

Any kayak can capsize. Tip one beyond its final stability point, and it will go belly up. Folding kayaks give you generous amounts of stability to play with, and they tolerate your inattention to balance and the action of the sea around you. But they all have a tip-over line; cross it and you'll land in the drink.

As a folding kayaker, you need to test the level of stability your boat allows so you can gain confidence in it. Bracing is, of course, one way to feel out your boat's fine line. Even though your ordinary paddling in a foldable hardly ever needs even a slap brace to restore its balance, you should occasionally do some brace strokes anyway. This practice will help you get a feel for how much your boat will heel before bracing is necessary.

Other drills can also give you a sense of balance and stability. You can do things in a folding kayak that you would never dare in a rigid one, as you will learn below. These drills will build your confidence in your boat and prepare you for self-rescue—and even the rescue of others.

Rescues performed in folding kayaks differ from those of rigid boats. The reentry methods are remarkably easy, almost intuitive, as you will also see below. However, you do have to watch out for some common errors that would test even a foldable's ability to support your reentry.

CONFIDENCE DRILLS

How stable is your foldable? Following are some confidence-building drills that can be done in a single or double by either paddler.

IF YOU WANT TO ROLL A FOLDING KAYAK

Rolling is not critical with folding kayaks since they don't tip easily. Still, anything can be rolled given the right amount of leverage and technique, and folding kayaks are no exception. That includes singles as wide as Nautiraids and doubles as wide as Kleppers. For the most part, however, rolling a folding kayak is a circus act. Most likely you will not be able to rely on a roll if capsized, with the exception of sleeker foldables such as the Feathercraft Khatsalano.

However, if you want to practice rolling a folding kayak and already have rolling skills, you need to do several things. First, in most folding kayaks the paddler fits loosely in the cockpit. Many folding kayakers prefer it this way; the comfort of a roomy cockpit may have drawn them to a foldable in the first place.

So you'll need to do something to fit more tightly in the cockpit. Some folding kayaks come with hip pads or bars that will help you fit tightly. Feathercrafts have optional hip pads and several other models, including the Klepper Alu-Lite and FirstLight models, have bracing bars that come as standard equipment. If your boat lacks these, then tie some side bags to the frame alongside you in the cockpit to snug up against your hips. This will give you more hip-flick control in the rolling process.

You should also move your foot pedals a few notches closer than for general paddling. If your boat doesn't have foot braces, you'll have to improvise something—try using gear or an airbag to press your feet against.

When you're going through the roll process, don't rush it. Most books on hardshell kayaks instruct you to do a roll slowly and calmly, and this slowly-does-it approach is even more important for folding kayaks. When a folding kayak rolls back up, it does so more slowly than a hardshell because of friction from the fabric skin and hull. If you go slowly, you give the kayak enough time to roll up.

Before you try any of these drills, make sure you and your boat are set up properly. If your boat has an open cockpit, give yourself more room to move around by leaving off the spraydeck. Be near shore or with another boat that can help you. At first, try to do these drills in relatively calm water until you gain confidence to move into wavier conditions. Remove all loose things from your kayak so if you do have a spill, you won't have to chase after your gear as it floats away.

Be prepared for any prolonged immersion. Hypothermia is always a danger, so proper clothing is essential. Dress with long sleeves and pants or a wet suit, even if the water is warm. Rescue drills can also bang you around a bit, and such clothing will protect you from that. (For more on protective clothing, see the sidebar on pages 82–84.)

Most important, fill your boat up with all the flotation you can. The built-in air sponsons aren't enough; get float bags to fill the underdeck portions. (For more, see pages 79–80.) Float bags will help keep your boat higher, so it will take on less water making it easier to empty.

Drill #1

Lift your body completely out of your seat. To do so, support yourself with your hands on the coaming or washboards. Most paddlers have sufficient arm strength to perform this confidence builder. It makes getting in and out a lot easier, especially when you do have a spraydeck attached, and particularly if you have long legs. And it will help you do the push-off start (see the sidebar on page 107) for getting off the shore quickly.

Drill #2

Get on your knees. The hardest part of this drill is not to scratch or bang yourself up on the crossribs, seat, or fittings. (That's why it's best done with long pants and a long-sleeved shirt, or even a cushiony wet suit.) Get into a squat, then onto your knees, and move forward a bit in the boat.

Drill #3

Turn around in your seat—totally around. Some people are very limber and can do this easily. If you're not quite so limber, try turning around one step at a time. Keep low, twist your upper body to one side, lean on your forearm, and quickly get your lower body turned around. You should now be facing backward with your body somewhat stretched out. Now, tuck your knees up and raise your upper body as much as you can while still feeling comfortable.

Drill #4

Crawl out onto the back deck a bit. (You can do this as an extension of Drill #3.) You may find yourself in this position during a self-rescue, so it's excellent practice. Make certain to get a good grip on the coaming on both sides of you, balancing your weight on both hands. Keep low and crawl just a little way onto the back deck to get a feel for the position and how secure you are.

Drill #5

Change boats while on the water. This trick can be done with hardshells but is incredibly easy in folding kayaks. It's not only a confidence drill but also a technique worth knowing. You may someday have to switch boats on open water if someone in a single is hurt or feels ill. Switching the individual to a double may be a good safety measure.

First attempt this drill with at least one double. Here's how to do it with one single and one double.

Get the boats side to side, facing in the same direction, with their cockpits next to each other. The front paddler of the double and the single paddler should grab the coaming of the opposite boat. The back paddler of the double sits up on the back deck and throws one leg over the back deck of the single. The single paddler can now move into the back seat of the double. If you're the paddler who's switching boats, remember to keep low, crawl over to the other boat on your belly, and then turn your body around into the seat when your legs are in that boat's cockpit.

Next, it's the turn of the paddler hanging out

Switching between doubles.
(Dan Chu)

on the back deck to be seated. The paddlers presently seated in the double both hold the coaming of the single boat. The person on the back deck of the double shifts his or her weight to the single boat and rolls over, belly first, onto the back deck of the single, facing the stern. Then he or she crawls, feet first, into the cockpit and then flips into a seated position.

Drill #6

Stand up. Yes, stand up. It's amazing how few folding kayakers are willing to try this. This is one drill that will impress hardshell kayakers who have a hard time even turning around in their boats. You may want to do this in steps.

First, just lift yourself off your seat into a squat position while gripping the coaming or washboard on either side of you. Keep your feet spread out to each side as much as possible to give you a wide base for balancing yourself. Be careful in a Klepper not to get your foot caught under the edge of the keelboard, a distinct possibility if you're wearing sandals.

As you get more confident, stand up all the way. Do it for a moment if that's all you can manage. The objective is not to hang around standing in your boat, but to prove to yourself how well your boat will balance. A double folding kayak offers as stable a platform as a floating dock, particularly if someone is sitting in the other seat providing ballast. Regular-size singles are a little hard to remain standing in, unless you're extremely agile. The mini-foldables will tolerate only a quick stand-up—and an even quicker sit-down.

SELF-RESCUE SKILLS

If you look at other sea-kayaking manuals, you'll find reams of detailed information on rescues

The ultimate confidence test. (Sean Coffey)

after a capsize. They suggest that if no other boats are around to give you a hand, you should self-rescue using a paddle float, or better yet, know how to Eskimo roll.

But here you are, the proud owner of a folding kayak that will not Eskimo roll easily, and you're feeling a bit intimidated, maybe somewhat less of a sea kayaker than everyone else around you, rolling their hearts out.

Don't be concerned. As a self-rescue technique, rolling is not what it's cracked up to be. After an unexpected capsize, few people who have learned how to roll will succeed in using it to come back up. They blow their roll, have to wet exit, and do a reentry with a paddle float; i.e., they have to get in like the rest of us. Eskimo rolling requires lots of practice in all kinds of conditions before it becomes a dependable self-rescue method. Only paddlers who are willing to put in considerable amounts of time can claim to have a fail-safe, "bombproof" roll. They represent a very small percentage of the paddling population.

Your simple moves for self-rescue in a capsized folding kayak are easy to learn and hard to forget, and they don't require precise timing or holding your breath. Self-rescue for doubles and singles will be covered first. Then you'll learn how to participate in a group rescue.

Any rescue, whether assisted or done without outside help, should be thought of in three "gets" (which are expanded upon later):

1. Get the boat right-side up (assuming it was hull-side up).
2. Get yourself back in.
3. Get the water out.

Depending on how much water you have in the boat, you may want to get #3 before you get #2.

GET THE BOAT RIGHT-SIDE UP

This can seem the most daunting of tasks when you're neck-deep in water and a bit scared. Wearing a PFD is a must, because to get the boat cockpit-side up again, you're going to have to push upward. Without the buoyancy of your PFD, every application of upward pressure would only push you underwater—not right the boat.

Here are three techniques for your practice sessions. See what works best for you. The first is probably the only workable one with a fully loaded single or double. The others will work for light loads in either type of boat.

Over the Hull of the Boat

For the first method, begin by heaving yourself over the belly-up boat from the side, then reach over to the far side, try to grab the coaming, and, with a snap of your upper body, pull the boat toward you. If done right, it will break the suction and get the boat upright with only a little water in it. It has to be done quickly; a slow flip-over will scoop up lots of water, especially if your boat has an open cockpit without a spraydeck.

If you're trying this method in a double, you have two choices. For the first, both of you get on the belly-up boat and proceed as above. (Remember to time the pull-over maneuver so that you do it together; use a signal if you have to.) If both of you can't participate in the pull-over, have one partner assist from the other side—helping find the hand-holds, pushing up, and so forth.

In the Upside-Down Cockpit

The second method borrows from how capsized canoes are sometimes tossed right-side up. It will

Getting ready to enter the zone of silence.

work for either a single or double foldable kayak. Dive under the boat and poke your head into the cockpit. You'll have a huge air pocket where you can breathe and calm down in what is termed a "zone of silence." Then you (and your partner, if in a double) will push up forcefully on one coaming side (be sure to agree which one) while pulling on the opposite side to keep it from sinking and scooping up water.

A Hybrid Method

The third approach is generally for doubles, although it's workable in a single. For a double, both paddlers should be on the same side of the boat. One reaches under to get a grip on the coaming on the opposite side. At the same time, both people push up on the closer side to begin flipping the boat. As the boat starts to go up, the first person pulls on the opposite coaming to keep it from submerging and scooping water. In a lightly loaded single, you might just be able to push the boat over right-side up. As it is going over, grab the opposite coaming to move it quickly toward you so it doesn't scoop water or get away from you.

No matter which of these three methods works best for you, try these additional tricks to get the boat righted more quickly: try rocking the boat a bit to break the suction seal created by the air pocket; try to break the seal on the side that will be rotating up through the air; and try to maneuver the boat so the side that will be going up is pointed toward the wind, because the wind may help flip the boat over. At least it will decrease the resistance to righting.

GET BACK IN

Here's where the differences between doubles and singles are really evident. The methods below take advantage of the fact that there are two of you in a double, and one can steady the boat while the other climbs in. In singles you don't have that luxury. In either situation, these hints should ease the task.

Now that the boat is righted, try to keep it pointing into the wind—its most stable position —so it won't tend to swing around or away from the entering paddler. In the instructions on doubles below, the rear person reenters first to start operating the rudder or using a paddle to control the boat from the best steering vantage point. A sea anchor would also be useful to keep the boat pointed into the wind.

Make certain that your pant legs aren't ballooned with water, a distinct possibility if you wear paddling pants that cinch at the ankles. That extra water weight won't help when you try to climb out of the water and into your boat.

Keep your body as flat as possible at all times. This even applies to your body position in the water as you attempt to enter your boat. If you have your body straight down in the water, you will be pulling the boat over and down, which is dangerous. By keeping your body parallel to the water's surface, you'll glide yourself in with the force of a swimming kick, with little tendency to upset things. Also, when you finally are up out of the water and on your boat, remain low and flat. This will keep the center of gravity (yours and the boat's) as low as possible to prevent tipping. If you use the over-the-deck approach, crawl on the deck until you're in a position to twist your body into your seat.

Reentering Doubles

If you are in a double, you have several options. Try them to see which one would be most workable for you in an emergency.

Have one paddler hold the bow while the other gets in. If you're the person holding the bow, hoist yourself slightly up on the front deck while the rear paddler gets in from either the side or back. If the boat has a rudder, the rear-deck entry means coming in from the rear quarter, not straight over the back. Then you get in from a front quarter or straight up the bow.

Have one paddler on each side of the boat. The rear paddler climbs in from one side while the front paddler, who is still in the water, holds the opposite coaming. Then the front paddler gets in while the rear paddler low-brace sculls to the side opposite where the front paddler is getting in.

This second method may have several advantages over the first one. The boat is extremely secure when the first paddler is getting in because the other paddler is on the opposite side, a great position for preventing a recapsize. It doesn't require as much crawling on decks, which is not an especially stable activity.

Reentering a Single Foldable

Getting back into a single folding kayak is easier than into a rigid one. Except in very rough conditions, you can dispense with the need for a paddle float to steady the boat. You have two approaches for getting back in sans paddle float.

Over the back deck. This is known as a *cowboy* rescue as it resembles how an old-time Western movie hero would mount his horse from over its rear flanks. Get alongside the rear of the boat and face front. Grab on to both sides of the boat and hoist yourself onto the back deck, still facing forward. Your legs should be straddling each side with your feet in the water to act as outriggers and lower your center of gravity. Keep your upper body low to keep your center of gravity down. Now, with your hands reaching

Over the stern self-rescue in a double.

Self-rescue in a single from the side, without paddle float.

forward, pull yourself along the deck. When you have the trunk of your body over the cockpit, lean your head back to keep your center of gravity low, and then bring your legs in and drop into your seat.

This method can be difficult if your boat has a rudder with steering cables running along the deck's surface. Also, when you are over the cockpit, it is hard to drop in without raising your upper body somewhat. But if you do so quickly, you should be all right.

From the side. This position offers you a greater amount of stability and avoids any deck cables. Get aligned in the water alongside your cockpit, with your belly down and legs and feet stretched out behind you horizontally toward the bow. Grab on to the coaming on the near side, and then try to grab the far-side coaming. If you cannot reach that far, get that hand at least onto the back of the cockpit.

Your flattened-out body should be almost parallel to the boat. Start kicking your feet to bring them to the surface. Continue kicking to help lift your body out of the water as you pull yourself up with your hands. Aim to put your head and upper shoulders over the back deck. Now start crawling toward the stern until your feet and legs can drop into the cockpit. Keeping low, twist your body into the seat. The confidence drills should have helped you get the sense of balance you need for this.

Paddle-float method. If conditions are exceptionally rough or you don't feel you have a good sense of balance at the moment, use a paddle float. The various kinds of paddle floats inflate differently, so be certain to figure out yours on land. In general, you inflate a paddle float about half to three-quarters full, and then place one blade into the paddle-float pocket. Now it's ready to use. Inflating the float will be easier if you can throw yourself over the cockpit before doing it.

Self-rescue with paddle float.

The beginning and end of the paddle-float reentry resembles the over-the-side method covered above. Line yourself up alongside the cockpit. Place the paddle float at a right angle to the boat, with the other end across the back of the cockpit. Hold it there with one hand grabbing both the coaming and shaft and the other hand on the paddle about level with the side of the boat. The float will be acting as an outrigger, which will help you pull yourself up on the boat. If you have trouble lifting yourself up onto the boat, put one leg over the shaft to raise your body half way out of the water. Continue to pull yourself up until you get right over the cockpit, similar to the previous method. Then twist into the cockpit in the direction of the float.

No matter how you get yourself back into the boat, you'll probably want to rest there a minute to get yourself settled down.

GET THE WATER OUT

If you capsize where no other boat can lend assistance, and if your boat is full of water, you should try getting some of the water out before you climb back in. On the other hand, you may have been able to capsize and right your foldable

Sea Socks

One of the best ways to deal with water that may get into your kayak is not to let it enter in the first place. A sea sock—a waterproof fabric bag that fits over the coaming of a cockpit—will do the job. You sit in the sea sock in your kayak. It will give you a generous amount of wiggle room within your cockpit and yet not cling to your every move.

It works in two ways. The sea sock is small enough that in the event of a capsize it could not take on much water. Plus, air pressure from the inside of your boat tends to press out against the sea sock, which helps keep the sea sock from filling up.

If you capsize and have a sea sock attached, there isn't much water to empty out. The little bit that does get into the sea sock can be expelled by simply reaching into the cockpit and turning the sock inside out, dumping the water out.

The trouble with sea socks is that they hinder your access to things you may need when out on the water. Since they must be tightly attached to the coaming to work properly, they are difficult to remove and reattach if you need something.

Only Feathercraft and FirstLight offer sea socks for their models as standard equipment. The socks work well because of the rigid individual coamings the companies use. However, it is possible to devise your own sea sock for an open-cockpit folding kayak. You can attach it to the same ring in the spraydeck your spray skirt attaches to. It won't be quite as watertight as closed-cockpit kayaks such as Feathercraft singles but it should work well enough.

awkward and inefficient. Keep in mind that a double boat is capable of holding about 150 gallons of water (a single holds around 80 gallons). That's an awful lot of pumping to do from alongside your boat. Here are two methods that work to get water out in a hurry:

Get the boat on its side. This method works well if you are on a day trip and not carrying much weight in gear. Folding kayaks have wonderfully buoyant sponsons; take advantage of this unique feature to get lots of water out quickly. Putting the boat on its side places it on one of its sponsons. The sponson will lift the cockpit out of the water, and bilge water will come pouring out. At most, what you'll have left to contend with when you're back in is a few inches of water.

Climb on the back deck and rock the boat. Get on the back of the boat once it is upright. In a double, one paddler does this and starts rocking up and down, with the front person at the bow pushing up and steadying the boat. The rocking action can get a third of the water out of a totally swamped boat quickly as the water sloshes back and forth and out the cockpit toward the rear. You can also do this with a single boat to get some water out if completely swamped.

There are times when you might not want to attempt to do these steps even if your boat is totally swamped. You might be getting blown into a shipping lane or onto a rocky shoreline. If that is the case, get back into your boat right away.

Unlike a rigid kayak, a folding kayak is extremely stable when filled with water. Since the air sponsons run along the perimeter of the boat, they act like a life-preserver ring to stabilize the boat. Rigid kayaks have their flotation at the ends (watertight compartments), which makes these boats want to spin like a barbecue rotisserie; they are notoriously unstable when swamped.

In a folding kayak you can just paddle off, even with virtually no freeboard and water continuing

without scooping up much water. In either case, here's how to proceed.

Whatever you do, don't try bailing or pumping from an in-the-water position. It's too to lap over you. You can even paddle the boat totally submerged. It is not the fastest way to paddle a kayak, but you will be able to move out of harm's way. Being in the boat with your spray skirt on will keep you warmer and prevent the cold from sapping the strength you need to pump out water.

If you have added extra flotation at both underdeck ends of your kayak in the form of air bags or waterproof storage bags, you're in even a better position. The air sponsons will stabilize your kayak from rolling over like a swamped rigid kayak, while the extra flotation will give you a few inches of freeboard so water does not keep washing over you.

Pumping and Bailing

Getting water out with a pump or a bailer is better done from inside your boat. If your boat is very full, be prepared for the process to take half an hour or more including some rest periods.

Generally, a bailer will move more water faster than a pump. Scooping and emptying a bailer is less tiring than the pistonlike push and pull of a hand pump, but you should plan to have both. A bailer will work well if conditions aren't bringing more water in. If seas are breaking over the deck, you may not be able to bail.

To deal with such conditions, first tighten on your spray skirts. Then push your pump down along the front of your body into the top of the skirt and into the cockpit. Now as you use your hand-pump, more water will not come crashing into your boat. In a double, take turns pumping, or pump at the same time if you have two pumps. It's important to keep waves from hitting you broadside, so keep steering into the direction of the sea and wind. Again, a sea anchor would help keep you pointing into the wind. With adequate flotation, you'll be floating high enough not to take on too much water, and you'll have fewer cubic feet of water to expel.

Electric pumps are another alternative to

What happens if swamped and you don't have extra flotation.

hand pumps. These work while you use your hands for better things than pumping, such as paddling. They're not the speediest things in the world, but they do work, completely emptying a double in around twenty minutes to half an hour. (These were discussed on pages 80–81.)

GROUP RESCUES

Having another boat around, a single or a double, greatly aids a rescue. It can even help in flipping the capsized boat over, getting most of the water out, and getting the occupants back in. You should learn how to participate in an assisted rescue from the perspective of both victim and rescuer.

Make certain to heed the five points in the First Things First sidebar (see page 145) so that you have your rescue priorities straight. Also watch out for other factors mentioned earlier, such as the victim's pant cuff gaskets sealing up water in the legs, making reentry extra difficult.

Flipping the boat over and getting water out are part of the same procedure, so they will be discussed together. Assisting victims back into their boat will follow.

Flip and Empty

The first step is to get water out of the capsized boat fast so you can get its paddlers back in. The steps are a takeoff of the methods used for self-rescue, only more quick and effective. Here are a few suggestions:

Get the capsized kayak on its side, alongside and parallel to the rescuing kayak. If the victim's boat is a folding kayak, you can help get it to ride up on its sponson. The victim pulls up onto the deck of the rescuing boat and pulls on the coaming of the capsized boat to get it to spin toward the rescuing boat. As seen earlier, this will get out plenty of water in a hurry. If the victim's boat is a hardshell, this procedure will be somewhat more difficult unless the boat has flotation bags at either end or watertight end compartments. Give this method a try anyway, because it certainly won't hurt.

Get the two boats perpendicular to each other, with the victim's boat bow facing into the rescue boat. With the victim's boat still upside down, the rescuer pulls the bow up on deck a foot or so. The rescuer then rocks the victim's boat while the victim puts full weight on the stern of the capsized boat to push it down. This motion will force water to run out through the cockpit. The victim's boat is then flipped right-side up. It will have very little water in it.

There's a danger that the weight of the flooded kayak could crack something on your deck. It happens to the decks of fiberglass kayaks during rescues, and it could happen to your foldable. The top bar might crack or bend. Weigh this potential damage against the urgency of the situation. You can reduce this danger by pulling only a small part of the capsized boat onto your deck and having the person in the water do most of the work. If you feel strong enough, you may just grab the bow while it's alongside your boat rather than dragging it onto your deck. If the rescuing boat is a folding double, you may want to pull the bow of the capsized boat between the two paddlers since this is generally the strongest part of the boat. By the way, hardshellers call this the TX-assisted rescue, since one boat being pulled across the other resembles the letter T.

Use two rescue boats to do the emptying. If you have two or more boats, you can do what is termed the H-I two-boat-assisted rescue. The two rescuing boats line up side-by-side, facing in the same direction. The victim's upside-down boat is floated between the two, bow toward rescuers. The two rescuers lay both of their paddles perpendicular to, and spanning, the space between them, thus forming the letter H. The bow of the victim's boat is lifted onto the paddles (like the letter I), something like how it's lifted onto the rescuer's deck in the one-boat rescue. The victim, however, has greater leverage to push and twist the capsized boat because he or she can half sit on the bow of one of the rescuing boats.

As the victim's boat is pushed farther onto the combined paddles, more and more water will pour out through the cockpit opening. Seesawing it up and down will leave the boat almost dry. As the emptied boat is pushed back into the water, quickly flip it right-side up to keep the cockpit area from sucking up water once again.

Getting Back Aboard

To get the victim back in, place the now-emptied boat parallel to yours. Any two boats that are rafted up or held together become a very stable platform. Your body weight enhances the foldable's steadiness even more.

Start by having both boats pointed in the same direction. If you're the rescuer, grab the cockpit coaming of the victim's boat near the back with both hands. Lean into your grip on the other boat; it won't bite you. You now have a platform that is 5 to 6 feet wide and will hold through just about anything, as long as you're not timid about using your body weight to keep the platform together.

Or you can opt to span the two boats with your paddle. Place it behind you and have it lying across to the back of the other boat's coaming. If both boats were rigid kayaks, you would have to do this just to keep both boats stable, but you don't have to when yours is a foldable. The paddle, however, might serve as a useful gripping point for the person in the water to pull up on when reentering.

Reentry is identical to that of the self-rescue. So if you're the victim, remember to stay flat on the water almost parallel to the rescuing boat, pull yourself up at a low angle toward the rear deck, get your legs into the cockpit, spin around, and you're rescued.

Only this time, as the victim, you'll have extra help getting in. For example, as you start lifting yourself out of the water, the rescuer can grab the back of your life jacket or seat of your pants to help you get out. The rescuer can also help pull and aim your legs into your cockpit or steady you as you turn around into your seat. The rescuer

could also assist you in bailing, reattaching your spray skirt, and so forth.

FINDING REALISTIC PRACTICE CONDITIONS

Find places where you can experience 3-foot waves coming at you quickly. The locations, if picked carefully, offer a relatively safe environment if you heed the warnings below. Moreover, you will be able to find these ideal conditions fairly close to home.

Where to Look

Find a river that runs into tidal waters, or a narrow split of water or a bay. The river must have an incoming tide or flood current at some time during the day.

Locate an area just offshore where there is a fairly wide band of shallow water (6 to 10 feet: shallower depths are also OK). A key factor is having deeper water farther offshore. Determine

FIRST THINGS FIRST: FIVE RESCUE POINTS TO REMEMBER

Be decisive. Use the rescue method that first comes to mind and do it fast. A better method may eventually occur to you if you start weighing options and jogging your memory, but don't hang around deciding. Do something right away.

Check the condition of the people in the water. If you and your partner in a double are turned over, the first thing to do is check if your partner is OK. Ask, "Are you all right?" If someone else is in the water and you're the rescuer, establish the condition of the person. Speak calmly; this will help keep the swimmer calm.

Forget about loose, floating gear. Attend to the people. Get them back in their boats,

and then worry about that floating hat or lunch bag.

But do worry about paddles. If you go over, make certain you hang on to your paddle. If other paddlers are being rescued, retrieve their paddles immediately, as long as doing so doesn't hinder the rescue effort.

Make sure no one remains in the water long. While you're emptying water from a rescued boat, try to get its occupants out of the drink and on to the deck of another boat, at least until they can get back in their own boat. Your goal is to reduce their exposure time in the water to avoid hypothermia.

what the shoreline in the area is like. What you want is a gentle shore free of piers, cliffs, boulders, and the like.

Look for an area that is likely to have heavy motorboat traffic farther offshore. Strange as it may seem, *you will want this traffic.* Clearly, it should be far enough away from you not to run your kayak over, but close enough to provide wave action.

When and What

Your next concern is timing. What you want as you consult your clock and the tide and currents tables are times during which boat traffic will churn out wakes large enough to simulate wave action. You will often find that the wakes will rise to 3 feet or more as they approach shallow water. Moreover, they can be quite powerful, and may even have breaking crests if they get high enough. Also, their frequency is relentless, and the distance between the waves is shorter than most coastal waves, forcing you to act quickly and decisively.

The best times for testing your rescue mettle are when the current and tide are coming in. These conditions will tend to cause higher wakes as boats go down the river against the current, and you won't be pushed out to sea by the tide.

This is the next best thing to a surf zone for testing your rescue skills. You'll see how well a paddle float will work, and you'll see how well you can hang on to your paddle, how well its inboard blade will stay under a deck bungee cord, and so on. You'll even learn that you can use these waves to help get back in your boat. For example, as a wave passes under your boat and you are on the shore-side of the boat, the boat will drop as

you rise. As you do, it will help you drop into the boat instead of having to hoist yourself up and in. You'll also find out what it feels like to get hit again immediately with more waves as you try to settle into your boat. It's a good learning experience that will give you more confidence in your ability to deal with rough seas.

Be Careful . . . Really, Really Careful

Make certain that the conditions you choose to practice in are pushing you and your boat toward shore. You don't want to be in the water while the movement of the water is pushing you into motorboat traffic or out to sea.

For example, the shoreline configuration may cause an eddy to push you out near the top of a cove, even though at the center of the cove you get pushed toward shore. If so, choose another spot farther upriver where the flood current is not wrapping around and turning you toward the middle of the river.

Winds coming from the shore can cancel out the effect of the wakes and move you into boat traffic. Be careful.

Most important, take all the precautions you can in order to be as safe as possible—starting with your kayak. Make certain you have it loaded to the brim with extra flotation. If possible, practice with at least one other kayak to help you if things go wrong. Wear your PFD snugged tight and zipped up. Have on a wet suit even if paddling conditions seem to call for just a T-shirt and shorts. The wet suit will prevent you getting scratched up as you climb into your boat. Also, even in warm water, you will get chilled and hypothermic with any prolonged exposure to the water.

Part Three

Using and Enjoying

Folding kayaks demand little and deliver a lot. They adapt to your needs, not the other way around.

Transport a foldable anywhere in the world by every means from camel to Concorde. Carry it around in its bag or keep it assembled if you wish—your pick. This section of the book will show you how to pack away your foldable to minimize risk to parts and skin during travel.

To enjoy your folding kayak, you will need to learn the easiest ways of assembling it. This section will provide tips and insights that will make the process less of a vexing chore.

Use your folding kayak in ways beyond paddling. A foldable is flexible in spirit, not just in structure. Have an urge to sail? No problem. Folding kayaks are born to hoist canvas and move with the winds. Want to camp? Foldables swallow up gear for weeks of adventure along your favorite water trail or coastline. Have it your way—fish, hunt, row, scuba dive, snorkel, bird watch, take pictures. In part 3 you'll get practical information that will help you enjoy the wide range of activities available to you in a folding kayak.

Accept the boat as it comes from the factory, or customize it to fit your needs. Fiddle, make changes, add doo-dads. Your foldable is adaptable. This section will show you modifications that you may find handy, and it will tip you off to ways to keep your boat young. Maintenance? Surprisingly little is needed to get scores of years of service from one.

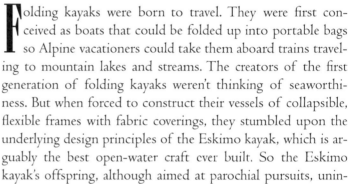

Chapter Eleven

Traveling with a Foldable

Folding kayaks were born to travel. They were first conceived as boats that could be folded up into portable bags so Alpine vacationers could take them aboard trains traveling to mountain lakes and streams. The creators of the first generation of folding kayaks weren't thinking of seaworthiness. But when forced to construct their vessels of collapsible, flexible frames with fabric coverings, they stumbled upon the underlying design principles of the Eskimo kayak, which is arguably the best open-water craft ever built. So the Eskimo kayak's offspring, although aimed at parochial pursuits, unintentionally became globetrotters able to be taken and paddled anywhere.

The concept of a folding kayak is mind-boggling. From just a cubic foot or so of portable storage space a fully formed seaworthy vessel unfolds, capable of transporting one or two people and all their gear along any waterway in the world, no matter how fierce its seas or remote its reaches. Folding kayaks have been carried by camels across Middle Eastern deserts, by dogsled out to fresh ocean leads off frozen Arctic coasts, and by horseback to high Sierra lakes. A folding kayak even traveled by llama to a mountaintop lake in the Andes to set an altitude record for paddled craft.

You needn't go to such extremes to enjoy your folding kayak. You can release its potential for pleasure in temperate zones or in any easy-to-reach tropical

Biking with a mini-foldable. *(Klepper)*

paradise. And you needn't burden four-footed animals to find your own special world; planes, trains, and cars will do just fine. So will a mountain bike.

But before rushing off to the airport or train station, you should take some travel lessons from the school of hard knocks. Learn how to transport your foldable so that it arrives at your destination in the exact number of pieces it's supposed to.

BY PLANE

Let's start with planes, since they're what folding-kayak wanderlust is now most associated with. Air travel will transport you the farthest from your home with your foldable, and it will open up your broadest horizons, putting you alongside some beckoning shore within a few hours. Add a few minutes for assembly, and you'll be ready to paddle or sail off on an adventure of exploration and personal discovery.

The airport is a good place to learn how to transport your folding kayak by other means of conveyance as well, because flying your stored-away foldable puts it at the mercy of its most rigorous testers—airline baggage handlers. If you can prepare your bags for airline baggage check-in, where they disappear into the dark hole at the end of the conveyor belt, then you can prep them to survive anything.

Folding kayaks have passed muster in air travel with flying colors. They've been kicked, shoved, abused, even tossed from on high, and they've still arrived in the right number of pieces. Several air travelers have retrieved their boat bags and found them adorned with tire marks; the bags had fallen off the baggage carts and been run over. Remarkably, the boats could still be assembled without problems at the kayakers' destinations.

The funny thing about air travel with foldables is just how few people take added precautions in packing yet get away with it. The parts are just shoved in, the bags are zipped up or tied off, and they're handed over to the vagaries of the baggage system. Yet they usually arrive in fine shape.

But why press your luck? Here are some simple precautions to take before traveling on airlines with your foldable.

Ready to board a small-engine plane, Bahamas.

Check with the Manufacturer

Even if your owner's instruction packet didn't contain additional information about packing the kayak for travel, the manufacturer may have it available through customer service. The company may even offer some add-on products that will help.

But be careful about one piece of advice. At one point, one manufacturer suggested that you could use the large flat boxes specially designed to carry bicycles on airplanes to pack your foldable. It even provided elaborate plans on how to lay the kayak's frame members and skin inside the box. Be warned that these boxes have been known to break and spew parts. Such a box is meant to carry a 30-pound bike, not an 80-pound double boat. Baggage handlers are not ready for the unaccustomed weight of your boat and may simply fumble the box. If you plan to use a bike box, you'll have to make arrangements with the airline prior to your trip, and they'll require your early arrival and charge you extra.

Follow the Three Key Principles of Packing

Some items need extra protection, others don't. If you understand the principles, you're well on your way to happy packing. Here are the three cardinal rules.

The hull can take care of itself and of some other parts, too. Hypalon and other materials used for a boat's bottom are gluttons for punishment. You need do nothing in particular to protect them.

Take advantage of the hull's toughness to shield other parts of the boat, starting with the deck. Roll or fold up the skin so that the textile deck is shielded by the tougher hull. Depending on the particular boat, wherever possible place frame members within the enfolding hull.

Return frame members to the mass from whence they came. Wooden frame members came from a tree trunk, aluminum ones from metal bars and ingots. If you pull wooden frame members together in a tight bundle, you return them to the strength of a log. Ditto for aluminum and for any other synthetic structural material.

For example, when packing long wooden frame parts, lash them together mercilessly so there is absolutely no wiggle or play, even if you have to bend some flex out of them. Don't worry; they'll spring back later. Aluminum tubing parts have far less chance of bending or crinking when tied together to form, in effect, one thick tube.

Some manufacturers provide you with separate straps to lash parts together in this way; if yours has, use them. If not, buy some or tie everything together with cord. If a bag has external straps, tighten them. If not, get some external straps, because they'll help snug frame parts into one fat parcel that can withstand plenty of punishment.

Ends of long pieces and fittings need protection. You don't want the end of an aluminum piece to get dented. If either the male or female end gets pinched, you may not be able to mate them. Even boats with wooden frames incorporate tubing to join ends. Cushion these ends with any combination of the devices suggested below. The fittings used to connect crossribs to long pieces, though strong, also can suffer damage that would call for repair or replacement. Again, use cushioning. In some models, you'll be able to sneak the ribs inside the hull.

Or you may want to try another approach toward protection: keep the more susceptible parts out of the checked baggage system. The oval bag that carries Klepper crossribs is small enough to take on board as carry-on luggage. This eliminates one whole set of parts from your precautionary measures. Camping stores usually have inexpensive versions of this oval bag that can accommodate other foldables. You can also place the ribs in a regular suitcase mixed in with your clothing.

Nautiraids don't lend themselves to this since most of their crossribs are attached to long parts.

Cushioning

You have a lot of choices in how to cushion parts from damage in transit. You can pick up some specialized materials or use items that serve a double purpose.

Some people use packing materials such as bubble wrap or corrugated cardboard. This works fine for packing protection, but once you reach your destination you'll need to find a home for it. If you're flying to a friend's vacation home or back to your hometown, this material probably won't present a storage problem. But when flying to an isolated take-off point, you'll have to do something with the specialized packing material so it's available for your return flight.

In that case, you'll be better off with cushioning that isn't so specialized. For example, towels, which you're probably planning to take anyway, can be used to protect the ends of long bags. Shove one tightly folded towel down to the bottom and wrap another at the top of the ends. Or you can use articles of clothing to do the job. If you're going to be camping, you could use small pieces of closed-cell foam, which will also come in handy as camp seats. Be careful that you don't use so much cushioning that you won't be able to get your two-piece paddles into the long bag.

With any boat that comes in one bag, like the Feathercraft, you may want to shove clothing or towels in here and there. This will help round off the bag and protect end pieces, including the ends of the four-piece paddle.

If you feel a need to wrap crossframe members, you can usually find room to wrap foam sleeping pads around these. The same goes for long parts.

If you find that the cushion material hinders packing away parts, try thinner dimensions of the stuff. You don't really need a lot of padding. Re-member, many folding-kayak travelers don't bother with padding and do just fine. You're trying to add an extra measure of protection, not build a bomb shelter.

Loose Ends and Other Thoughts

Here are some loose ends to deal with, literally and figuratively.

Loose straps and strings. You'll want to keep any shoulder harnesses from getting caught in the baggage conveyor belts. If they can be removed or zipped away, do so. If not, lash them in place by tying several belts or cords around the bags.

If your bags tie off, as do Kleppers and some older Nautiraids and Folbots, make sure to secure the knots. First double-knot them and then put tape over the knot. This will prevent them from coming loose, allowing parts to spill out. And the tape will discourage any sneaky fingers from opening your bags in transit.

Airline baggage limits. Some airlines limit the number of bags that you can check for free, and above that number they charge you for excess baggage. If you have a foldable that is in one bag, it's not a problem. If you have one that comes in several bags, though, you may get hit with the extra charge. Your first option is to find out which airlines have the more generous baggage limits. Another option is to double up your bags by buying a bigger bag that can carry two smaller ones within. (Feathercraft offers such a bag; it protects the basic carry bag and allows you to put other gear in along with it.)

Mark your bags. Occasionally an airline has been known to lose a kayak bag. Firmly tie luggage tags on the bag(s) with ¼-inch nylon cord.

Be careful not to put too much information on any tag. Leave your home address off the label since thieves sometimes note this information and alert cohorts that you are away. Use your office address and phone number, and also put this information on the inside of the bags in case the luggage tags come off. You may also want to consider stenciling your name and phone number on your bags.

You should also check about insurance. Your homeowners insurance may cover the loss of your boat in transit or may have provision for a rider that covers it. Insurance companies vary in what they cover, so check with your insurance carrier.

Customs. If you're traveling abroad, you'll have to deal with the U.S. Customs Department and the customs bureaus of other countries as well. Different countries vary in how they treat a disassembled boat being transported inside a bag. And within any country, one customs officer may be harsher than another. There are no hard and fast rules.

When dealing with customs, the less said is probably the better. Put on a nonchalant smile as if everyone traveled with a boat these days. It's just another personal item like a tennis racket—only bigger. However, if you are pressed to explain what's in the bags, be prepared with descriptive information. Make clear that this is your personal sports equipment that will leave with you when you exit the country. You intend to use it in the meantime, while staying at some luxury hotel. This shows that you are going to be enriching the local economy with your spending. Be careful about mentioning camping; campers may be looked upon as deadbeats who don't spend much locally.

Be prepared to open a bag and show its contents. If questions persist, it's a good idea to have with you some photos showing how the boat is assembled. These should be personal photos, not a manufacturer's brochure. A professional brochure could be interpreted as sales literature intended to help you sell the boat in that country, which would either be a no-no or require you to pay import duties. You may want to show the customs agent this book as an illustration of what folding kayaking is all about. (But *not* this page!)

Lastly, make certain to have your bill of sale with you. It could come in handy when returning to your home country to show that you bought it there, not abroad.

Shipping. Instead of carting your boat with you through the airline systems, you may want to consider shipping it ahead. The cost of shipping a folding kayak via United Parcel Service (UPS) from the U.S. East Coast to the West Coast is around $60, depending on the weight and size. If you ship it a week or so in advance, the boat is sure to beat you to your destination. This will save you the hassle of dragging it through airline terminals on both ends, getting the stuff into cabs, and so forth.

To package your folding kayak for shipping, it's best to use the boxes that it originally came in. However, you could get away with using the carrying bags themselves. In a sense, they are duffel bags, and UPS will accept them as such for delivery.

BY CAR

You have three main choices when it comes to traveling by car. You could carry your boat in its bags inside the car, tie the bag or bags on the roof, or tie the assembled boat onto your roof rack, just as you would with any other type of cartop boat.

Your kayak is always best off inside your car. This keeps it out of the elements and relatively safe from theft, especially if it can fit into your trunk. Even the largest of the doubles will fit into almost any car trunk, even that of a subcompact car. So generally you won't have to put the disassembled boat on your roof unless your trunk is loaded with all your other gear. A disassembled boat will need to be put together, but that is a fifteen-minute process once you get good at it. (See chapter 16 for tips on speedy assembly.)

A cartop boat will have to be untied and lowered, and since that will take you a few minutes anyway, it's not much of a time savings over the assembly process. And when you first place it on the roof you have to make certain it's fully secured, even locked. More and more rigid boats are being stolen from roof racks. You would have to protect a cartop foldable just as you would a rigid boat.

It's OK to cartop a folding kayak. This certainly won't hurt the boat. You could drive thousands of miles at top speed with no negative effect—except on your gas mileage. Cartopping is sometimes handy at the end of a long day when you're tired and don't want to wait for your boat to dry. Carrying it on a roof rack will dry it thoroughly in the rushing air. If you want to cartop your assembled foldable, here are some pointers on how to do it.

Getting It On

Foldables are loaded onto the roof of a car just as rigid boats are. If you're strong enough and your roof is low enough, start by getting your foldable up onto one shoulder.

The way to pick up a single boat is to stand alongside the cockpit. Crouch down. Pull the boat onto your knees. Place your arm into the cockpit and swing the boat onto your shoulder. Use your other hand to help balance the boat. Stand at the side of the car with the cockpit facing away from it. Lift it onto both roof-rack bars at once, if you can, or first onto one bar, then onto the other. This procedure works well with a light mini-foldable.

If you have a heavier single foldable, a high roof, or both, start by placing a car mat on the ground alongside the car, about even with its rear bumper, and place the boat alongside the car, with its stern on the mat. Pick up the boat from around the middle toward the bow, pivoting it on its stern (protected by the mat from abrasion). Put the front half up onto the front roof-rack bar, and then lift the stern end and put it on the rear bar.

With doubles, both partners hold the ends of the boat and lift the boat from the ground. They can try to lift it all at once onto both racks or put it on one rack at a time.

If you're having trouble getting your foldable

Cartopping a foldable.

up from alongside the car, try it from behind the car. Have the boat angled 45 degrees from a point about half the length of the boat from the rear bumper. Put a mat on the ground at the stern. Lift the front and pivot the stern on the mat until you can get the bow onto the rear bar of the roof rack. Go to the stern and start lifting the boat onto the rack and pushing it forward until it slides onto the front bar.

Tying One On

You should use a roof rack unless you're cartopping occasionally for only a few miles and only at slow speeds. An assembled boat that's just tied onto a bare roof with only a blanket protecting the boat and the roof top will tend to slip off to one side—or come flying off.

If you already have a roof rack, you can purchase special kayak cradles that fit onto the roof-rack bars. They offer an added measure of protection as do the windsurfer-rack pads that are made of nylon-covered rigid foam. If you use just the pads, an additional worthwhile investment might be a kayak stacker-bar set. Stacker bars go in the middle of the roof-rack bars and keep the boat from sliding around when the car is traveling at high speed. The stacker bars also give you a good place to tie the straps that secure the boat to the rack.

Carry your cartopper with the cockpit facing skyward. This is its strongest position and will put less stress on the kayak deck than carrying it upside down would. Pointing the bow toward the front of the car helps reduce wind resistance.

Use webbing straps to secure the boat at both roof-rack bars. Also put one line from the bow to the front bumper and a similar line from the stern to the rear bumper. The end lines will keep the boat steady and are added security in case a strap breaks or a buckle slips.

The roof-rack straps should be tightened hard, even to the point where they indent the sponsons. The end lines should not be guitar-string tight. You should be able to roll the line around a bit of your finger with little effort.

Locking it on. Get a bicycle cable lock set. The cable should be coated so it can't scratch the boat. Lash the cable around the stacker bar or the roof rack, and then work it into the cockpit and wrap it around a rib, gunwale, or anything it can go around. This will secure it against all but the most determined of thieves.

BY TRAIN OR BUS

Folding kayaks were made for travel on trains, but few people still use them this way. Few people travel by bus with their kayaks either because the car has become the primary land conveyance for foldables.

If you do use public transportation to carry a foldable in its bags, use the same precautions as for carrying your boat in a car trunk. You may not need to do any special packing because the bags will be handled mainly by you. On a train you'll place them in overhead racks. For bus travel, they'll go into the lower storage area, placed by you or by someone who knows you are watching closely to see how the boat is handled.

However, you have to ask yourself how far you'll have to carry the disassembled boat. You may have to cover long distances through terminals and out onto the bus or train platforms. Two people of average build can carry a disassembled double boat and enough camping equipment for a week's trip. One person can't duplicate that feat, especially with the camping gear.

If you're making overnight trips alone, you'll need a boat cart. Folding-kayak manufacturers offer carts that can carry one of their boats either assembled or in its bags. The carts vary in how easy they are to use. They have the advantage of being able to be folded away into your boat when you paddle off.

You can supplement the boat cart with an or-dinary collapsible luggage cart for carrying your camping gear. You may wind up pulling one cart and pushing the other, but the carts will help you get to a train that will start you on your weeklong camping trip.

Chapter Twelve

Sailing

Don't let anyone kid you; if you want to move under full sail at top speeds, you're better off in a sailboat. No kayak can match its sailing performance. But a kayak, particularly a folding one, can take advantage of the wind, even tack into it pretty nicely. What's more, it will give you the underlying thrill of sailing as you search for wind, find it, and hang on for the ride. You might not be moving as fast as a sailboat, but, being so close to the water, you certainly will have the sensation of speed as bow waves break over the deck and you see the water rushing by.

A sailboat is much better at what it does because it's dedicated to that pursuit alone. A sailboat has a deep keel or centerboard that allows it to hold position in crosswinds and to point higher into the wind than a kayak with its puny leeboard. Even the smallest sailboat carries at least 100 square feet of sail and can be rigged in all sorts of exotic ways. Kayaks, on the other hand, hardly ever carry more than around 50 square feet of sail area because any more would invite a capsize.

But folding kayaks have several things going for them. If you're becalmed, you can paddle until you can find wind and take off again. Try doing that in a sailboat. You can sail a kayak in shallow waters in which a sailboat's deep centerboard would run aground. You can beach a kayak for exploration. And of course, your folding kayak, sail and all, can be packed away in small bags for transport or storage, something you can't do with a sailboat.

Kayaks offer one other advantage that affects some people. If you get seasick on regular sailboats as they roll sharply from one side to the other, then the sailing kayak is your remedy. A kayak doesn't even induce a smidge of this common ailment because you're so close to the water that your pendulum of swing is much smaller and lower. On the pitching deck of a sailboat, your body can be 6 feet and more above the water's pitching surface.

Folding kayaks are in keeping with the tradition of the great sailing canoes of the nineteenth century. Sailing canoes were among the fastest methods of transportation without the aid of motors. Foldables were almost from their very beginning built with sailing in mind.

Sailing is something you can do very well with a folding kayak, better than with most hardshells because a foldable gives you a wider platform. All foldables have hull shapes that feature hard chines (angular as opposed to round-bottomed hulls) that help counteract heeling. Contrary to popular belief, heeling (running with the boat tilted up on one side) hurts your performance and opens you to the risk of capsize.

As mentioned in chapter 5, sails are available from the folding-kayak industry and from aftermarket producers. You have two basic choices in sail types: those capable of tacking into the wind, and those considered downwind rigs, albeit with some ability to go sideways to the wind.

UPWIND SAILING RIGS

To simplify sailing lessons for a full-range sail capable of going into the wind, this chapter focuses on two types of rigs, the Klepper S-4 and the Batwing from Balogh Sail Designs. The S-4 is typical of the type of sail rig that incorporates a jib and mainsail. This type of traditional upwind rig is also found on older Folbots, Pouchs, and other boats. The Balogh Batwing is a racier rig that uses a cambered windsurfer-type sail with no jib. The design dates back to a batswing sail seen in the nineteenth century on sailing canoes. Any similar sail adapted from the windsurfing world would work in a like fashion.

Klepper S-4 rig.

SAILING THE S-4 RIG

The Klepper S-4 rig is a classic in every aspect of the word. It's been around for half a century and has a very traditional gaff-rigged mainsail. Here are several things to keep in mind when sailing the S-4 rig.

It's a lot of sail that can easily overpower you. The S-4 carries 48 square feet of sail, enough to get an unaware or cocky paddler into trouble.

Even highly experienced kayak sailors have run into trouble with the S-4 when caught in heavy winds with gusts off nearby highlands.

Thousands of people have learned to sail the S-4 successfully. If the rig didn't work for the ordinary guy, Klepper couldn't have continued selling it all these years. Kids and octogenarians with little experience have sailed it. The secret to becoming proficient at using the S-4 is that you can learn to sail it one component at a time before trying the full-blown rig. There are mini-sets of rigs within the system, and this allows you to expand your knowledge of your foldable and how it functions under various wind conditions while using increased amounts of sail.

Rig Possibilities

Let's look at the S-4's components, the sailing range of each, and various combinations. The sail has a gaff-rigged 32-square-foot mainsail with a 16-square-foot jib. Until recently, Klepper also offered the M-I, a 10-square-foot drift sail. The M-I has been discontinued, but is still used by many kayakers. The other components, besides a rudder, are a crossbar and leeboards that attach to the coaming. Here are some of the many sail combinations you can try.

Jib alone. Jib sailing is fairly easy, as discussed later in this chapter. With leeboards, you can almost beam reach with the jib alone; i.e., go about 90 degrees off the wind. Some people just jib sail all the time, getting a boost when going downwind or going off at an angle of 90 degrees or less.

M-I drift sail alone. This is strictly a downwind setup, with some play possible to 30 or 40 degrees off dead downwind. You need pretty steady winds to make this setup worthwhile and luck that the wind is going precisely where you want to head. The drift sail has a boom that attaches with a hook to the mast and ties off to the top and bottom of the mast.

Jib with the M-I as mainsail. This is a pretty neat combination that's not likely to overpower you. It gives about 26 square feet of sail all told, about half that of the full mainsail and jib. Because it has a boom, you get some of the advantages of a mainsail but without the gaff to catch wind in awkward directions, and therefore less possibility of a spill. But 26 square feet is not an awful lot of power for a double kayak, so you'll go ahead slow but steady. You can tack with this rig setup, going to windward as much as 40 to 45 degrees, depending on your skill and other factors.

Jib with full main sail, the S-4 setup. Here is the full 48 square feet of sail area. It has three battens, a boom on the foot or lower part of the sail, and a gaff that swings up from the top of the mast when the main is raised fully. It's a lot of sail. You can perform the full range of sailing possibilities: run with the wind, reach in various directions, and go to windward.

Special Tips and Doo-Dads

The S-4 has prompted the use of many homemade devices and approaches that make sailing it easier. Bill Lozano of Atlantic Kayak Tours of Saugerties, New York, is an innovative paddler who put a lot of thought into the S-4 rig, fine-tuning it so it's a lot easier to sail. His ideas make it possible to assemble the rig quickly while under way and fairly easy to strike it when the weather changes or when you want to switch to paddling. Moreover, the customized setup allows unencumbered paddling, which isn't true of the stock S-4 setup as it comes from Klepper. Here are several of his suggestions.

Go without the leeboard and crossbar attached. These can encumber the paddling of the person in the front seat of a double and certainly will stymie anyone in a single-seat folding kayak. For the most part, your boat won't slip sideways much if you're running flat and not beating into the wind. If you absolutely need the leeboards, you can attach them on the go while in the water.

Don't bother having the battens placed in their pockets in the sail. Instead, just have them handy somewhere in the boat in case you decide it's going to be a day of all sailing. Having the battens in place makes it difficult to keep the mainsail in a tight roll and ready on deck where it won't interfere with paddling. The battens contribute only a small degree to sailing power, certainly not enough to warrant their interference with paddling.

Place a hook on the port mast shroud and a loop on the starboard, or vice versa if you like. Shrouds are guy lines on both sides that help support the mast. They attach to D-rings on the deck, so they get in the way of paddling if the mast is kept in place. The hook and loop allow you to pull the shrouds closer to the mast and out of the swinging room of the paddle in front, yet the shrouds still give enough support to a mast not carrying sail.

Make certain that the main halyard is tightly attached to the omega fitting on the gaff. If you don't, the gaff will not be truly vertical. Instead, it will be leaning to one side or the other, complicating sailing and risking a capsize.

Don't follow the Klepper method of lashing the mainsail to the mast. Klepper calls for running one continuous line through the eyelets on the luff or forward part of the sail, looping around the mast between each eyelet. Klepper calls for either a simple way or a more complex sliding wraparound non-knot, but always with a continuous line. Instead, just tie short pieces of line to each eyelet and tie off as many as you want to the mast. Most of the time, you can get away with one or two lashed to the mast. This speeds getting the mainsail in place and greatly simplifies striking the rig and putting it away in a hurry if a storm is brewing.

When rolling up the sail, you can easily create a tight package without needing to put it in a bag. While the rear person switches to paddling, the front person can roll up the sail tightly by wrapping the mainsail sheet (control line) around it. When it comes to hoisting the sail again, the back person can do the unraveling while the front person puts up the mast or works on various lines.

Work out such divisions of labor beforehand. What are the duties of the front person when switching from paddling to sailing? What are the duties of the back person? Are they the same when striking sail and switching back to paddling? The S-4 has a reputation for requiring too lengthy a setup and knockdown process. Teamwork and split duties can cut the time to a few minutes.

The Control Panel

Bill Lozano's most important little device, what he calls a cleat board, is worth its weight in gold to any S-4 sailor. The board is made out of ½- or ¾-inch plywood, and all you need is about 10 inches by 4 inches, which you'll cut down a bit. The board contains four clam cleats with fairleads. The cleat board is mounted on deck just ahead of the front person and close to the mast.

The two outside cleats—marked In and Out—control running the jib tack (lower front end) in and out from the bow. The jib that Klepper supplies has a snap hook that the company intends to be hooked directly to the deck fitting on the bow. Modify this by running a continuous line through that deck fitting and back to the In and Out cleats on the cleat board. The jib-tack snap hook is attached to a loop about halfway along that continuous line. Using this modification, you can opt to pull the whole jib toward you and store it in one of the paddle pockets. Why? Because even if the jib is lying flat on the deck, it can catch water in heavy waves and pull over your kayak. The importance of being able to bring the jib in and out while

Control board for a double.

Control board for a single.

under way cannot be overstated. It is essential to your safety.

The two cleats in the middle of the board are marked J for jib and M for mast and control the jib and main halyards. By releasing the J cleat, you immediately cause the jib to fall down onto the foredeck without having to undo any lines. Likewise, pull the line on the M cleat and it will loosen, pay out quickly, and lower the mainsail. Both the jib and main halyards run through a pulley at the bottom of the mast and, of course, to a pulley at the mast top. This control panel with its cleats provides a key to safety when sailing the S-4 and getting full enjoyment of it even while under way.

Sailing Tips When Under Way

Beyond the usual advice on sailing any small boat, advice that you either already have heard or can pick up from a book, class, or friend, there are some things to keep in mind when sailing the S-4.

When letting out the mainsail, be careful not to let it out too far. Don't let it press against the shrouds. That's as far as it can go anyway, but you don't want to let it get to that point. If you have it resting against the shroud and a gust of wind hits, you have no more room to pay out the sheet (the line in your hand) that is controlling the boom. You could tip over.

Do let out the mainsail until it flutters, and then pull it back in a bit to a taut position. So much of this is feel, but by doing it this way you can quickly get the feel of the wind and its power.

Try to strike a balance between wind and rudder. This is true of sailing any small boat, but, again, it's trickier in an S-4-rigged folding kayak. You want to work the right amount of wind into the sail (so it's as taut as you feel comfortable with) with the main sheet and the rudder, but you don't want to over rudder. If you do, the boat will stall and either lose power or play some losing games with the wind in which you can capsize, depending on wind strength and the boat's angle of heel.

Try to keep the boat running as flat as possible. A boat that is heeled over is losing speed. Again, it's a matter of balancing forces. Either slack the sail to keep the boat flat or hike your body out on the coaming or special seat to maintain a flatter running position. You can also sit on something that will allow you to lean over farther than you can from the regular seated position.

A reduced sail area kept taut is better than a larger sail area sheeted out. Unfortunately, the S-4 does not come with reefing ties or zippers. You have to add these or, awkwardly, roll some of the lower part of the sail around the boom. That's why using something like the M-1 rig as a mainsail can sometimes make a lot of sense.

SAILING THE BALOGH BATWING

The Balogh Batwing is a fully battened, camber-induced sailing rig that is revolutionizing kayak sailing. It's an easy rig to strike and works well in the open cockpit arrangements of foldable kayaks. Unlike in a sloop setup, which generally has a jibsail out on the foredeck as well as a mainsail, the Batwing has only one sail to get down, and it's close at hand to the cockpit. When you uncleat the halyard, the battens drop the sail almost like venetian blinds into a neat package that can be stowed away or tied off quickly.

Balogh Sail Design has come up with a major innovation in its patented Balogh Outrigger Stabilizing System (BOSS). The outriggers were originally conceived as "training wheels" for beginners to learn sailing without risking a capsize.

The system certainly serves that function but has become much more. Seasoned sailors are using BOSS for greater performance to windward and to achieve higher speeds.

Square foot for square foot, the Batwing, with its airfoil cambered construction, is more powerful than anything else around for kayak sailing. Under ideal conditions this is great, but that power must be respected. When the wind picks up, be quick, not tardy, to reef—that is, reduce your sail area. You'll actually move faster and have a safer time of it.

The BOSS outrigger setup allows for greater boat speed under heeling conditions as well as when sailing in stronger winds, but don't get too cocky. Know your own limitations as a sailor. Offshore winds can put you well out to sea before you know it. Tacking back against such strong winds can be a long, drawn out experience.

Below are a number of tips designed to get the most out of the Balogh Batwing. They would apply to any other similar rig that uses a cambered, battened sail.

LEFT: Balogh Batwing on single Klepper with BOSS. RIGHT: Balogh Batwing on Nautiraid double. *(Dennis Stevens)*

Balogh Batwing schooner-rigged Klepper double. *(Dennis Stevens)*

Tighten Up All Lines

The first point to watch out for is the downhaul that pulls down the bottom of the sail and snugs it to the mast. Under most wind conditions, the downhaul should be pulled tightly; manhandled, it won't break anything. The idea is to pull it tight enough to smooth away any sail wrinkles that run perpendicular to the luff, the leading edge of the sail.

The second area that needs tightening is the battens. Here the objective is to get out any wrinkles that run perpendicular to the battens themselves. Tightening the battens is appropriate for wind speeds from moderate to gale. The exception is light winds. In light winds, too much tension cups the sail in the leech area, where the wind will catch and the boat will stall. Looser is better when the winds are light.

Select an Appropriate Sheeting Point

This is a crucial detail for getting the most out of your Batwing. First, the sheeting point is where the sheet or controlling line is held, and it should be approximately 6 to 18 inches aft of the clew (the back, lower corner of the sail) when the sail is in a midships position. This is the most efficient place from which to control the sail, giving you the most power out of your Batwing.

Second, that sheeting point should be mechanical; i.e., not just your hand. Use a pulley or cleat. It should not be tied off, but a stopper knot can be tied at the end of the sheet to prevent it from running out through the pulley, if that's what you're using. There's an exception to the position described above. If you decide not to use the BOSS, have the sheeting point farther aft. This position delivers less power but more safety, which is especially important protection from unexpected gusts. It gives the sail a greater twist that allows it to spill off any excessive air fairly automatically, so you don't have to be highly attuned to anticipating gusts or to reacting quickly. It's more forgiving if you're going without outriggers.

Use Finesse, Not Force

The Batwing is a high-performance sail that must be handled with subtlety, requiring a feel and touch for the varying wind and sea conditions.

Finesse is the key, something that experienced sailors who come from more traditional sails have difficulty grasping. Such sailors almost invariably oversheet; i.e., pull too tightly on the sheet controlling the sail. When they do, they stall the airfoil on the Batwing and lose, rather than gain, power.

The Batwing is a radically different type of sail. It's highly efficient, and it has a short outhaul. A sail's outhaul is the distance from mast to back of the sail.

Achieving Various Points of Sail

When sailing, keep an eye on the telltale attached to the upper leech to help your sheeting control. The telltale should be streaming back horizontally in line with the sail. If it's wrapping around the other side, you're sheeting too tightly, so sheet out a bit. If it flutters in front of the sail, you're too loose with your control, so pull in some on the sheet. Also keep your rudder as straight as possible; hard ruddering stalls the boat.

Sailing downwind. The telltale reading doesn't apply when you're sailing straight downwind, but you should not be going straight downwind, because this course doesn't give you your best velocity made good. When you want to go downwind, tack in a series of broad reaches (45 degrees off downwind). The exception to this rule is very light wind, when you might as well go straight downwind.

Off the wind. When the clew moves forward in an off-the-wind maneuver, you should pull down and out with the sheet to get more power. Basically you follow the clew. If it's moving into a down and forward position, you follow or mimic this with the sheet control.

Upwind sailing. When going upwind, don't head directly into it, which is called "pointing too high." Kayaks are lightweight boats with little inertia, so waves can slow them down and stall their forward motion. Even if the Balogh sail is capable of pointing well up into the wind, this will not give you the best velocity made good. You're better off close reaching and tacking than trying to go too close to the wind.

You may want to try what some paddling sailors term "motor sailing." Since you don't have a motor, you paddle to supplement the sailing as you move into the wind. At that point you are working with apparent wind, not actual wind. Paddling moves you enough to feed more air into the sail as you go upwind, thus getting more speed out of the sail. It's a classic symbiotic relationship. The sail is giving you speed between paddling strokes, and your paddling is feeding air into the sail.

DOWNWIND SAILING RIGS

Downwind sailing rigs are much less complicated than their upwind cousins and are favored by paddlers who are looking for a boost only part of the time. Downwind rigs offer several benefits:

- **Cheaper to buy.** Downwind sails are about a quarter of the price of upwind sailing rigs.
- **More stowable.** You can take one along without much fanfare because it takes up less room in your kayak. Downwind sails have less canvas area, and their masts are often thinner and shorter.
- **Easier to rig up.** You have fewer lines to deal with when setting up the rig. Hardware requirements are minimal, and very little customizing is necessary to fit a downwind rig to your boat.
- **Simpler to sail.** Sailing downwind is less complex, as you can only do so much with a downwind rig.

There is a catch. Performance tends to be modest. In most cases, you won't be able to achieve the speeds you can with a full-range rig.

You also are limited in where you can go in relation to the wind's direction. Some downwind rigs can only go within a narrow range of 20 degrees on either side of straight downwind. Others can sail up to 45 degrees off straight downwind, or broad reach. Still others can beam reach or sail almost 90 degrees to straight downwind.

To simplify lessons for using a downwind rig, the following descriptions look at two types: the Balogh Twins and the Klepper jib sail. The Twins is one of the better downwind rigs because it is so powerful and versatile. Several imitator rigs on the market operate in a similar way. The Klepper jib is a classic setup, and lots of similar rigs are around. Jib sailing has quite a few advocates because of its simplicity and surprisingly good performance.

Other types of downwind sail rigs use kites and parafoils that don't require masts. Their uses are very specialized, and they offer little control.

SAILING THE TWINS

The Twins rig has a superficial resemblance to a classic design, the Ljungstrom rig, in that it is two triangular mainsails sewn together at their luffs. But the Ljungstrom is mostly an upwind sail, and the Twins is a downwind sail with some upwind capability. Unlike the Ljungstrom, the Twins uses sprit booms under each sail half. The booms are attached to the clew, and they lead nearly perpendicular to the mast.

The Twins rig looks like a child's kite being flown upside down. It carries the widest part of the sail fairly low on the mast, where it is least likely to destabilize your kayak if hit by a gust. The dihedral or two-planed sail is self-trimming. Bridle lines run from the clews to a 2-foot-long bridle bar attached to a single sheet. This allows easy one-

hand adjustment of the sails. The Twins rig ranges in sizes from 20 to 40 square feet. The 30-footer would be a good compromise, giving adequate power to a double foldable but not overwhelming any single you might want to switch it to.

You'll find several sails on the market that resemble the basics of the Twins rig. Or you could make a primitive version that will work in fundamentally the same way. Here are the driving lessons for using this type of downwind rig.

Setting Up While Under Way

This is a maneuver you'll want to get proficient at performing. The Twins and its look-alikes are meant to be used whenever wind opportunity knocks; for example, when a good following wind blows up or when you're 60 degrees or so off the wind's direction.

If you're in a double, the front paddler takes out the disassembled mast parts and feeds the hoops carefully on to the lowest section of the mast. Practice this on dry land so you know beforehand how it should look and how the pieces go on.

Meanwhile, the back person assembles the other two sections. These are then attached to the bottom section, which already has the sail hoops attached. The front paddler then crawls forward a bit to lift the mast and drop it through the mast partner and into the mast step on the kayak's floor. The front paddler hoists the sail with the halyard line and ties it off on a cleat, then pulls down on the downhaul line and ties it off.

If winds are gusty, don't hoist the sail to the very top of the mast. This will keep the largest part of the sail low and out of the way of gusts. However, the downhaul should be pulled down tightly, similar to how it is done with the Batwing.

Sailing with the Wind

When sailing relatively straight downwind, you use the Twins with its two halves opened up.

When the two opened halves form a straight line, you get the maximum amount of downwind thrust.

The Twins sail doesn't have to be absolutely perpendicular to the line of travel of the boat. You can let its straight line come slightly to one side, which will work only for a few degrees off straight downwind.

You can slow down by simply letting loose on the bridle sheet. When you do, the two halves no longer form a straight line; instead they form an angle of about 150 degrees. This will slow you down. To depower completely, just let the sheet out all the way until the bridle strikes the mast. The two halves will have folded out in front of the mast where they will catch absolutely no wind.

Sailing Closer to the Wind

The Twins rig has a trick up its sleeve that allows you to sail with the wind on your beam. You simply fold one half over the other to form

Jib sailing.

a single triangle. This cuts your sail area in half but gives you something that looks like a mainsail. In this position it resembles the Klepper M-I drift sail.

To get the most out of the doubled-over Twins, a single boat should always use a leeboard, which helps it resist being pushed sideways by wind coming from the beam. You almost don't need a leeboard as long as you are short of a full beam reach, say, up to 60 degrees off straight downwind. Doubles can often get away without leeboards when approaching a beam reach.

As in the case of the Batwing, finesse is needed for subtle rudder control and sheet control. Keep the rudder as straight as possible to avoid going into a stall or losing what you are gaining from the wind's force on your sail.

Don't oversheet, or pull the sheet too tight. Pulling tightly on the sheet works when going straight downwind with the Twins fully opened, but it doesn't give you more power when the sails are doubled over. Let the sheet out a bit, and then pull in slightly. You shouldn't feel like you're holding the leash of a dog that wants to chase a rabbit.

All the time you're working with the sheet, keep fiddling with the rudder to get just the right angle to the wind. There are no hard-and-fast formulas. It's a feel that comes with time.

JIB SAILING

While the chief purpose of a jib is to work with a mainsail to improve its aerodynamic efficiency, you can sail quite well with the jib alone. There are some provisos, though.

Jib sailing appears to work better with double boats than with singles, because anything more than the smallest of jibs tends to overpower singles. For example, the Klepper jib can be scary under certain circumstances in a single. The bow will want to dive under, and the wind whipping around so far in front of you may give you the feeling that you lack control. Paddlers who like to jib sail often find some way to cut down the area of the Klepper jib, or they replace it with a smaller custom-made jib. Doubles seem to thrive on the regular jib.

You need to use leeboards for reaching. With the wind's force ahead of the mast, there is a greater tendency for the boat to slide than when the wind is hitting directly at or at an angle to the side of the boat.

To switch to jib sailing while under way, you pretty much have to have most of it already in place. You must have some way to get the jib in position, something like the setup mentioned above for the S-4. And you'll want to keep the mast in place. You can install the leeboards when you need them.

You can reach impressive speeds with a jib, especially in broad to beam reaches when you are operating 45 to 90 degrees off straight downwind. Going straight downwind requires a trick or two. Here are some pointers on sailing these ranges.

Downwind with a Jib

The Twins rig has sprit booms that can hold the sails wide open. On a jib you don't have such a device. To expose the greatest amount of sail surface to the wind, you need to extend the clew, the back corner of the jib, out to one side. If you push on it with the end of a paddle, you'll get some extra extension. Push out with the paddle's blade end, not a shaft end, which might slip and tear at the sail cloth. Make certain to hold the sheet out to that side, too, as far as you can comfortably extend your arm.

Reaching

Broad and beam reaching require a delicate balance of rudder and sheet. Let the sheet out until the back of the jib flutters. At that point, sheet in a bit. Just as in other light-craft sailing, you'll need to play with the rudder's angle to get it just right; that is, producing the most power from the wind while still heading the boat where you want to go.

Chapter Thirteen

Camping

One of the most pleasant features of a folding kayak is how well it adapts to camping. Not only can you take a foldable halfway around the globe, but once you arrive, you can enjoy kayaking for more than just day trips.

Folding kayaks are voluminous enough to carry a payload that could see you through a month's journey. Their payload weights generally run higher than those of comparable rigid kayaks, and loading up a foldable doesn't compromise its seaworthiness. Even the mini-foldables can carry a week's worth of gear safely. You can stretch this to several weeks if you know how to pack small and light.

You can load large items through the cockpit area so you don't get stuck working through the small hatches as in some rigid boats. The crossrib structure in the cockpit area provides perfect tie-on points for placing plenty of gear around you that you may want to grab in a hurry. The long rods and keelboards along the inside bottom offer convenient nooks for keeping round objects from rolling around. It's almost as if the frame concept was created with camping gear in mind.

Getting ready for a camping trip.

Taking out gear.
(Walther/Klepper)

HOW TO LOAD A FOLDABLE

Just because you *can* carry everything but the proverbial kitchen sink doesn't mean you *should*. And, as easy as it may be to shove items anywhere, you should also be thinking of proper trim, access to the rest of your gear, and other considerations. In the long run, you'll have more loading space if you put some thought into what you're doing. Your boat will also perform better under changing sea and wind conditions.

Optimizing Available Space

The beauty of packing a folding kayak is that you can get a sneak preview of how everything will fit in. How? Simply make the frame of your boat without its skin covering. That's the size and shape of the loading space you have available. See what can fit where and how you can get certain items into particular spots. Here's the step-by-step approach to use after you have the fully assembled frame in front of you.

1. Measure the opening at each rib and the space between them. These extremely valuable measurements will tell you if, for example, a certain bag can be slipped past a particular rib opening and down into that end of the boat or not. Knowing the space between ribs will tell you if a certain dry bag can be secured lengthwise in that area.

You could make a sketch of the frame with these measurements or simply use the sales literature or assembly instructions from the manufacturer. One or the other should have a picture of the full frame. Just write in the dimensions.

2. Pack your gear bags and place them into the naked frame. Start with any waterproof bags you may already have. Don't rush out to buy new bags until you determine what you may need. Sea trim will be discussed later in this chapter, but for now, place items where they best fit. Make certain that bags that you locate in an end section can actually be shoved there from the cockpit area.

Don't forget the storage area that is available around you inside the cockpit. For now, use cord to tie items into this area. Sit in the boat to make sure you have enough room for yourself. Check that the rudder cables won't snag on anything.

3. Mark the bags and sketch where they belong. When you mark bags, indicate not only the area in which they fit but also their relative weight. H, M, and L, for heavy, medium, and light, will suffice. This is valuable information for trim. Make certain that your H bags can fit immediately in front and behind the cockpit section. If an H bag can't, plan to reduce its size until it will.

4. Establish how you might load bags into the ends of the boat. You may want to prepack the ends when you make the frame, before inserting the frame halves into the skin. Such difficult-to-reach end space should be reserved for emergency items that you won't need in a hurry or on a regular basis, such as the hull patch kit. Many Feathercraft models have hatches you can reach through to position awkward items. And more and more models of folding kayaks, such as those from Folbot and Nautiraid, have zippered decks, and zippers are an available option on Kleppers. Otherwise, use a half paddle to shove items in toward the bow or stern.

5. Think about how you will unload the ends. You may want to create a pulley and cord system for retrieving bags placed deeper in under the deck. Attach a cord or strap to the bags stowed in the ends. Secure the strap or cord on a nearby rib and use it to haul the bags out when unloading. Again, hatches and zippers on many models simplify getting to the ends of your boat.

Loading for Best Trim and Stability

Never load any kayak by just throwing things in. You must consider such things as the boat's stability, its best trim for certain conditions, and protection from water damage. Here are some of the more important points.

Pack light. This is the first commandment of sea-kayak camping. When looking at all that empty space in a foldable, it's awfully tempting to load it up to the brim. Avoid the temptation. When you think about loading in extra items, consider the effect of the added weight. A heavy boat requires more energy to paddle because it rides deeper in the water and creates more drag. A heavier boat will be more difficult to turn and maneuver. Also, a heavily laden boat is harder to deal with while launching and landing.

A good philosophy to have about any camp-ing trip is to pretend that you're going to have to backpack the weight of everything. Make believe that all your gear must fit in a 6,000-cubic-inch backpack. Obviously, kayak campers don't really have to carry it all on their backs, nor are they limited to the size of a conventional backpack. But that imaginary backpack is a good place to start. Build up from there with essential gear, rather than starting with the double's potential 700-pound payload and the copious volumes its interior can absorb. You'll be happier in the long run.

Load for anticipated sea conditions. Generally, you load a kayak with about 50 percent of the load on either side of the boat's center to balance the boat. Some boats behave better with a slightly heavier rear, say 55 percent of the load. But sea conditions often get in the way of such ideal weight-distribution schemes.

If your weather radio tells you that the wind and seas are likely to be coming from behind you on the course you're taking that day, place more of the weight behind you than you normally would. This will counteract the bow's tendency to dive when swells and wind propel you forward.

If you anticipate that wind and current will be coming at you throughout a good portion of the day, put a greater proportion of the weight in front. This will keep the bow down and prevent it from catching wind and slowing you down.

Wise placement of your heavy bags may be your best and easiest way to achieve the appropriate trim, but you don't want them too far forward or back. They should be placed immediately in front of or behind you. The very ends of the boat should contain the lighter gear.

Use the space around you as much as possible. You have plenty of space to load gear in the cockpit area, the center of the boat. Keeping gear weight in the center is the ultimate trimming method for many reasons. Your steering is least affected when your boat is center-loaded, especially in beam winds. Neither end is likely to resist turning or, conversely, be prone to swinging around when you don't want it to. Center-loading also contributes to stability and, in a capsize, will make it easier to right the boat. A folding kayak allows center loads whereas a rigid boat doesn't, and this feature helps make foldables such good packhorses.

Consider using bags as seats and seat backs to make double use of their space. Ordinary dry bags used for holding clothing and other items are OK but may have you sitting too high. A better type is one with a one-way purge valve through which you can expel air from the closed dry bag. The best types are ones with long inflation tubes that are sold as combined flotation-storage bags for underdeck use. But you can sit on the smaller sizes of these and use the inflation tube to blow in or expel air while under way for comfortable seating and height adjustment.

Avoid deck loads. Consider yourself fortunate if you don't have D-rings with which to attach loads on top of your deck. If you do, avoid the temptation to use them for excess gear that you cannot fit inside the boat. Follow the rule: "If not inside, leave aside."

Deck loads are dangerous because they can catch beam winds. They raise your effective center of gravity, which reduces the inherent stability of any boat. In a capsize, they make it almost impossible to get the boat upright again, and they can get in the way of your reentry. If you have D-rings, use them only to secure something light, like a paddle float and hand pump.

Keep heavy items low in the boat. For example, the floor of your foldable is the place to locate your water supply, which weighs a lot. Consider storing water in flat bags, sometimes called water sacks or desert bags. One of these will hold 3 gallons of water in a space only about 6 inches high.

Water sacks not only keep your center of gravity low but also act as ballast.

When you're tying items inside the cockpit area, don't locate heavy items too high up the sides. If you have a tent in this area, keep it on or close to the bottom of the cockpit, alongside you or your legs. Reserve higher tie-ins for the lighter items, such as sleeping mats.

Protect everything in waterproof bags. Some people make the mistake of protecting only clothing and sleeping bags. They think that tent poles and nylon-covered sleeping mats can survive getting wet. They can't. Aluminum tent poles, for example, are not made of the same marine-grade alloys as folding-kayak aluminum frames, which resist saltwater corrosion. The same goes for stoves. And, while a nylon-coated mat might not absorb much water, its surface will stay wet and be annoying in a tent.

Try to use small- and medium-size waterproof bags. Larger bags are harder to slide in past the ribs closest to the cockpit, and some won't fit at all. Smaller bags can easily be placed in the underdeck areas, and when they're loaded around you in the cockpit, they won't take up the room you'll need to sit comfortably. Smaller bags are also a good insurance policy for your gear. If you have three small bags in place of one, and a bag tears, you have water penetration in only a third of that gear, not all of it.

Tie and lash everything. You don't want loose items that could float free in a capsize or get in your way as you climb back into your seat. To keep gear contained in the front and back underdeck sections, try running webbing straps in an X pattern across the ribs leading to these sections. Bungee cords will also work.

Provide yourself with easy access to everything. An earlier section suggested pulleys and tie-on cords to retrieve items that are farther under deck.

Another method for easier access is to use the long carrying bag that comes with some of the foldables. For example, the Klepper long bag is narrow enough to fit well into the underdeck area in front of you. While it is not waterproof, you can load it a third full with smaller items in zippered plastic bags, and then shove the long bag into the bowels of your boat as far as it will go. Push it in with a paddle. Then load some larger, heavier items into the rest of the long bag. When you land, pull these one or two bulkier or heavier items out first, and then yank on the whole bag to retrieve the rest of the load.

CAMPING CONSIDERATIONS

Camping from a kayak lets you extend the adventure over days and weeks on the water. But, assuming you know how to load your boat correctly for prevailing conditions, what other points should you consider?

There are many. Three key considerations are where to camp, what equipment to have, and how to move your loaded boat and gear around on land when you have to.

If you're lucky, you'll have a series of legal campsites strung along your route at the right distance from each other to provide you with a good paddle each day. If not, you'll have to try another approach for your nightly encampment.

For kayak-camping equipment, backpacking gear will do, but you may want to add some special items made for camping out of your kayak. Moving your boat and gear on land can be made easier if you follow certain pointers.

Commando Camping

Camping these days has some new realities. A half century ago, you could pull up just about anywhere and find a spot to camp. With the advance of civilization, you now must be sensitive to the rights of property owners and to local laws. You don't want to ruffle anyone's feathers.

You can still find attractive touring areas where camping is permitted. In other areas, several designated scenic sites might work into your paddling mileage schedule. Be thankful that such places exist. You can help keep them open by practicing low-impact camping techniques that preserve their pristine beauty and reduce maintenance costs.

Many wonderful paddling areas just don't have such camping available. To enjoy them for more than just a day trip, you'll have to engage in a shadowy procedure few of us who are responsi-

Commando camping near the Big Apple. The boat was later moved out of sight.

ble citizens ever wish to do—commando camp. It's not legal, so you're not setting up for the night as you would in an official campsite. Instead, you camp in the least obtrusive manner you can so no one need know you were there. You're taking your chances. But for many stretches of shoreline that you're likely to paddle, if you don't take this chance, you're not going to sleep that night, and perhaps not for several nights thereafter. Here's how to commando camp with the least risk to you and least disturbance to others.

To ask or not to ask. Asking permission seems to be the antithesis of commando camping, but it's really your first rule. Size up the situation.

If you're in a remote area but there's a home nearby, you should ask politely about camping possibilities. Chances are highly in your favor that, being so remote, the owner may welcome someone to talk to, especially someone in a folding kayak who probably has a tale to tell. Besides, if you don't ask or advise the remote home dweller of your presence, you probably would be spotted anyway; such individuals are acutely aware of what goes on around them.

If you're in a more populated area, you're probably better off not asking, especially near a private home. Vacation-home owners usually don't want anyone around them to share the natural wealth of the spot or may be concerned about liability. Year-round residents are a toss-up.

Likeliest spots. Some areas offer better commando-camping prospects than others. Large state or provincial parks work out OK if you don't camp near the more heavily traveled walking trails. Avoid camping near a road where a passing ranger could spot you. Railroad rights-of-way along coastlines and rivers are also good choices. Railroad detectives no longer patrol that property or bash in the heads of wayward hoboes. Abandoned industrial sites are likely candidates, although they're not very glamorous.

Do avoid municipal parks, roadsides, and village outskirts. Also avoid camping near navigational aids such as range markers and lights. The Coast Guard levies heavy fines for obstructing the operation of these devices.

Set up late, leave early. Whatever you do, don't set up camp in broad daylight if you are trying to commando camp. If you find a likely spot in late afternoon, hang out as if you are just taking a rest. Check out the site. If it's suitable, casually prep the site a bit by kicking away stones from where you'll place your tent. Paddle away for a while, circle back when it's getting dark, and then set up. Plan to leave at or before first light. Not only does this help you avoid being spotted, it's also a practical way to paddle on long trips. Getting off to an early start means you can get a lot of paddling in that day. If the weather turns sour later in the day, you'll have gotten in at least some mileage before being forced to halt. You'll be surprised at how easy it is to get an early start without breakfast, and then have breakfast maybe three hours later at your first stopping spot.

Hide your tent and boat. If your tent is bright orange, meant to draw rescuers' attention after an avalanche, don't dismay. You can cover it with an olive-drab tarp. Pull your whole boat away from the water's edge and into the brush or among the trees. If it has a bright colored deck, turn it over to reveal the black or gray hull, which will not draw as much attention.

Show little light, make less noise. You should never carry a bright Coleman lantern on any kayak camping trip, and you're even less likely to carry it when you don't want to announce your presence. A bright light would attract curiosity, and then someone could object to your presence or cause you trouble. Keep your sounds low. You don't have to whisper, but commando campers don't yell out to one another to get something from the boat.

No fires. This is the strictest no-no. Nothing will get you into more trouble than building a fire in an area you don't belong in. The smoke is likely to attract the attention of any official or property owner, and then they're likely to be upset and demand that you leave immediately—even if ordinarily they'd be disposed to let you camp. Some paddlers think it's OK to make their fires below the high-tide line, but it's not. A fire is a fire in the eyes of most onlookers, no matter where it's built.

Camping Equipment

Here's a list of camping gear that's practical for kayak touring. Chances are that much of what you already have can be adapted for camping from a kayak. Or you may decide to buy some gear made especially for kayak camping.

Tent. You may want a larger tent than you'd ordinarily carry in a backpack. The larger size can be useful for drying gear. Also, in the paddlers' damp environment, that greater space helps disperse body vapor and preserves a sense of dryness. To do that, the tent should have adequate ventilation.

When buying a tent for kayak camping, keep in mind that it should fit nicely between the ribs in your foldable so its poles won't get bent out of shape. As a rule, any tent will work if its poles break down to lengths of less than about 22 inches for a Klepper, 18 inches for a Nautiraid, and about 28 inches for the rest of the foldables. Otherwise you'll have to lay the tent poles on the rest of the gear. Opt for a tent with a full fly cover, because mist rising off fresh and salt water will wet the lower parts of the tent proper if its rain fly does not cover them well. Make sure the tent provides good ventilation, or too much moisture will build up inside. Lastly, consider color. If possible, get an unobtrusive gray or green, not a bright blue or bright orange.

Tarp. You'll want a rain tarp. Not only can you get protection under it during rain, it will also keep lake mist and ocean spray from chilling you as you eat dinner. If you hole up in the middle of the day to wait out a change of tide or wind, a tarp can keep you from frying in the sun. A 10-by-10-foot tarp is quite versatile, and you can set it up to protect two people.

Sleeping bag. You can usually get by with a

Camping in the Bahamas.

much lighter bag than you may think. In warmer months, you'll be generating so much heat at night from having been in the sun all day at a high activity rate that you and your partner will be little furnaces inside a tent. If you get chilled, use warm clothing to increase the warmth rating of your sleeping bag.

Be careful with down. If a down bag gets wet it becomes useless, so you'll always be worried about keeping it dry. Opt for a synthetic bag. Many new fillers are being developed that have almost the same compressibility, weight, and warmth as down, and the best part is that they retain their insulation properties even if they do get wet.

Stove. Choose a stove that's easy to light and maintain. The fewer parts, the better. You might be camping in sand, which can work its way into mechanical parts and cause the whole stove to fail. Butane stoves perform extremely well. Some butane-mix canisters even work in air temperatures close to freezing. The cans present a disposal problem for backpacking, but in your foldable you have the room to carry them out.

Food. You may want to think twice about planning gourmet meals. Some kayaking manuals devote many pages to foraging for food along the shore that you can cook with pastas and grains, but foraging takes time at the end of the day when you're tired and daylight is fading. Such items require extensive cooking time, and that uses up fuel—which increases the amount you must plan to carry in the first place.

You're better off with nutritional one-pot food that only needs to be heated, not cooked. Freeze-dried camping food can taste wonderful at the end of the day. Hunger adds a very tasty sauce to any food that's put before a famished person.

Water. You'll need a way to carry plenty of drinking water. Kayak touring differs sharply from backpacking in that you won't have trails with drinking-water sources every so many miles. If you plan on saltwater touring, you'll need to carry 1 gallon or more of drinking water per day per person. The cost of desalinators can be prohibitive for all but the most dedicated of expeditions.

For a freshwater environment, you can find a relatively inexpensive water-purification system that will relieve you from having to carry the weight of all your water. If you're paddling on large freshwater lakes, you could take your chances by drinking lake water, but be sure to lessen your risk of ingesting bad bacteria by collecting your water well offshore before you land.

You won't need to use your precious drinking water for cleaning up. Sand and gravel will work for cleaning plates and pots at the shoreline. When you're freshwater paddling, the water is safe enough for bathing. Even in salt water, you can take a good bath if you use one of those camping soaps designed for salt water. Dry yourself quickly after emerging from any salt water to keep the salt crystals from drying on your skin and irritating it later.

Extra line and paper. Make certain that you tie off your boat well. Wind waves, boat wakes, and rising tides can snatch any loose boat from shore, even if it was originally left a few boat lengths up from the water's edge. Even though it's a lot of work, get your boat well onto high ground and tie it off as though it were still in the water—for total peace of mind.

Write your name and your itinerary on a piece of paper, and place it inside a Ziploc bag inside your kayak somewhere it can easily be seen. If your boat ever strays from a beach with a passing wake, you'll have a better chance of getting it back or of someone summoning help for you. In a worst-case scenario—a capsize in which you lose your boat and swim to shore—the itinerary notes may direct searchers to where you are likely to be. Leaving this note is a good idea not only for camping but also day trips, in case you are separated from your boat.

Uninvited guests. You won't want to discover uninvited guests—like mice, snakes, scorpions, or spiders—when you're already a half mile offshore, so always cover your folding kayak. If it has a spraydeck, leave it on; attach the spray skirts and tie them closed. This should keep out any stowaways.

Be meticulous about removing any opened food and crumbs from your kayak. Such savory items attract rodents and other beasts that can make mincemeat out of your canvas deck.

PACKING YOUR KAYAK WITH GEAR

You can get a surprising amount of gear into any kayak, regardless of the boat's size. You just have to cull down your gear and find a place for it. Below are some examples, starting with the smallest of boats, a mini-foldable, followed by a slim regular-size kayak, and then a double one. All happen to be Feathercrafts, but other models of like size can accommodate the gear and have it placed similarly.

What a Mini-Foldable Can Carry

Here is a way of packing a mini-foldable such as the K-Light for a week or more of camping. Of the minis, the K-Light isn't the one with the most internal storage space. Still, you have a surprising amount of space in the K-Light if you know how to use it efficiently, pick proper dry bags, and use these well. The illustration opposite shows one way to pack a K-Light that would help you carry about 50 pounds of camping and paddling gear, food, and 22 pounds (almost 3 gallons) of water.

To make good use of the very ends of the K-Light, do the following: roll up its carrying bag into a tight package, and then preload it into the stern prior to inserting the rear frame half into the hull. This bag fits perfectly in this area without protruding into the skin or into the next compartment.

For trim purposes, place an equal amount of weight in the bow end, about 3½ pounds, as the carry bag in the stern. Here is where proper dry bags come in. Stick with small- to medium-size flat bags (i.e., without defined round bottoms, although round-bottomed ones work too in some places). The dry bag in the bow end can carry a tarp and a sleeping mat flattened out. Put the bag on its edge so that it's in line with the keel of the boat and not pressing out on the skin and push it into place with a paddle. It slightly protrudes into the next section.

For the second bow section, first remove the foot pedals for access, and then insert a round-bottomed medium-size dry bag. A round-bottomed bag works well to store cookware and a stove since these items don't lend themselves to flattening out. This bag also holds food. The weight of this bag and its contents helps in trimming the boat.

At and around where your legs are in the cockpit area, carry flat, 1-gallon water bags and several canteens. Also have a small dry bag with day-use items such as a paddle jacket, a long-sleeved warm top, and socks. A deck bag can hold other items such as rain pants, an emergency kit, and snacks such as energy bars in case you want to eat lunch while on the water.

The rear section between the rib at the back of the cockpit and the stern rib is quite large. At the very rear of this section, place three flat bags lengthwise. One bag can hold most of your clothing, another a light sleeping bag and pillow, and the third bag a light one-person tent. In the leftover area between this trio of bags and the back-of-cockpit rib, you can place various items—such as walking shoes, extra socks, notebook, candle lantern, flashlight, and spare glasses—in a small round-bottomed bag.

A small dry bag with kielbasa, pita bread,

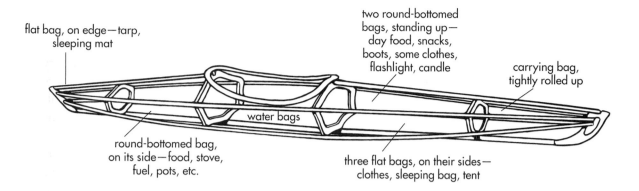

flat bag, on edge—tarp,
sleeping mat

two round-bottomed
bags, standing up—
day food, snacks,
boots, some clothes,
flashlight, candle

carrying bag,
tightly rolled up

water bags

round-bottomed bag,
on its side—food, stove,
fuel, pots, etc.

three flat bags, on their sides—
clothes, sleeping bag, tent

Placement of camping gear in a mini-foldable for a one-week trip.

peanut butter, and more energy bars—i.e., regular lunches—can also be stowed in this area. You can also squeeze loose items such as a mesh bag for hauling gear up a beach and an aluminum 1-liter wine bottle in this area.

Right behind you can place another gallon of water held in a flat water bag.

Clearly, there are alternative ways of loading the boat. You can get extra food into nooks and crannies in the bow area, which can easily hold another twenty to thirty freeze-dried dinner packets as well as more food in Ziploc bags in little spots.

What a Regular Single Can Carry

When the Feathercraft Khatsalano was first designed, it was thought of as a day boat and not for camping. But Doug Simpson, one of the owners of Feathercraft and cofounder, managed to stash some 140 pounds of camping gear during a two-week winter test run of the prototype boat. On pages 178–79 is a list of exactly what he carried in what size bag and where in the Khatsalano. Just by way of comparison with another Feathercraft single that is meant to carry lots of gear, the K1, here is how much more could have been placed in the latter. Instead of just one #10 stuff sack (10-

liter capacity; the numbers used in the table correspond to the volume in liters that can be accommodated) in the bow area, he could have placed two of them. And he could have shoved one #20 and an extra #10 instead of just one #10 in the stern compartment. He also would not have had to wedge a #20 bag between his legs as he had to in the Khatsalano.

What a Double Can Carry

On pages 180–83 is a cargo list that Feathercraft used in the shakedown cruise of its Klondike double. The gear totaled around 310 pounds. The list should give you plenty of food for thought for packing double folding kayaks of similar size and shape, such as the Folbot Greenland II, Klepper Aerius II, or the Nautiraid expedition doubles.

The Klondike gear covered a two-week winter trip along the exposed coast of British Columbia north of Vancouver Island. The trip took Doug Simpson of Feathercraft and a friend through conditions that sometimes saw 45-knot winds and 15-foot seas and involved some surf landings, dreaded by loaded-kayak paddlers. The Klondike lived up to Feathercraft's expectations.

(*Note:* the volume of bags and containers is in liters; e.g., 5 L for 5 liters. Weights are in grams.)

Packing a Single for Two Weeks

LOCATION	ITEM	CONTAINER	WEIGHT (LB.)
bow hatch (i.e., loaded through hole)	small float bag	–	0.5
	tent pegs	black stuff sack	1
	repair kit	purple stuff sack	1
	Therm-a-Rest pad	yellow stuff sack	2
	stove	blue #5	3
	spare water bag	blue	0.5
	two large stuff sacks for equipment	–	1.5
	flotation bag	–	0.5
bow cockpit (i.e., loaded via cockpit)	clothing, fleece pants, toilet paper	black #10	2
	sleeping bag	purple #20	5
	first aid, toiletries	green #5	2.25
	one pair gum boots	separate bags	5.25
	day pack	–	2
cockpit area	water bag (ahead of seat)	blue	13
	clothes (between legs)	yellow #20	5
	1 liter water (port seat sling)	–	1.5
	EPIRB or personal locator beacon	–	1.5
	smoke flare (port seat sling)	–	0.25
	tow rope (starboard seat sling)	–	0.75
	sponge/cockpit cover (aft of seat)	–	0.5
	sea sock	–	1.5
	spray skirt	–	1.25
stern (i.e., loaded via cockpit)	accessories	purple #5	3
	food	green stuff sack	9.5
	food	blue stuff sack	7.75
	food	blue stuff sack	13
	rain jacket, pants, rubber gloves	purple #5	3.25
	two extra stuff sacks and four garbage bags	–	1
	small clothes bag	yellow #10	2.25
	two flotation bags	–	1
stern hatch (i.e., loaded through hole)	fuel container	–	2
	tent poles	yellow stuff sack	2
	two-person, four-season tent	blue stuff sack	7.5
	mess kit	blue stuff sack	2
	headlamp, candle lantern	clear #5	2
	candles	green stuff sack	0.5
	large stuff sack	–	1.5
stern deck (i.e., carried on rear deck)	Sea Wings	purple stuff sack	1.25
	pogies, etc.	blue stuff sack	2
	sea anchor	black stuff sack	1.5
	pump	–	1
	fishing rod and reel	–	2
	spare paddle	–	2.5

LOCATION	ITEM	CONTAINER	WEIGHT (LB.)
bow deck (i.e., on front deck)	compass and chart	–	1
wearing/at hand	Gore-Tex dry suit	–	4
	fleece sweater and pants	–	2.25
	fleece socks and polypropylene socks	–	0.5
	cap or sou'wester	–	0.75
	neoprene boots	–	2
	life jacket, lighter, firestarter, flares, sea seat	–	3.5
	fanny pack, lighter, flashlight, etc.	–	1.5
	VHF radio	–	1
	paddle	–	2.5
Weight of all gear			**139.25 lb.**

PORTAGING AND OTHER LAND MOVEMENT

Every ship must come to shore, and so must your kayak. How do you move a gear-laden kayak, an object that may weigh half as much as a compact car? If you're traveling from one lake to another, what do you do about portaging? You have several options—besides breaking your back.

Land Movement of Boat and Gear

A good boat cart is worth its weight in gold. Most of them can be rolled right into salt water because they're made of corrosion-resistant materials. If you're planning to buy a cart, get one that has wide wheels that won't sink in soft sand under a heavy load. You can help your cart negotiate the more difficult terrain by partially emptying your boat until the cart is easier to manage.

Keep some bags handy to stuff gear into as you unload at the shoreline. This means fewer trips back and forth to your campsite. The bags that your foldable came in are ideal for this job, and you'll have them along anyway. Mesh bags also work well.

Boat fenders are another tool for moving your boat on shore. You'll need three tubular fenders that you can keep deflated in your boat and then inflate when you need them. Use them as the Egyptian pyramid builders used rollers to move stone blocks. Place one fender under the bow, one dead center, one toward the stern. As you roll the boat on the front two boat fenders, take the one from the rear and place it in front of the boat. Roll the boat onto it and continue the process with the others in constant rotation. You may be able to get by with two rollers, but three are better and easier to work with.

PVC 4-inch-diameter water pipes will also work well as rollers, but they weigh more than boat fenders and take up more space. If you can cap the ends, you may use the pipes to store small, loose items within the boat.

Portaging

It certainly makes good sense to have a handle on portaging. How else can you enjoy the many strings of freshwater lakes and rivers that interlace North America and parts of Europe? You have several choices:

Wheel your foldable on a boat cart. This is certainly one of the easiest and handiest approaches. Your boat can traverse quite rugged terrain on a boat cart. The wheels on the two best carts, Klepper's and Nautiraid's, are large, tough, and give

PACKING A DOUBLE FOR TWO WEEKS

WHAT FRONT PADDLER PACKED

LOCATION	ITEM	CONTAINER	WEIGHT (GRAMS)
bow end	candle lantern	stuff sack	120
	2 975 mL fuel bottles	—	1,805
	rubber boots	2 stuff sacks	2,270
	medical repair kit	5 L dry bag	1,835
	soap	plastic bottle	175
	toilet paper, 2 rolls	5 L dry bag	465
	pots, with lids; cutlery	stuff sack	1,470
	soap, scrub pad	—	17
	fish kit	stuff sack	2,825
	1 large storage bag (K2 skin bag)	—	535
	1 extra-large storage bag	—	660
	gas camp stove	stuff sack	510
Weight in bow section			**12,687**
bow cockpit, at feet	large fly	15 L dry bag	2,470
	sleeping bag	stuff sack	2,575
bow cockpit, under calves	food	10 L dry bag	4,765
	water	partial 10 L water bag	8,000
bow cockpit, starboard seat sling	heavy fleece sweater	5 L dry bag	760
	binoculars	5 L dry bag	725
	water bottle	1 L	1,060
	8 in. fry pan	—	340
bow cockpit, port seat sling	water	1 L	1,170
	spinning reel, 6 candles	5 L dry bag	2,825
	lunch bag, empty when set off	5 L dry bag	110
	rain jacket and pants	5 L dry bag	835
bow cockpit, underneath seat sling (sling in raised position)	clothing in 2 dry bags (6 pairs fleece socks, 3 pairs polypropylene socks, 1 Polartec 100 tights, 2 long-sleeved polypropylene shirts, 4 bandannas, 1 long-sleeved cotton T-shirt, 1 Polartec 200 pants, 1 Polartec 100 long-sleeved shirt, 1 pair wool gloves, 1 Polartec 100 balaclava, one towel, one pair fingerless gloves, one pair nylon shorts)	15 L dry bag 15 L dry bag	1,965 1,930
	accessories (2 latex ankle seals, toothbrush, glasses, hairbrush, scissors, 4 pencils)	stuff sack	200
bow cockpit, between legs	accessories (flashlight, vitamins in top pocket, 4 spare garbage bags, wallet, duct tape, 1 partial roll toilet paper stolen from motel, 1 hand-made wool toque, 1 kalimba [hand piano] in foam case, 1 journal, 2 novels)	15 L dry bag	3,000
bow cockpit, inside sea sock, clipped to D-ring	EPIRB	—	780
	sponge	—	50
Weight in bow cockpit			**33,560**

WHAT FRONT PADDLER PACKED (continued)

LOCATION	ITEM	CONTAINER	WEIGHT (GRAMS)
bow deck	mesh pouch	–	100
	neoprene pogies	–	160
	nylon pogies	–	120
	water	700 mL	780
	pump	lined to deck	485
	paddle leash	–	20
	sea anchor	stuff sack	720
Weight on bow deck			**2,385**

WHAT FRONT PADDLER WORE

LOCATION	ITEM	CONTAINER	WEIGHT (GRAMS)
	life jacket (6 skylight flares, 1 parachute flare, diving knife, 2 compasses, sea seat, Swiss Army knife, whistle, spare wood compass mount)	–	1,715
	nylon dry suit	–	995
	other clothes (Polartec 200 tights, Polartec 100 shirt, Polartec 200 shirt, nylon shorts)	–	2,250
	fleece socks, neoprene boots	–	800
	paddle	–	1,310
Weight of gear worn for front paddler			**7,070**
Weight of gear for front paddler			**55,702**

WHAT REAR PADDLER PACKED

LOCATION	ITEM	CONTAINER	WEIGHT (GRAMS)
mid-cockpit (ahead of feet)	1 L food cup with spoon	mesh bag	335
mid-cockpit, port side (beside legs lashed to gunwale and chine bars)	food	10 L dry bag	5,260
	food	10 L dry bag	2,950
mid-cockpit, starboard side (beside legs lashed to gunwale and chine bars)	food	10 L dry bag	3,425
	food	10 L dry bag	4,070
Weight in mid-cockpit			**16,040**
stern cockpit, under legs	water	10 L Dromedary sack	8,000
	water	10 L sack	8,000
stern cockpit, port seat sling	food	10 L dry bag	4,030
	rope	stuff sack	300
stern cockpit, starboard seat sling	food	10 L dry bag	3,605
	fishing kit (handline, Buzz Bomb, pliers, cord, knife with cord, stuff sack for fish)	stuff sack	1,005
stern cockpit, under seat sling	water	10 L sack	8,000
	Therm-a-Rest pad	15 L dry bag	1,280
	garbage container	10 L dry bag	45
Weight in stern cockpit			**34,265**

Packing a Double for Two Weeks (continued)

WHAT REAR PADDLER PACKED (continued)

LOCATION	ITEM	CONTAINER	WEIGHT (GRAMS)
stern, main compartment	four-season hoop tent	25 L dry bag	4,640
	clothes (2 pairs fleece socks, 1 pair Helly Hansen socks, 1 fleece balaclava, 1 Polartec 100 tights, 1 nylon shorts, handkerchief, 1 nylon pants, 1 long-sleeved polypropylene shirt, 1 Polartec 100 shirt, 1 cotton T-shirt, underwear)	20 L dry bag	2,610
	sleeping bag	20 L dry bag	2,080
	food	10 L dry bag	4,130
	hatchet	–	810
	extra-large storage bag	–	660
Weight in stern main compartment			**14,930**
stern end	tent pegs	stuff sack	455
	repair kit (three cans glue, Hypalon, Poly-Tech, pack cloth fabric, sandpaper, sponson fabric, Leatherman tool, wire, epoxy stick, neck and wrist gaskets for dry suit, duct tape)	5 L dry bag	1,200
	rain jacket and pants (extra bushwhacking rain pants)	5 L dry bag	1,585
	gas camp stove with 22 fl oz. fuel	5 L dry bag	1,325
	small fly	5 L dry bag	1,055
	accessories (large Ziplocs: toilet paper, 4 candles, 2 lighters, fire starter, harmonica, #3 cord, spare Ziploc for spent batteries, film)	10 L dry bag	2,380
	(large Ziploc, spare first aid: Band-Aids, triangular bandage, adhesive tape, gauze pads, lighter)		
	(small Ziplocs: 4 rolls film, vitamins, 10 AA batteries, 4 AAA batteries, 2 lithium camera batteries, 1 headlamp bulb, 1 flashlight bulb, money, wallet, keys, spare rechargeable radio battery, mini-compass)		
	(small stuff sack, emergency fishing gear: 3 Buzz Bombs with rubber bumpers, hooks in film canister, leader line on plastic spool		
	journal, novel, pens, marker	5 L dry bag	950
	(small Ziploc: pens, cloth labels)		
Weight in stern end			**8,950**
mid-deck	chart, 4 cross-deck shock cords	–	310
	(1 sheath knife, small compass mounted with shock cord, paddle leash)		
stern deck	mesh pouch	–	100
	neoprene hood	–	100

WHAT REAR PADDLER PACKED (continued)

LOCATION	ITEM	CONTAINER	WEIGHT (GRAMS)
	neoprene mitts	–	200
	watch with barometer function	–	55
	VHF and binoculars	5 L tethered dry bag	1,000
	water	700 mL bottle	105
	pump	lined to deck	485
	four-piece spare paddle	stuff sack, tied over stern hatch	1,140
inside sea sock (all items clipped on to D-ring sewn to sock)	dry bag for lunch	–	110
	heavy fleece sweater	5 L dry bag	755
	water	1 L bottle	1,170
	sponge	–	50
Weight in sea sock			**5,580**

WHAT REAR PADDLER WORE

LOCATION	ITEM	CONTAINER	WEIGHT (GRAMS)
	life jacket (3 flares, sea seat, lip balm, nylon pogies, plastic jar with waterproof matches, fire starter, small knife)	–	1,225
	Gore-Tex dry suit	–	1,815
	other clothing (Polartec 100 fleece suit, one-piece swim trunks, polypropylene shirt, fleece socks, polypropylene socks, neoprene boots, neoprene gloves, nylon hat)	–	2,075
	dry pouch (dark glasses, lip balm, whistle, toilet paper, tide tables in Ziploc, fire starter lighter, Swiss Army knife in Ziploc, 5-pencil flare set in Ziploc, flashlight, nylon skull cap, watch, small compass)	–	520
Weight of gear worn for rear paddler			**5,635**
Weight of gear for rear paddler			**85,400**
Weight of total gear			**141,102** (141.1 kg/310.4 lb.)

adequate ground clearance, though Nautiraid's has a slight height advantage. Take care with where you place the cart on the boat. You want to locate it at a point where you're not holding the entire weight of the kayak in your hands but not so far toward the center of the boat that you scrape the bow or stern on the ground.

When carting your boat up hills, you should be on the downhill side of the boat, holding it as low as possible. From this position you can foresee any ground rubbing and avoid it. You also get the best leverage and control. When going downhill, reverse the position so you're uphill of your boat. If you are downhill, you won't be aware of rubbing, and most hull damage from carting occurs going downhill with the person in front. However, the recommended position offers less control and braking; take care not to have a runaway boat! On the flats, pushing offers you more control, and it's easier on your shoulders.

Balance is another issue when using a cart for portaging over rough terrain. Lashing the boat firmly to the cart frame will help. You can never get it too tight. Cinch several sets of straps around the boat, and then snug up the straps some more. If possible, place all heavy objects just above the cart. This means you may have to do some quick repacking, but it's worth it. You won't feel the weight as much, and the heavy objects won't throw you off balance.

Be a beast of burden. Even if you're used to portaging a canoe, portaging a folding kayak is much tougher. You don't have a handy place to put a yoke and shoulder. If you decide to lash on paddles the way you would with a canoe and place these on your shoulder, you're in for an uncomfortable portage. Because folding kayaks are flexible, they transmit more up and down force onto the paddle shafts, which will jar your back. Extra padding might help.

Another solution is to use a yoke shoulder band. Here's how to make one. If you're portaging a Klepper single, cement back to back two bands of Hypalon repair material approximately 3 inches wide and 22½ inches long. Use either the repair cement meant for patches or Barge cement, which won't come apart. Before applying the cement, place a strip of ¼-inch nylon cord at each end so that it's encased by the Hypalon bands, creating a bead at each end.

To use this band, let a bit of air out of the sponsons and slip the band's ends under the coaming and into the underside groove, similar to the way the beaded hem of the Expedition tuck-under spraydeck fits. Then reinflate the sponsons. What you have is a much softer, flexible shoulder harness that moves with the flexible boat. The band forms to your back, distributing not only the weight but also the pressure. You carry it very much the way you would portage a canoe.

If you're portaging a double, you can do it somewhat the same way as you would carry a tandem canoe. One paddler carries the boat upside down, with his or her head against the rear seat. Pad the rear seat by tying in place something like a floatable boat cushion. The other paddler guides the carrier from in front. Or both paddlers can put their heads into the boat to disperse the weight. The taller paddler should be in front so he or she can see what lies ahead.

Fold your foldable. When you must move from lake to lake or around inhospitable parts of a river, why not take advantage of a folding kayak's foldability? It takes an average of ten minutes to knock down a folding kayak and about fifteen minutes to make it again. Even if it takes you twice as long, you're still looking at just fifty minutes of work. If two of you are paddling a double, one could disassemble or assemble while the other portages gear.

Most carrying bags for folding kayaks have padded shoulder straps and other comfort devices. If you're not happy with the bags that came with your folding kayak, look around for an external-frame backpack that could carry your folding kayak bags reasonably well. When not in use, the frame can be lashed to the rear deck. Being so light and open, the frame will neither raise your center of gravity nor catch crosswinds.

Chapter Fourteen

More Fun with Foldables

Folding kayaks are misnamed; they should really be called all-purpose kayaks. They offer many possibilities in a small package, like the many facets of a cut diamond. Foldables will accommodate your needs as they have for thousands of paddlers before you. And people still keep coming up with new ways to enjoy the built-in flexibility of these versatile vessels.

Why are folding kayaks so much more adaptable to a wide range of uses than other small craft? It's hard to say what accounts for their ability to do your bidding, but a number of possibilities come to mind.

For one, folding kayaks have been going strong for nearly a century with remarkably little change in their basic design. Hundreds of thousands of people have gotten their hands on these vessels and studied them. Under such scrutiny, folding kayaks have been used for activities that range from the broadly appealing to the bizarre.

But there's more behind the phenomenal breadth of service than just the exposure of time. Stability and seaworthiness also underline the folding kayak's adaptability. The stable platform allows you to attempt many activities you wouldn't dare try in other small craft. Its open-water performance lets you move quickly over great distances in rough conditions, thus broadening your ability to do the things you want. You're not confined to a small area.

Another reason may be the take-apart skin-and-frame construction of foldables. One proven principle of creativity is that the more you have to work with, the more you can innovate. There's something about having all those parts and pieces and the process of assembling them that gets the creative juices flowing.

Whatever the reasons behind the phenomenon, folding kayaks work for more than just paddling, sailing, and camping, as discussed earlier. Here's some more fun you can have in a foldable.

FISHING

People have been fishing from foldables since they first emerged from the factory floors of Bavaria. The combination of folding and fishing is a natural fit.

Folding kayaks adapt equally well to freshwater and saltwater fishing. You can carry one into remote areas on horseback or on a human's back, wherever sparsely fished waters beckon. Once there, your luck is likely to be better away from the shoreline, and you can roam from spot to spot quickly. In salt water, rugged conditions are less likely to affect the single angler alone at sea in a foldable than in any other type of small vessel.

You can fish from just about any of the foldables, but the open-cockpit doubles seem to be ideal. These give you the most room to deal with the paraphernalia of the sport.

You can catch all kinds of gamefish. Weight?

As much as you can handle. Large catches in a foldable have included a 100-pound halibut, which is about as much as any one person can deal with. But you can also go for smaller lake gamefish with light tackle and flies. You can cast fairly easily from one of these boats.

Trolling works well in a folding kayak. Many anglers consider the average paddling speed to be ideal for this type of sport. What seems to work best is about 50 feet of line out and with varying trolling weights, depending on whether you're after bottom feeders.

Here are some tips on fishing in a foldable.

Be careful with sharp knives and hooks that can do damage to your boat—and yourself. Be particularly cautious with a gaff, and keep a cork on the sharp parts until you're ready to bring a catch aboard. You may be better off with a net, depending on the size of fish you're after.

Secure tackle boxes and other objects. One easy method is to place self-adhering Velcro strips on your boat and gear. You can also use webbing straps. Fishing poles can be put into paddle pockets or pushed under the deck either in front or behind your seat. Some folding kayaks have built-in mast partners that make a good place to park your rods. The mast partner also functions well to hold a trolling line high, as is done on larger

Fishing from a double. (Feathercraft)

vessels. The pole top being high in the mast partner makes the troll more lively, more likely to attract fish than one being towed behind from a low position.

Avoid soiling. To protect your boat from fish blood and entrails, carry along large plastic sheets or garbage bags. Line the area in front of you with the plastic, because this is where you're likely to toss fish and where you may have to deal with them. To secure the loose sides of the sheet, run bungee cord or line from the front of the coaming to the back. Water bottles and other heavy objects can keep the bottom of the sheet down and in place.

Keep all your work within the confines of the cockpit. You can keep a bait bucket between your legs, and anything you catch can go into a basket in front of you. Don't put such baskets on the front or back decks; deck loads are risky business and can capsize you faster than anything else around.

NATURE WATCHING

Folding kayaks live up to their ancestral Eskimo legends of stealth in tracking wildlife. Because they're extremely quiet, modern foldables can move you up close to wary birds and animals. Their flexible sides absorb and silence any ripples and small waves, and their bow wakes are equally smooth and silent. The accidental slap of a paddle against the side of a foldable makes far less sound than it would against a rigid surface.

Stability and portability help for observing nature. The latter, as in the case of fishing, allows you to pack in to remote waters where you find nature at its best. Stability is critical in getting close to what you want to observe. As you draw near, you can put down your paddle and drift without having to keep your paddle ready for a brace stroke. You can even lower your body pro-

file by dropping down partially into your cockpit, and you can keep your arms inside.

Preparing yourself and your boat is fairly simple. Make certain you have nothing shiny showing that could reflect or transmit light. To further silence your boat, you can cover the coaming of an open-cockpit boat with rubber hose. To do this, simply slit the hose and place it along the length of the coaming in any spot where your paddle shaft might hit. Then, to get your body farther down inside the cockpit, remove your seat temporarily and sit on light padding.

Get yourself good binoculars if you don't have a pair already. In rigid kayaks, you probably wouldn't want to use anything more than 6X or 7X power since the shaking of the boat blurs the image. But in a more stable foldable you can make use of 10X power. To help you see in low light, get 8 X 50 or 10 X 50 binoculars.

PHOTOGRAPHY

All the advantages that foldables offer for nature watching carry over into good photography. And you can get better shots in a folding kayak than you can in a rigid kayak because you can put down your paddle and focus your attention entirely on the shot.

Some photographers use tripods in open-cockpit foldables, being careful with the leg points and the inside of the hull. Most people find that doubles are the best setup for photography; one person does the shooting while the other paddles and positions the boat for the shot.

You can use your ordinary camera equipment in a foldable, but take precautions not to get it wet. Several types of waterproof storage containers are made just for cameras. The hardshell boxes from Pelican and other manufacturers are probably your best bet, better than the soft storage bags. The boxes are quicker to open when a good photo opportunity presents itself, and they can be closed fast if water starts to slap into the boat. Soft storage bags have to be rolled and unrolled, an operation that can take a few valuable extra seconds to perform. The hardshell boxes also will do a better job of protecting the camera equipment from hard blows. Always tie the box or bag to a rib in your foldable with some webbing strap. Also have a dry cloth handy to wipe camera surfaces that accidentally get splashed.

Varying levels of water-resistant and waterproof cameras flood the market. Before you buy one, read the instructions to be sure it will do what you want. Watch out especially for the zoom lens of a water-resistant camera, because a bit of salt on the extended zoom can gum up its operation. Immediately after using any camera, wipe it clean and dry with a cloth. Even if a camera is weather-resistant, treat it as you would an ordinary camera. Consider the feature a fallback, not a fail-safe parameter.

Waterproof cameras generally live up to their billing, but even so, be careful with them. Wipe off salt periodically, using a clean cloth dampened with fresh water. Be especially careful with your lenses. You're likely to keep the camera ready inside your boat without a case, but any water splashed on the lens will dull the sharpness of your photos. And saltwater crystals can permanently etch the lens. Make sure it can float when it's loaded with film and the batteries are installed. If you already own the camera, you could test how well it floats in your bathtub. If it sinks, get a flotation collar or neck strap.

SNORKELING AND SCUBA DIVING

Snorkeling and scuba diving are great water adventures that lend themselves to the use of folding kayaks, particularly the open-cockpit doubles.

Foldables offer the snorkeler or scuba diver a good diving platform, they're easy to exit on the water, and they're easy to reenter.

Many militaries use folding doubles for their covert diving activities. One partner is designated the paddler, the other the swimmer/diver. Both people have mountains of military hardware packed around them in addition to the diving gear needed by the swimmer/diver. In civilian use, most double paddlers take turns diving. And of course you could also go solo.

To get started snorkeling or scuba diving, put on your fins (and weight belt, if needed) while you're still inside your folding kayak. You'll have enough clearance for this. Roll out and drop over the side as you would from a rubber raft, but watch that your fins clear the cockpit's opposite coaming.

For scuba diving, you may find it easier to get into the harness and air tank once you're in the water and alongside the boat. Even though you have enough room to put on a scuba tank in the boat, your center of gravity would rise and, as you go over the side, your boat would be less stable.

Smaller scuba tanks may be your first choice because they'll fit easily between the ribs alongside your legs in the open cockpit area. Larger tanks are better reserved for solo diving from a double, when the tank occupies the seat of the other paddler. Measure the space between ribs on your foldable to check the size of the space. Placing a foam mat on the floor of your foldable will protect the scuba tank's regulator if the tank gets dropped into the boat.

After diving, get yourself back inside the foldable by starting from a horizontal position in the water alongside the boat. Kick with your fins to propel your body into the boat, similar to self-rescue reentries explained in chapter 10. Don't try to come in from a vertical position, with your legs down deep in the water, or from a position directly perpendicular to the boat.

Rowing a Klepper double in Bavaria. (Walther/Klepper)

Spear fishing goes hand in hand with snorkeling and scuba diving, so if you're using a spear gun or sling spear, be careful of the fabric and hull of the boat. Follow the fishing guidelines covered above for other ways to protect your boat and gear.

ROWING

Yes, you can row or scull a folding kayak, but it must be a double with an open cockpit. The preferred rower is the Klepper because of its solid keelboard. Don't fool yourself into thinking that a folding kayak when rowed will be as speedy as a racing scull. The latter is made just for the sport of rowing, while a folding kayak is an all-around vessel that can be adapted to be good at it.

If rowing is your preferred mode of moving through the water, you'll be able to cover a lot of it in a foldable. A Klepper has even been rowed around Cape Horn.

Several oar setups are available, but the best seems to be the Oarmaster from Martin Marine. It has a sliding seat unit and outriggers that support the oars without any modification of the

Oarmaster by Martin Marine. (Michael Skott)

boat's coaming. The whole unit weighs 26 pounds and will work with a 9-foot, 9-inch set of oars. To fit the apparatus into the Klepper, you'll need to add a 14½-inch by 52-inch baseplate; ⅜-inch marine-grade plywood will do, but ½-inch would be better. You'll also need special track sliders from Klepper. The whole unit lifts in and out quickly.

MOTORING

You can attach a motor to any open-cockpit double foldable, and you have your choice of either a quiet electric motor or an efficient gasoline-powered one.

Why have a motor? If you have some physical problem that prevents you from sustained paddling, you could still enjoy the advantages of a folding kayak. Or if your adventure calls for going upstream for a long distance against a heavy current, you might opt to use a motor. Or you might just want a backup for your paddling.

Sailing kayakers are also starting to add motors to their large array of on-deck equipment. The kayaking schooner rigs have two sails, two masts, leeboards, outriggers, hiking seats, and more. All this extra gear makes it difficult to get a paddle in the water. A motor allows the sailor to move along without wind until conditions improve. If winds become too strong to tack against effectively, kayak sailors can switch to their motors to get back home.

An electric motor is ideal for fishing because it makes very little noise. The electric motor of choice appears to be the Minn-Kota 35Na, which is powerful enough to move you steadily for a good part of a day. This particular model weighs only about 12 pounds, but then you have to add the weight of the motor mount plus the marine battery to furnish power to your motor. Electric batteries need occasional recharge.

If you're interested in a gasoline motor, you have plenty of choices among what are considered dinghy or trolling motors. Choose one that weighs no more than about 15 pounds so it won't destabilize the boat when used on a counter-weighted motor mount or in conjunction with sailing outriggers. At that weight, there are several motors on the market that are between about 1 and 1½ horsepower. A gasoline motor will give you greater range than an electric motor due to the latters need for recharging, and you can bring enough gasoline for hundreds of miles of travel without overloading your boat.

Either motor will work well as long as you know its limitations. You probably are not going to move faster than a normal, healthy crew paddling a double. Motors are failure-prone, like anything electrical or mechanical in a marine environment. Such motors work well for their intended use on the back of a dinghy or small rowboat, where they're protected from splash by the boat itself. On a foldable, the motor is mounted about a foot and a half off to the side of the boat, where it gets exposed to all the waves, including your own boat's wake. Constant splashing can foul the air intake and exhaust, and even the most insulated motor can short out and drown.

Motoring to find wind.

PADDLING WITH KIDS

Having a foldable when paddling with a child aboard has some great advantages.

Stability. Other types of boats, including hardshells and canoes, don't offer the extra measure of safety you get in a folding kayak. Its greater stability helps protect your precious cargo from harm. Sudden movements by a child, enthralled by something she or he sees, won't have you all in the water. You don't have to admonish a child to be still all the time, which can discourage him or her and dampen the experience.

Room. A child can crawl around and move easily from one parent to the other. It is easy for a child, when sleepy, to lie down. This goes for most folding double kayaks, which have large open cockpits.

While open-cockpit foldables are the best choice for trips with children, don't rule others out. On page 186, you'll see Doug Simpson of Feathercraft in a double Feathercraft with his son Evan, who was about three or four at the time.

Safety

Following are a half dozen or so things you can do to keep your child safe and maintain your peace of mind. These will help both of you get the most out of your adventures afloat and make memories that will last a lifetime.

Make your intervals on the water short. This is a must with children of almost any age. Even though there's extra room to move around, kids get bored and tired of being in one spot, so you need to do some careful trip planning. You should have a good idea of how far you are likely to be able to paddle in an hour or two and make certain that this will put you in a spot where you can readily pull out. Preferably, your stopover place should have some attractions that may entertain your child, such as a beach to collect shells or rocks to explore.

Create things to do. Make certain the experience is a fun one for your child. There are all sorts of ways to go about this. Since you are on the water, why not take advantage of it? Let your child fish or troll with a small net. Don't make things too hard on yourself.

Another fun thing to do, especially if there is more than one boat (such as when one parent is in a single), is to have pretend races. In hot conditions, have water fights using your hand bilge pumps; the splashing will cool all of you off.

Don't forget to build some education into the experience. You can do this in a number of ways. There are all sorts of children's books about whales, seagulls, starfish, etc. Read from these while at home and let the child know that you will soon be out in the midst of this interesting world. Bring the book along if the child wants to. Some larger plastic baggies will hold most books. If the book is particularly outsize, a chart case will work well. In fact, having a chart case in which coloring books and other such paraphernalia can be stowed is a good idea.

You can also get a child interested in some of the tools of kayaking. Children are often fascinated by charts and compasses, and they learn fast. Assign them a task such as helping you identify where various objects on a chart can be found while on the water.

Children also can learn about ecology and the delicate balance of the world around them. The transitional zone between land and water is a great place to begin. Ecology is often taught in kindergarten and other lower grades and also featured on educational television, so use your paddling trips as an opportunity to follow up on what your child is learning.

Set up your kayak with your child in mind. Make certain that the child can see, which means you'll need to work out some kind of seating arrangement that allows this. If a child is kept down inside the cockpit walls, he or she is not going to enjoy the experience much. Also, make the child comfortable with padded seats and the like.

A PFD is a must, for yourself and your child. It is amazing how many parents will put a PFD on their child but not wear one themselves. This isn't particularly safe. Consider tethering your child to your boat or to you. This is a tricky subject. In the event of a capsize, you risk entangling yourself or your child in the tether. Weigh this against losing the child overboard.

Dress your child warmly. It is easy to forget that a child naturally tends to be more easily chilled than an adult. Also, a child, even if he or she is moving around a lot, is not keeping as warm as someone who is paddling and generating heat. Even small children can be outfitted with cold-water gear if you are inclined to push the season a bit into colder conditions. You can even have a neoprene bunting suit made for a baby.

Use sun protection. Since sunlight reflects off water, you are more exposed to the sun while paddling than when on the sunniest beach. Children's—and adult's, for that matter—delicate skin should not be exposed to such strong rays. Use protective clothing and plenty of sunblock, and try to do most of your paddling when there is the least amount of sun exposure (usually between 10 A.M. and 2 P.M.).

Modifying Your Foldable

Folding-kayak owners always seem to be on the alert for modifications to improve what they got from the factory. Whenever two Folbot or Klepper owners meet, one of the first things they do is compare what they've done with their boats. They poke their heads in, look over the deck layouts, and comment on specialized equipment and the like. It's almost a ritual dance.

Even if you think you have two left thumbs and can barely get a stamp to stay stuck on an envelope, sooner or later you'll be bitten by the modification bug. Folding kayaks will bring out the resourcefulness in you. Each time you assemble or knock one down, you'll probably have a thought or two about changes you may make.

One reason for such thinking is money. Some modifications that you can do yourself can save you the cost of buying an item from the manufacturer. Anything you can do for yourself will reduce the effective cost to you of enjoying your kayak.

For another, no one manufacturer has the answer to everything. You may like a feature on some other company's boat, and in many instances, you can adapt it to your own boat with make-do materials or by buying the components from the other company.

But most important, kayaking is a very personalized sport. No boat, no model, no matter how well thought out and designed, can meet the demands of every individual. Fortunately, folding kayaks, with their skin-and-frame design, lend themselves to tinkering and customizing to suit particular needs.

Below are some modifications that have been tried by other paddlers. These ideas come from the pages of *Folding Kayaker*, my bimonthly newsletter that offers tips and insights on using and enjoying folding kayaks. Some of the modifications are from readers of the newsletter who, like you, saw a need and figured out a way to meet it.

As you read through the modifications, keep an open mind. The kinds of approaches used to come up with the particular solutions may suggest new ways you may look at any special situation you are facing. Remember that while necessity may be the mother of invention, it is simplicity that often fathers it. During the industrial revolution, some of the best developments were simple, not complex, answers to a need.

Here is a story attributed to Thomas Edison that you may want to keep in mind. During the development of the light bulb, there was a point at which some of his associates were trying to calculate the volume of gas needed to fill their odd-shaped glass bulb. They worked with their formulas for the volumes of spheres and cylinders but were stymied by the bulb's tapered shape. Edison happened to walk in on his vexed associates and asked what the problem was. He then simply picked up the glass bulb, walked over to a sink, filled the bulb with water, poured the water into a measuring beaker, and said, "Gentlemen, here is your volume!"

RUDDER IDEAS

Rudder fixes rank second as folding-kayak enthusiasts' most sought-after modifications. (What's first? What you sit on!)

Also, paddlers are often not happy with the way their rudder controls work. For example, some find the stirrup controls in Feathercraft's doubles and in Nautiraids awkward. Some of the modifications below show how to make improve-

ments. The first fix is an old one that has been around for years, a well-kept secret that Klepper isn't quick to divulge.

Reversing a Klepper Rudder

The Klepper rudder, despite its claim of being designed with sailing in mind, is actually a so-so performer in that endeavor. The Klepper rudder's pronounced horizontal profile tends to cause drag and slow down a boat under sail, almost to a stall if the winds are weak. Solutions such as the balanced rudder (see opposite) were offered, but the easiest solution is to reverse the rudder blade in its bracket, which will make it act more like a balanced rudder as well as plunge deeper in the water for better control.

All you need to do is punch or drill out the rivet that holds the rudder blade in its bracket, flip the rudder blade totally around, and then reinstall it. Some people, such as Wayne Hall of Anchorage, Alaska, who have tried this have replaced the rivet with a stainless steel bolt, lock washer, nut, and Nylok nut. With such a nut and bolt, you can always switch back to the factory configuration for shallow waters or paddling.

Wayne reports: "The reversed Klepper blade worked great! The boat turned much quicker and with much less apparent drag. I was able to tack successfully at much slower speeds, and the pressure I had to put on the rudder pedal was negligible. Steering was also more controllable in higher waves. The only drawback was that the blade could not be lifted as high as on the stock setup. But the new setup did lift the blade well above the keel of the boat, and it definitely cleared the water. Also in its uplifted position, it did not catch as much wind as before."

When the Klepper rudder is in its factory position, it tends to run shallow when under way with little bite. In big waves, the rudder will often be out of the water.

After the rudder has been modified to be used

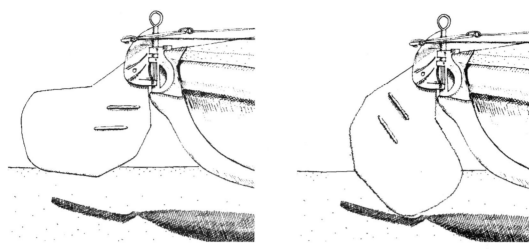

LEFT: Rudder in factory position. RIGHT: Rudder in modified position.

in a vertical position it gives you more bite in the water. *Note:* It does act like a balanced rudder; i.e., one with a portion of its surface ahead of the rudder's pivot point.

The Balanced Rudder

This idea was created by Mark Balogh of Balogh Sail Designs and David Valverde of New York, and it's primarily aimed at achieving a better rudder for sailing. A balanced rudder prevents stalling a kayak under sail, and it does so by putting 20 percent of the rudder's surface ahead of the pivoting point. Sailing enthusiasts who have used one say, "It's like changing from manual to power steering in a car." When paddling a double, it also has practical application for use in turning. This is especially true when using larger rudders like those on the Klepper and Folbot. The balanced rudder is deeper in the water, so in waves it's less likely to ride in the air and more likely to bite into the water.

The balanced rudder shown next page can be fiddled with for Kleppers and similar foldables. The idea is that you need to get up to, but no more than, 20 percent of the swept area of the blade forward of its vertical pivot axis. This balanced area uses the water pressure generated by the boat's movement to help turn the blade.

With this setup, you can use a larger blade without needing to exert excessive steering pressure, particularly at high speeds. The 20-percent limit is critical; any more and you would lose rudder feel at your feet. More important, the blade will swing quickly to one side and slow down or stall the boat. Another advantage of the balanced rudder is that you can use the rudder as part of the lateral plane of the boat without inducing too much pressure into the steering system. This allows you greater flexibility in where the center of effort of the sail rig is in relation to the leeboard. If the sail plane is substantially aft of the leeboard, then such a balanced rudder becomes a beneficial part of the lateral plane of the rig without adversely affecting steering.

It's important to hold the rudder down at higher sailing speeds. If a balanced rudder kicks partway up because of speed pressure, it loses its balanced area and, because of its large overall size, becomes difficult to turn. To keep the rudder down, use a bungee-cord arrangement. A bungee

Balanced rudder for sailing, designed by Mark Balogh.

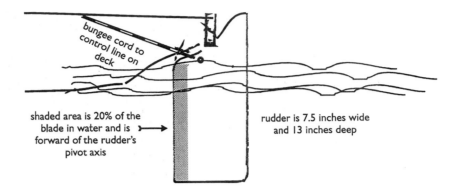

bungee cord to control line on deck

shaded area is 20% of the blade in water and is forward of the rudder's pivot axis

rudder is 7.5 inches wide and 13 inches deep

or shock cord is knotted into a hole in the rudder and run back about halfway to the cockpit, where it's tied to a piece of line that leads to a cam cleat within easy reach of the cockpit. You can then adjust the pressure tighter for heavy winds, looser for light winds.

T-Bar Rudder Control

This is a simple, do-it-yourself modification that harkens back to some rudder controls seen back in the 1920s and 1930s. Most recently Folbot has changed its rudder control to this system. Adapting the Folbot rudder control is a good ex-

ample of how the astute tinkerer can borrow ideas from what you find in other makes and models of folding kayaks.

The illustration shows what it looks like on a Folbot. A foot control consisting of a horizontal bar rotates around a vertical post. The horizontal bar has the rudder cables connected to its ends. The vertical post, which is clamped at the top and bottom to the frame, fits most easily if it's located in the opening of a crossrib, but you could also have it set away from any crossrib. To do so, make the vertical post's base attach to a plate connected to the keel and possibly chine bars.

Rudder Pedals

Bill Longyard of North Carolina, who travels frequently in Europe with his Folbots (see how to order his videos in the appendix), has come up with a pedal system for his Folbot Aleut and Greenland II. These replace an older awkward system of heavy rails that are time-consuming to set up and attach to the frame. What he has is simplicity itself, and it also weighs less than the factory system and packs easily.

The pedals are ⅛-inch aluminum plate with a series of ½-inch holes drilled down their sides. These holes accept the ⅜-inch aluminum stub-tubes that are fitted to the front of the ⅛-inch Dacron control lines. The various holes allow for

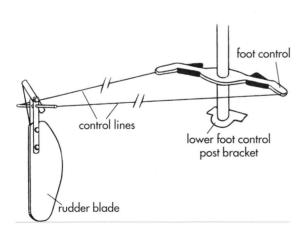

foot control

control lines

lower foot control post bracket

rudder blade

T-bar rudder control.

fine adjustment of the pedal position, while the Dacron line can be retied for coarse adjustment. The stub-tubes have $\frac{3}{16}$-inch holes drilled in their centers, through which the line is fed and tied. The knot stays out of the way inside the stub-tube.

Bill used aluminum aircraft hinge riveted to the top of the pedal with aluminum aircraft rivets. Stainless steel piano hinge (or brass, though not brass-plated steel) would also work, as would short stainless bolts using Nylok (self-locking) nuts. He cautions to make sure you have no excess bolt thread past the Nylok once everything is tightened down because it could scratch your hull fabric. The pedals permanently mount to the cross frame of his Folbot Aleut, and this saves space as well as time since there is one less thing to assemble.

Bracing Boards and Bars

You need something to brace your feet against if you want to be an efficient paddler; otherwise you won't have a powerful forward stroke. Some folding-kayak models do not have a good place to brace your feet, and they lack pedals except for operating a rudder. You can modify this yourself by making a bracing device either in board or bar form.

Board-type foot brace. A number of individuals have made the board type of foot brace, and some of the designs have been elaborate. Others are fairly simple. You can base your design on what Nautiraid offers as an accessory, which is generally hard to find.

The foot-brace board consists of a section of plywood that attaches to the keel rod. A block of wood attached to the top of the board provides a place to brace your feet. You can make adjustments for different paddler heights via webbing straps. The base itself is made of ⅛-inch marine-grade varnished plywood. It is about 6 inches long and 10½ inches wide.

Rudder pedals modification.

Bracing boards, bottom view.

Bracing board, top view.

On the underside is a set of parallel rails running the length of the plywood base. The rails are just far enough apart to form a channel that corresponds to the Nautiraid's keel rod. A small Velcro strap is attached here and goes under the keel rod to keep the bracing board from lifting out of its position.

The actual bracing piece runs across the top surface of the plywood base, and it is against this that you brace your feet. An adjustable webbing strap setup attaches to the bracing board and runs back to the crossrib at the front of the cockpit. This way you can adjust the bracing board position for different-size paddlers.

Bar-type foot brace This type of brace does not attach to the keel but rather is suspended from nearby long side pieces of the frame. The Klepper Alu-Lite and FirstLight models have something like this.

If you want to make one yourself, start with a short length of PVC 1-inch pipe. Run two webbing straps through the pipe. One webbing strap attaches to either the gunwale rods or the chine rods to hold the bracing bar in position, and the other comes toward the cockpit area. You attach both sides to points close to you using Fastex buckle loops. To adjust for different paddlers, adjust the Fastex buckles.

You will have to figure out what lengths of webbing straps will work for your particular kayak.

You could use cord instead of webbing and use slip knots or sail-line tensioners for adjustment. For comfort, use foam pipe insulation around the pipe.

Hand Tiller and Secondary Steering

David Valverde has come up with an interesting hand tiller, as seen in the accompanying photo. It rides on the mast for the second sail on his schooner setup and uses the same basic tubing incorporated into Balogh's BOSS outrigger system. It gives him a good, reliable tiller that won't hang up and is easier on the hand than the one from Klepper. Valverde also has fitted a similar tube at the bottom of his front mast to act as a foot control bar in case he needs to steer from the front seat.

MODIFYING SEATS

Your bottom and back are not the same as those on the next person, and kayak seats are proof positive of this. What a friend finds heavenly, you may experience as a time-warp trip back to the

Hand tiller on a schooner rig.

Spanish Inquisition. Some seats are downright skimpy and uncomfortable for just about anyone.

If you are having problems with the seating, your first step should be to experiment with what the factory has provided with your kayak. For example, see if there is any built-in adjustment you can make. After trying this, then you can start considering modifications.

Varying the Seat Pitch

You may try making a modification that would change the pitch of the seat bottom itself. Sometimes paddlers experience leg cramps or have their legs fall asleep while paddling. The solution is often to provide more support to the hamstrings, which helps relieve pressure on the sciatic nerve. Raising the front of the seat bottom can achieve this. The solo seat that Klepper sells for older models (see next page) has such a raised front of the seat bottom, with a rise of about a ½ inch or so. This angles your legs slightly differently.

To accomplish the same effect with your present seat bottom, you could try to duplicate how Klepper does it by mounting the seat bottom on a piece of plywood that is tilted upward at the front by a piece of lath wood. For example, you could pitch the seat bottom on the Folbot Greenland II and the Aleut in much the same way with a piece of plywood that is tilted up at the front. The same goes for some of the Nautiraids that have a seat cushion for a seat. The only problem you may find in doing this, however, is that the flat seat cushions on Folbots and some Nautiraids do not have enough anatomical curvature to hold your butt from sliding off if the seat bottom is pitched upward at the front.

Extending the Seat Bottom

You could also extend the seat bottom a few inches to give you more support in the hamstrings, which will also relieve pressure on the sciatic nerve. For example, with Feathercraft seats

you can slip a hard plastic board between the lower seat sling and the actual seat bottom, with the board extending beyond the front of the sling. You will need to secure it in some way with cord or Velcro.

Seat Backs

Folding kayak seats vary in how much they support your back, particularly your lower back. Lumbar support is critical for many people. Folding-kayak companies are improving on the stock seats all the time. For example, Feathercraft offers seats with an inflatable lumbar pad that you can adjust as much as you want through varying degrees of inflation. But if you have an older model, you are not out of luck.

Bob Snider of Spokane, Washington, hit on an idea that may just be the ticket for those who can't find comfort even with Feathercraft's original seat. He has worked out a way to attach a product from Cascade Designs called the Back Rest, which is an 8-by-16-inch self-inflatable pad similar to the company's well-known Therm-a-Rest sleeping pads. The pad is 2½ inches thick fully inflated, but you can inflate it to lesser thicknesses if you so desire.

Bob's setup is shown in the illustration. The

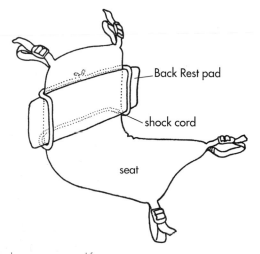

Back Rest pad

shock cord

seat

Lumbar support modification.

Solo seating.

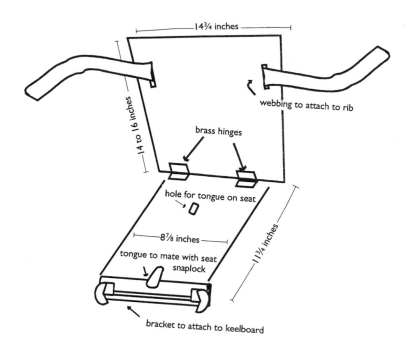

Back Rest pad is held in place with shock cord tied together in a continuous circle that is looped over one side of the pad, and then around the back of the Feathercraft seat to loop around the other side of the pad.

Bob positions it low so it forces him to sit perpendicular in the boat, and it keeps him from slouching and sagging in the seat, which is tiring over a long day. But here is where it can prove to be a godsend for anyone with lower back problems: In that position the Back Rest forms an excellent lumbar support. Since the pad is inflatable, you can adjust it to the stiffness needed to give you the optimum support you require.

Solo Seating for Older Double Kleppers

Unlike other double folding boats with open cockpits, such as Nautiraid and Folbot, older Kleppers require special seats for optimum solo paddling. Klepper offers one as an accessory, but it has problems. First, it's expensive. Although the Klepper solo seat gives better lower-back support than regular Klepper seating, some people still report that it doesn't give enough overall support because its backrest is not particularly large. Then, too, the Klepper solo seat doesn't fold compactly, so it's a bulky item that adds to your load.

Below are a number of ideas on how to modify the Klepper seating. While these deal strictly with just Kleppers, note how various approaches are used. If you need to make changes in the seats of other makes of folding kayaks, similar approaches may lead to a solution.

A cheaper version. So, what to do? Make your own solo seat along the same lines as the one sold by Klepper. Some people have used a basic plan designed by Rodolfo Wazlawik of New York. The hardware runs less than $40. You'll need a piece of marine- or exterior-grade plywood. If you have to buy a full sheet, it adds to the cost. You can tailor the backrest to suit your breadth and height, naturally, within the confines of the cockpit area. The resulting solo seat is compact and folds down nicely. It also uses one of the regulation seat bottoms, which readily slip in and out. (The commercially available Klepper solo seat has a permanently attached cushioned bottom, which makes it difficult to fold up.)

You'll need to use some hardware available from Klepper. The most important is the keelboard bracket that Klepper has for attaching the rudder pedals to the keelboard as well as its solo seat. In addition, use a tongue fitting to mate the solo seat with the regular Klepper seat bottom.

Additional hardware can be purchased at hardware or cabinetmaker stores. You'll need brass, not brass-plated, hinges for connecting the backboard to the seat board. You will also need webbing and Fastex buckles, which you can buy at any camping supplier. The webbing fits through slotted holes that you make near the edge of the backboard for that purpose. It saves money, is unbreakable, and is ultimately a lot simpler. A seat cushion serves as padding for the backrest.

The woodwork does take time. You have to cut the various pieces to size, and then sand them and apply varnish or urethane. Then there is the precise location of holes and brackets. You also have to have a piece of wood to accommodate the keelboard bracket. And you should glue some rubber or carpeting on the bottom edge so it doesn't slide on the floorboard where it rests. (Klepper's solo seat is raised slightly from the floorboard, and some people have had a problem with breakage in this area. Resting the seat directly on the floor spreads the load of the paddler more evenly.)

Another approach to solo seating. The Klepper solo seat and home-crafted duplicates have some limitations. For one thing, they're all based on using the pedal/keelboard bracket. It raises whatever you have above the floorboard and, to accommodate the bracket, pitches any seat at an angle so that the front is higher than the back.

Here's a far simpler approach that will cost next to nothing. It requires half an hour of work, at most, and costs about $15 for a pair of T-fittings and an extra fitting tongue to place on the keelboard. To make this modification, you first have to determine the seat's best trim position for solo paddling a double. Sit on a boat cushion and paddle around from a seated position a bit forward of the normal rear seat. If the boat feels balanced, mark the seat spot. Then mark a spot on the coaming for the T-fittings that will hold the seat back. The best way is to measure the relative positions of the seat back and seat cushion in the normal rear-paddler location and duplicate this relationship at the solo-seat location.

At this point, cut a hole in the keelboard for the under-seat clamp that fits into the keelboard. Attach the new tongue fitting so it will mate with the snap fitting at the front of the seat.

Now comes a harder part, emotionally. Cut slits into the canvas where you have marked the coaming for the seat back T-fittings. Make a small hole, just enough for the T-fitting to hold the seat back. The canvas in that area has little or no stress on it, so your hole isn't likely to tear further. To be safe, however, add some fabric tape or duct tape around the edges of your cuts.

Now, anytime you wish to paddle your double solo, just move up both the seat back and the seat to the new position. Depending on where you place your solo setup, you may also have to adjust your rudder controls. To extend the cables, attach nonstretch sailing line to the end of the rudder cables to bridge over to the new foot-pedal position. If your foot pedals come too far forward on the keelboard where it narrows, you may not be able to secure the foot pedals properly. A piece of plywood attached to the floorboard with screws and wing nuts will remedy this. Then attach the foot pedals to the plywood with the clamps ordinarily used.

FEATHERCRAFT HATCHES FOR OTHER FOLDABLES

Feathercraft's deck hatches are the envy of owners of other folding kayaks. The hatches aid in loading and unloading gear into both ends of the boat, and they also help you make more efficient use of all that space since they allow you to reach in to arrange items into the areas between remote ribs. You can retrofit one to your boat as Richard Spener of Missouri did to his Nautiraid double and as several other paddlers have done to their Klepper Aerius IIs. To do so, use the basic materials available from Feathercraft—hatch cloth with bead, hatch coaming, and the hatch cover.

If you are considering doing this retrofit, remember that your biggest challenge is the risk you take in making the holes in your deck. Approach this with care, because you will ruin your boat if you don't. Once you've made the holes, your best bet is to have a professional sailmaker or shoemaker do the sewing. It's a fairly simple process for a professional to sew in the chimney-type base of the Feathercraft hatch system. The rigid coaming rim and the hatch cover are designed to come on and off in the normal assembly process.

Be careful where you place the holes. You want them in an area where ribs and top bars won't interfere with access. In modifying his Nautiraid double, Spener decided to have the hatches in a location that could provide double security against heavy wave action caving in the hatch. The holes straddle the top bars of the fore and aft decks. If something were to come crashing down hard, the bar would give some support to the hatch. Please note, however, that Feathercraft has had no such problem in either its testing of the hatches or under surf conditions.

SAGGING SPRAYDECK

Open-cockpit double folding kayaks are great for many uses, but paddlers have had one complaint about the arrangement since time immemorial. Invariably, the spraydecks used to span the wide

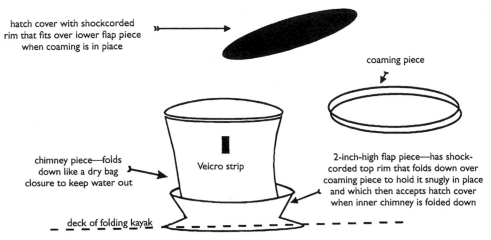

hatch cover with shockcorded rim that fits over lower flap piece when coaming is in place

coaming piece

chimney piece—folds down like a dry bag closure to keep water out

Velcro strip

2-inch-high flap piece—has shock-corded top rim that folds down over coaming piece to hold it snugly in place and which then accepts hatch cover when inner chimney is folded down

deck of folding kayak

This hatch assembly is standard on Feathercraft's latest models. The company will make these available to owners of other foldables who wish to add them at their own risk.

Feathercraft hatches for other foldables.

opening tend to sag. Water that pools in the area between the paddlers eventually seeps through. Some models are worse than others, and even within a model, you will see a range of fit. What to do about it? There are no sure fixes, but here are some things to try.

Batten Supports

This is one of the easiest and most certain solutions for improving a spraydeck that is made of nonstretchy material (such as Hypalon-coated nylon or polyester) and has come from the factory with too generous a cut. This method also will bolster spraydecks made of materials such as nylon or Cordura, which stretch when they're soaked.

Fiberglass sail battens, the material you'll be working with, come in various lengths, widths, and stiffness ratings. They're also available in uncut lengths, which you then can cut to size and add end caps to prevent the batten ends from tearing at anything on your folding kayak or scratching the coaming.

The way to apply them is fairly straightforward. Get or cut battens that are about ¾ inch to an inch longer than the distance between the sides of the cockpit. This allows the battens to bow upward and support the spraydeck. These are placed at intervals to lend uniform support. There are no firm rules as spraydeck materials vary in stretchiness and the generosity of their cut. You would want at least three between the two cockpit holes in the spraydeck, one or two in front of the front paddler, and one behind the rear paddler. Generally, a wider batten works better than a narrower one since it is less likely to twist and is stiffer, too.

The battens attachment can be simple or elaborate. Here are several ways to work with battens.

The simple fashion is to just jam battens under the spraydeck between the side coamings or washboards. The ends of the battens rest against the inside edges of the spraydeck, and sometimes this is enough to do the job without any permanent attachment. In any case, it is a good way to experiment to see where and how many battens you may need.

Sew in batten holders. These can vary from just simple end slots to hold the ends of the battens to full sleeves for the battens. These end holders or full-length sleeves keep the battens in place in the exact spots in which support is most needed for the spraydeck.

Add tensioning straps to the battens. This approach is used for hardshell spray skirts that have an implosion bar, which is similar to a batten. Webbing straps are sewn to the end holders or end-sleeves holding the battens as described above. Each end is connected to an adjustable buckle. To increase the upward pressure or bow of the batten, tighten the webbing straps. This brings the ends of the batten a bit closer together to raise its center and amount of upward bow.

A Stronger Solution

Gail and Robert Ricci of Vienna, Virginia, have come up with a stronger approach to the sagging spraydeck issue for their Feathercraft Klondike. They found that with the two-person spraydeck *in place*, water tended to pool on the deck between the third and fourth crossribs. To remedy this problem, they bought a length of ⅜-inch flexible PVC pipe, which they cut to fit just over the crossribs, and then wedged the ends under the coaming and above the gunwale bars. This fix keeps the cover slightly raised so water now runs off, rather than pooling in that spot.

This solution has an important advantage: The setup is so strong that it can support the weight of a person practicing reentry self-rescues.

CHEAP SPRAYDECK FOR KLEPPERS

Next to a sail rig, the Klepper spraydeck is the most expensive item you can buy for your boat. The Velcro-attached spraydeck with two spray skirts costs almost $350.

Matt Woodford of New Jersey found a way around the cost dilemma by making his own. The least expensive approach is to try to replicate the tuck-under version and the way its hem fits under the coaming. You could also use Velcro strips or snaps that fasten to both the coaming and spraydeck. But all these device-driven alternatives add to the cost. Besides, the tuck-under spraydeck has proved its staying power in all kinds of situations.

The factory version of the tuck-under seems to incorporate a cord sewn and glued into the hem of the deck for fitting into the groove on the inside surface of the wooden coaming. This cord hem could easily be replicated with some small-diameter nylon or polypropylene rope.

Another problem to solve is the hoop used to attach the spray skirt to the spraydeck. In the Klepper factory-built deck, the hoop is made of a flexible plastic material somewhat like a rubber hose but with articulated, curved grooves that do a pretty good job of securing the spray-skirt hem. It would be hard to find similar material already contoured for snugging on a spray skirt.

Other folding kayaks use a different form of hoop, and, like Matt Woodford, you may want to use this approach. Nautiraid has what seems to be a lightweight metal hoop sewn into the deck onto which you attach the spray skirt. It seems to be an uncomplicated approach. You may find a tough plastic hoop that will do the same. To get the hoops exactly in the right spot, which is critical, you'll need a template or true measurements of the factory deck.

The replica spraydeck requires considerable sewing, and for that you'll need a good sewing machine capable of stitching through several thicknesses of the material you'll use for the deck. That material should be fairly waterproof. Nylon pack cloth would be good as long as it's not too light. Consider material that weighs at least 8.5 ounces per square yard or a Cordura nylon that weighs 11 ounces per square yard. The pack cloth comes in 60-inch widths, costs $13 per yard, and is available from Campmor. To order, call 888-CAMPMOR (888-226-7667) or go to www.campmor.com.

Use an elastic cord at the front of the spray-deck so that it will fit snugly around the mast partner, the metal bracket with a hole in it. At the back of the coaming, sew in some grommets and shock cord to attach around the boomerang-shaped piece that closes off the back of the wooden coaming. To achieve a bead around the hem of the spraydeck, sew in some nylon cord. The hem then tucks under into the groove in the wooden coaming. This should work just as well as the factory version.

Use commercially available spray skirts. It would be hard to duplicate one for less than about $40, about what the standard spray skirt sells for.

PADDLE PARKS

Does your kayak have a handy way to "park" your paddle when you stop for a break? Folding kayaks such as Nautiraids and Kleppers do, while others, including Folbots and Feathercrafts, do not.

You can quickly get around this by simply shoving a paddle blade through a foredeck bungee, which will hold surprisingly well. For a secure place to park a paddle, however, you'll need more than that—a way to hold the shaft so it doesn't swing off deck. Randy Grepling of Evergreen, Colorado, has an interesting ap-

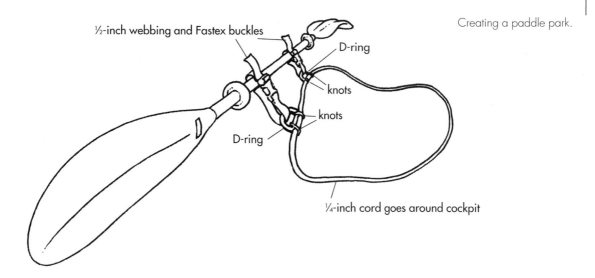

½-inch webbing and Fastex buckles

D-ring

knots

knots

D-ring

¼-inch cord goes around cockpit

Creating a paddle park.

proach that he set up on his Feathercraft K1 and earlier on a K2. It looks like it will work for just about any folding kayak.

The heart of his fix is a length of nylon cord that wraps around the kayak's coaming after the coaming has been attached to the skin. The cord is completely adjustable so that you can make it as loose or tight as you wish. Randy reports that the cord definitely does *not* get in the way of using a sea sock or attaching and detaching a spray skirt.

The paddle shaft is held in place using two Fastex snap-buckled webbing straps that are placed at knotted spots on the coaming cord. The straps are evenly spaced alongside you for quick access. Randy has found it to be relatively easy to snap and unsnap the buckles even when wearing neoprene gloves. If you wish, you can place the setup on either the right or left side of your cockpit.

While Randy uses the device for parking his paddle during breaks, this device could also hold a spare paddle if you don't already have a place to put one. An assembled two-piece spare located in this position is much easier to reach than a two-piece that is broken down and lying on your rear deck, the normal configuration you see on hardshells.

This setup is almost as good as the ones that

some folding kayaks come with. The difference is that these models also have paddle pockets into which blade ends go. If you use Randy's setup, you could mimic those pockets by just slipping the blade under a deck bungee. Or, if you wish, you could make a pocket using a flat ditty bag. The bag attaches to a deck bungee. Make certain it is large enough to accept the paddle blade so that it can slip in and out easily.

SPONSON INFLATION-TUBE MODIFICATION

The inflation tubes used to get air into folding kayak sponsons are generally not long enough if you want to top up air pressure. The situation arises when you assemble a boat, inflate the tubes, and then go paddling. Almost invariably the water temperature is colder than the ambient air temperature, and the sponsons deflate, sometimes enough to loosen the skin and cause speed-robbing drag.

The solution is to elongate the inflation tubes to something akin to what you find in Feathercrafts. To do so you need to find tubing that will mate with the existing one on your sponsons. Medical-supply shops and hardware stores tend to have this. Simply figure out the added length you need so that you can inflate the sponsons while seated in your kayak. Then, with the appropriate adhesive for such tubing, graft on an extension. You could, for added leakproofing, graft a short piece of larger-diameter tubing over the connection of the existing tube and the extension.

If you have a Klepper, why not improve the air stoppers while you're at it? Air stoppers are loose plugs that go into the inflation tube, and they often can get lost or separated from the tubing. You can replace these with an easy modification. Therm-a-Rest pads, among others, use Delrin valves as replacements for the ones on the air mattresses. These valves can be adapted to the inflation tubes on folding kayak air sponsons. The valves close and open by twisting them. The Therm-a-Rest repair accessory pack includes adhesive along with the valves, and this adhesive also works to graft tubes together.

DROOPING FEATHERCRAFT FOOT PEDALS

How many Feathercraft K-Light (and now Kahuna) paddlers have had their foot pedals fall down while paddling? Plenty. Here are some solutions.

Simple Solutions

Several owners have figured out a solution that is obvious: They drill a small hole in each foot pedal and run a cord through the hole. The cord is then tied to a gunwale bar on each side of the kayak.

Another solution that works is to place gear or an air bag so it presses on the back of the pedals. Some air bags used for extra flotation are big enough that they will press hard against the back of the pedals when fully inflated.

A *foot board*. For this fix, you basically create a foot brace that runs across both pedals. The virtue of this is that it not only keeps the pedals in position but also gives you more surface to press your feet against.

One way to accomplish this is to run a wooden rod between the foot pedals. The rod connects to the foot pedals through holes drilled in them; holding the rod in place are bolts and wing nuts.

Sam Davis of New York has an even better version of this, a *full plate* of plywood that runs across and attaches to the foot pedals. In a way this replicates the foam bulkheads some hardshell paddlers add to their kayaks for a full footrest bracing spot for their feet.

This is roughly the size and shape of the opening in the second crossrib. Sam drilled one ¼-inch hole in each foot pedal. These holes are ⅝ inch from the top of the foot pedals, centered. He used ¼-inch marine-grade plywood. It is secured to the pedals with ¼-by-1-inch bolts that secure with wing nuts.

Ruddering Foot Pedals

The solutions above will not work if you are using a rudder. The pedals need to move back and forth independently of each other, and a rod, board, or even cord would hinder this movement.

There is a way to solve that, but first the logic. The reason the foot pedals are falling or shifting in the first place is that they are attached to rails that are permanently fixed to the chine bars. It is the chine bar that is rotating down and shifting the position of the foot pedal.

Why not, then, put some sort of stopper on the chine bar? A logical placement would be in the vicinity of where the chine bar comes near either the first or second crossrib. Attach some sort of stopper to the chine bar, and then another to the crossrib. First try duct taping a small block of wood to the chine bar and then a similar small piece to the crossrib. Position the two so that if the chine bar slips, the stopper on it will meet the stopper on the crossrib.

Do not to drill holes in the crossrib in order to attach a stopper such as a bolt. The material used in the ribs of the K-Light and Kahuna is polycarbonate—not the high-density polyethylene used in other Feathercraft models—which does not take kindly to drilling. Drilling could lead to fissures and eventual breakage, and that is why the holes in Feathercraft's polycarbonate crossribs are molded in and not cut out later. Strap or duct tape something on.

D-RING PATCHES

It doesn't take a genius to see that the hull of a folding kayak is a lot stronger than the deck. However, people who choose to make additions to their boats tend to think "deck," not "hull," so they sew things onto the deck, a tricky job that requires a good needle, proper thread, some backing material, and crossed fingers. Why crossed fingers? Because the sewn-on patch or attachment could tear out under stress and heavy loads, leaving a compromising hole. As long as it's feasible and convenient, attach whatever you need to the hull.

It's a simple process that's as easy as attaching a patch on the hull after you've torn or gouged the material. The most common such hull attachments are D-ring patches, which have a variety of uses.

D-ring patches at the bow and stern on both sides of the boat are used to attach a handle for lifting the boat and pulling it ashore. Some folding kayaks, such as the Klepper Classic models, don't come equipped with bow and stern handles, so the D-ring and strap arrangement takes care of this. You'll find other uses for D-rings along the hull close to the seam with the deck. They can be used as tie-down points behind the rear seat for deck cargo, but remember to keep deck loads light for safety's sake (see chapter 13).

When you purchase a D-ring, get the smallest patch size you can. They come as small as 3 inches in diameter, and the D-ring itself can be as small as ¾ of an inch. These often can be found in any marine store that has an inflatable-boat department. You're looking for a patch made of the same material as your hull, which in most cases is Hypalon (Achilles is one brand).

To attach the D-ring patch, follow the instructions in your repair sheet on patching the hull, using the contact cement that's recommended. The process is simple. Sand both the patch and the area on the hull where it will be attached. Be aggressive, but not too aggressive. You want to buff off the sheen on the hull but not expose the core material beneath. Apply the cement to *both* patch and hull area. Wait for the recommended period, usually fifteen minutes or more, and then apply more cement to the hull area. Wait another fifteen minutes or so and repeat. After waiting another fifteen minutes, make certain it is still tacky. Now press the patch on, using a roller or dull putty knife to really press down and out toward the edges. It should be ready for use the next day.

EXTRA PROTECTION FOR HULLS

This idea comes from several sources—including a look at folding canoes made by Pakboats. These frame-and-skin canoes are worthy cousins to folding kayaks, and as folding craft they're well suited to paddling on lakes and shallow rivers.

These folding canoes are tough and rugged. What makes them able to withstand abrasion and contact with rocks in shallow water is the foam liner mounted between its vinyl skin and aluminum frame. It's made of closed-cell foam that not only cushions impact but also provides flotation for this open boat.

Most damage done to the hull of any skin-and-frame boat comes from the hull being caught between the proverbial rock and hard place. The rock is, well, any rock in any shallow water, and the hard place is the frame member against which the hull is getting caught, or rather, pressed.

If you find yourself using a folding kayak in shallow waters, you may want to place some closed-cell foam between the bottom of the frame and the hull. Run this foam up along the sides to the level of the first set of long pieces. Go for ¼-inch foam, because anything thicker may interfere with inserting the frame halves during the assembly process. Placing anything under the frame of your folding kayak, be it a Feathercraft, Folbot, Klepper, or Nautiraid, can radically change the lines and chines of the hull. And if you change them, you change how the boat reacts and balances because, in effect, you are rounding out the bottom. This is neither good nor bad, just something that will make boat handling different from what is normal.

The idea of adding some protective layer for special applications is not new. Klepper has long made a similar suggestion for paddlers using its boats in shallow rocky water. The company ad-vises placing an inflatable sleeping pad under the keel portion of the frame, and then partially inflating it.

THE ULTIMATE MODIFICATION

If you think you've heard of everything, here's the story of the fellow who was unhappy with the length of his double Klepper. Don Barch of California wanted a longer one, longer than the 17-foot regulation boat, so he added more than 2 feet in length to his existing boat to get the boat of his dreams. Indeed, it sounds like a crazy idea. What do you do to the frame to extend it? How do you get the skin apart to lengthen it? And with what?

Barch thought that the cockpit area was too small. Paddlers were too close and their paddles clanked, and there wasn't enough storage room between the paddlers. Barch was also unhappy with the bow of the Aerius II; he believed it tended to dive too much into waves, slowing down the boat and splashing water up on the foredeck. In his eyes the bow was too blunt.

To make his dream vessel, Barch decided that

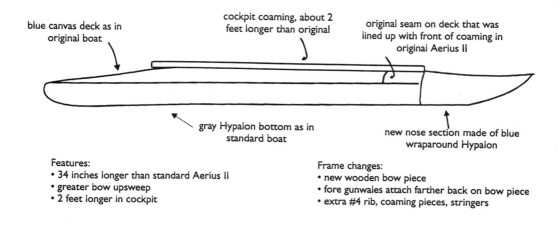

blue canvas deck as in original boat

cockpit coaming, about 2 feet longer than original

original seam on deck that was lined up with front of coaming in original Aerius II

gray Hypalon bottom as in standard boat

new nose section made of blue wraparound Hypalon

Features:
• 34 inches longer than standard Aerius II
• greater bow upsweep
• 2 feet longer in cockpit

Frame changes:
• new wooden bow piece
• fore gunwales attach farther back on bow piece
• extra #4 rib, coaming pieces, stringers

Nineteen-foot Klepper designed by Don Barch.

two areas needed work, the frame and the skin. In addition, any work on either of these areas would generate more work in other areas to compensate for new stresses, loads, and other fall-out effects.

Frame Changes

Attacking the wooden frame was the easiest part of the job and probably the area in which Barch felt most satisfied with the results. He did all of his major frame customizing at the bow half. He got rid of the standard bow piece and replaced it with a new, handcrafted bow piece made of oak for strength. It had the upsweep he wanted to see for riding over waves. The way he configured it, the gunwales no longer came quite as close together in front as on the standard setup but rather had a broader curve toward the bow. The stringers attached in somewhat the same way, mimicking the gunwales' new positioning.

The net effect of the new bow piece and the repositioning of the side pieces going to it was the addition of 34 inches to the overall length of the bow half of the boat. The stern half was fundamentally unaffected, except for some minor changes described below. With the greater length of boat, Barch added a second #4 rib in the cockpit area, which elongated the cockpit just as he desired.

Barch realized that greater length would put new stresses on the frame. To bolster things all around, he did two things to both the bow and stern keelboards. First, he fiberglassed the top of the boards that you see when you step into the Klepper, and second, he Kevlared the entire bottom of the keelboards. He felt that the combination beefed up the bottom of the boat for somewhat greater stiffness and strength. To finish up the reconstruction of the frame, Barch added extra stringers to span the greater length of the boat. He used wooden dowels to mate with the existing stringers via standard PVC plumbing-pipe sections.

He made some frame changes after experience on the water revealed some added stress points. The principal adjustment was at the stern where the stern piece mates with the rear gunwales. The mating brackets on either side were breaking free, so Barch put a metal plate on the stern piece and rescrewed the mating brackets to that. The new arrangement seems to be taking new stresses well.

Extending the Skin

Flush with his success redesigning the Klepper frame to suit his needs, Barch attacked the skin. It involved incredible labor and attention to detail, and it's the area where he's not totally satisfied with the results.

Here's how Barch proceeded. First, he worked on the hull. He removed the bow cap, a piece of Hypalon rubber reinforcement that fits over the front of the boat to act as a bumper. Underneath the bow cap is a seam joining the hull with the two sides. So the boat was opened at its nose.

Next was the deck. Barch opened a seam on the top of the deck along its entire length back toward the cockpit, leaving the boat open at the top in front.

Barch had a very simple solution for finding the material needed at both the hull and deck: He got blue Hypalon rubber material from a raft company and used it for the entire front of the boat, both hull and deck. The blue matched the color of the canvas deck extraordinarily well. The bow of Barch's boat had a distinct, almost 3-foot-long, blue nose that then flowed into the standard blue deck and gray hull.

The job was easy in theory, tough to execute. Barch used a sailor's awl to do the sewing by hand. Try as carefully as he could to gather the material evenly as he sewed along, he got a few wrinkles and what he termed a perceptible lopsidedness of port and starboard sides. The seams where the new piece met the regulation deck and hull were covered with the 2¼-inch keelstripping material available from Klepper. Potentially this created some drag, but not as much as might be expected.

Lengthening the Cockpit

With the top of the bow deck open, Barch was able to extend the cockpit to the length he wanted and have its front apex sewn together farther along the original foredeck. It was fairly easy to extend the wooden coaming. His vintage of Klepper had a coaming that came in three pieces, the front V and two extensions toward the rear, so he just made longer replacements for the two extensions. Some of the lopsidedness resulting from how the 34-inch bow piece was attached is visible in the cockpit area, and one side is looser here than the other.

What about the sponsons? Barch did nothing with them, so now they don't come up to the bow and stern ends as they would in a standard boat. But this is similar to the setup in earlier Folbot Greenland IIs, in which air sponsons didn't run the full length either.

Chapter Sixteen

Assembly Guide

If you purchase a folding kayak, you need to assemble it. Some people do it every time they go paddling as they have no place to leave one assembled. Others will leave their foldables assembled for long periods of time in a storage facility or garage; then they cartop the assembled kayak to paddling spots, knocking the boat down only in the off-season or for air travel.

But you will have to assemble the boat sooner or later. Assembly for most folding kayaks is not hard, but there are tricks that can help speed up the process. Also, occasionally some boats and a particular step may prove vexing; there are answers to such impasses as well.

The objective of this chapter is to help you get better at assembling your foldable and to deal with any adverse twists, including having a frame twist in the skin while assembling the boat.

And while disassembly shouldn't be hard, there are little tricks of the trade here, too. Use these, and you will be able to beat out an oncoming thunderstorm or disassemble your kayak while you still have daylight.

If you want to leave your kayak assembled for long periods of time, be aware that some models and makes can be left assembled for years; for others, you'll need to take some of the precautions given below.

HOW TO SPEED-ASSEMBLE ANY FOLDING KAYAK

This may not seem possible to those who are out there sweating through assembly and disassembly of their foldables, but

BE BRAINY, NOT BRAWNY

The following tip shows that you don't always have to follow the assembly instructions as provided by the manufacturer.

According to the instructions for Kleppers, connecting the bow and stern pieces to the forks on the keelboards requires you to pull the forks apart until prongs on the end pieces can slip into holes in the forks. This operation requires strength to get both prongs cleared into position. For most people, the time-honored way of doing it with the Aerius II is to slip your knee slightly between the forks to hold them far enough apart to slip in the prong fittings.

It has never been easy for weaker individuals to perform the feat with the Aerius I because the tension at the forks is even greater than on double Kleppers. In the Aerius Scout, it is even more difficult because there isn't any room to slip in a knee to hold things apart. The Scout is aimed partly at the women's market, so some remedy is needed.

The solution is fairly simple. Ignore the instructions that have you try to get both prongs lined up at their respective holes and instead do one prong first and then the other.

Use finesse, not strength.

manufacturers do not lie about how long it takes to put their boats together or the strength necessary to do the job. Their estimates, in fact, are on the conservative side and are beatable; i.e., you not only can bring your current time down substantially, but you can also shave five to ten minutes off the time the literature says the process will take.

Why should you work on assembly speed? Several reasons. It gives you more hours on the water—the less time you spend getting the thing together, the more time you have for paddling or sailing it. Long assembly times are a disincentive to impromptu trips and quick late-afternoon jaunts out on a lake or bay. Also, and perhaps more important, if you are achieving faster assembly times, it means you have undoubtedly licked those stubborn steps that can hang you up for what seems hours. When your assembly and disassembly times become predictable, you can count on catching a ferry or train after a day paddling without worrying about missing scheduled departures. Besides, quick assemblies and takedowns put you in control. (Plus they impress onlookers, which is always good for the ego.)

While manufacturers differ in how their boats are put together, and there are even differences among models within the same brand, there are some underlying principles that prevail in nearly all the foldables. If you grasp these principles and apply them along with the assembly and disassembly instructions that come with your foldable, you will be well on your way to greater speed and confidence in the process.

Tried-and-True Principles

Before trying to follow these, make certain to look at the Other Helps sidebar on page 217. The suggestions there are really your starting point. Then, read and take to heart the principles of assembly and disassembly outlined below.

The position-is-everything principle. Just like anything in life, you have to be in the right spot. It is always amazing when watching a basketball game to see just how some small guards pull down more rebounds than taller forwards. They've positioned themselves well and used their heads—not just their height.

The same is true in assembling or knocking down foldables. You have to be in the right position. Generally that means on your knees (use a seat cushion or PFD to go easy on those old joints) or crouched down low. Don't be in a standing position bent over from the waist (this is tough on your lower back). Be close to the work.

That position need not be a stationary one. The experts at the factory can often do everything from just one spot. They are that good at it. Don't try to do it their way, however. Move around to gain positions of advantage. Don't bend into any awkward reaching-out position. What you are looking for is a spot that allows you to apply good leverage and dexterity. Being on one knee generally works well.

How do you know that you have the right spot for a particular task? Easy. Try another position, say the other side of the boat. Is that side better for dealing with connecting some parts? If so, then make a mental note to switch to that spot when doing that particular process. It really is OK to jump around from one side to another. While it may seem time-consuming, it actually saves handfuls of minutes if the position shift leads to a smooth rather than chancy connection.

You may want to see if there are some other steps you could do on one side of a boat before having to bound over to the other side to do a repeat step there. Generally, though, there aren't many such shortcuts.

The umbrella principle. When people insert frame halves into the skin of their foldables, they don't seem to realize that what they have in their hands is virtually an umbrella frame; early German

Be in close, not standing.

Hug and squeeze frame half to insert.

brochures for foldables often called the frame an umbrella-like structure. The frame half is trying to expand out to the sides, which is how it helps keep the hull in tension, the same way an umbrella frame stretches out the material covering it.

Some frames don't snag up when they're put into or taken out of the hull. Others do, and when they do, the frame half either cannot be fully inserted or twists into an uneven, off-center position that can affect later assembly processes, such as proper connection of coamings.

WHAT'S POSSIBLE

If you take to heart the principles of assembly in this chapter, what assembly times can you reasonably expect for several popular models? Here is what ordinary people have accomplished, not factory teams. The times below start from an *in-bag position*, with the parts still in their bag(s).

Klepper Aerius II. Two people can assemble the basic boat in about seven to eight minutes.

Folbot Greenland II. Two people will take about ten to twelve minutes for the basic boat.

Feathercraft K-Light. One person can put together this boat in less than twelve minutes.

To ease the insertion process, squeeze that "umbrella" in toward its center. For example, with a Feathercraft, hug the open end of the frame half with your arms. Depending on the length of your arms, the lower stringers should be resting in your hands while the upper stringers are either along the inside of your forearms or in the crook of your elbows. Squeeze in on the frame with your arms while inserting the half. It will slide perfectly into position. If it starts going in crooked, you can adjust the angle by squeezing in some more on the tubes resting on the inside of your arms.

This works in the reverse direction, too. When removing a frame half, squeeze in the open end with your arms to reduce the outward pressure that is sticking the frame half in the hull.

The toothpaste-tube-and-cap principle. Often when it comes to dealing with assembly parts of a folding kayak, people tend to suspend precepts of physics that they use in everyday life. Simply put, would you try to remove the cap on a tube of toothpaste without holding the tube itself with your other hand? Of course not. Applying this to your kayak, use both hands when doing anything around your foldable. Grasp both pieces of the work. Steady or position a part with one hand while connecting another part to it with your other hand.

The biggest offenses against this principle seem to occur when dealing with aluminum tube

Twist frame piece to align.

connections such as those on the Feathercraft K-Light or the snap fittings on the gunwales of Klepper singles. For example, when connecting the center rods on a Feathercraft K-Light (those resting in the sling seat) to their bow and stern mates, people often fail to grab those bow or stern rods when trying to insert the center ones into them. What happens then is that the connection jams while only partly or halfway seated. About the only place where you can get away with not holding end rods when connecting center ones is in the Klepper Aerius I and Scout. The connecting point is under the deck, but you can usually slide the center rod into position while holding just one end. This has to do with the more generous tolerances in Kleppers at the joining spot.

The different angle–different order principle. This mainly applies to aluminum tube connections but is also applicable to the wooden frames of some models.

Some wooden frames, like Klepper singles, either the Aerius I or the Scout, often give people trouble when connecting the #2, 3, and 4 ribs to the gunwales. This is particularly true when the boats are brand-new and the gunwales have not taken a set, or curve, to them. What you need to do—using the two-hands principle—is grab the gunwale at the bottom and pull it in to twist it into an angle where the gunwale's fitting lines up properly with the mating fitting on the rib. It doesn't necessarily take strength, just leverage, which you'll have if you're in the right position. (Generally this is the opposite side of the boat, but as you can see in the photo opposite, sometimes the near-side position works, too). If this still doesn't work, then change the order of ribs you are working on. For example, see if it is easier to first attach the center cockpit. There is usually a prescribed order for a particular model, but, in the real world, wooden ribs and gunwales have a mind of their own, and you may find it easier to defy the suggested order of rib placement.

Try a different angle of alignment.

The same process applies to aluminum tube frames. In the Feathercraft K-Light, again using the two-hands principle, adjust the angle of connection. Say you are trying to move the slider at the center of the boat so that it bridges two tubes. (Folbots have a similar setup for their stringers at the center of the boat.) First see if the slider will simply slide fully into position without sticking partway. If it won't, then pull the aluminum tubes toward the center of the boat. Does that allow the slider to seat fully? If not, lift or lower the tubes slightly and try the slider again.

It's a matter of feel. (It helps if you were a safecracker in a previous life.) Use finesse and feel, not force. Try making the connection without looking; close your eyes and do it by feel alone. It's amazing how often your fingers can "see" better than your eyes when it comes to such delicate adjustments.

Whatever you do, don't ram the slider into position. It will likely only get stuck. If it gets stuck, don't waste energy trying to loosen it. Instead, move to another set of tubes and their slider. Getting others set up properly often makes the errant slider behave better when you go back to it.

The mountain-to-Mohammed principle. The idea here is to move bigger objects to smaller ones, a

Push rib down on rod for greater leverage.

common occurence when assembling or knocking down foldables. Some people have trouble snapping rods into their holders on the ribs. If you look at an assembly video, the individual is doing this with just finger pressure, but if you don't have that finger strength, or haven't gotten the hang of it yet, reverse the procedure; press the rib down against the rod to get it into the holder.

Doing it this way gives you a lot of leverage. With a full hand grip on the rib, you can use your weight to press the rib down to the rod. You can also do something similar when positioning crossribs inside the skin. This method can save you getting your knuckles scraped. If you reach around the rod to pull it to the rod holder, you can rub your skin against the underside of the boat's skin. Instead, push the whole boat down to snap the crossrib to the rods.

The remote-solution principle. Sometimes if you are having problems assembling a folding kayak at the middle, you can tackle it by doing something on a different area of the boat, somewhere that seems too far removed to have any effect.

For example, if you are finding it difficult to finish attaching the last bolt on the coaming of your boat, you can improve your prospects by lifting either end of the boat a bit. If you don't have a helper to pick up one end slightly, prop up an end on a life jacket. This relieves pressure at the center of the boat so that you can go back and finish what you were doing. This trick sometimes helps to disassemble the stringers on a Folbot where the slider bridges the central joining point of the aluminum tubes.

Speed-Assembly Instructions

Several sea-kayaking manuals state that assembling a folding kayak is "tedious" and thus put off some would-be buyers. However, putting one together needn't be a chore, and, if you put your mind to it, you can get very fast at both assembly and disassembly.

To start, make certain that all parts are labeled clearly. You may want to use bright colored tape to distinguish front parts of the boat from rear parts.

Figure out which is the best place to position your body in relation to the boat so you can do the most number of assembly and disassembly tasks from one spot. Time is lost by jumping needlessly from one side of the boat to the other.

Experiment to find the best position for your hands when attaching fittings, especially ones that may be giving you difficulty. Establish if there is some preferred order of rib placement, say, putting in rib #4 before #3. Camber and flex of frame parts may dictate this kind of order.

All of these steps taken together will almost guarantee that your assembly time decreases to the twelve- or fifteen-minute range for nearly all the foldables reviewed earlier. If two of you are assembling a boat, try the following speed-assembly method that is used by military special-forces teams who can't afford to hang around too long putting together their boats. The instructions are

OTHER HELPS

Get the assembly video for your model, if at all possible. The best way to learn how to assemble a boat is to see it done in person by a knowledgeable individual. The next best thing is the video; its pictures are worth thousands of words of written instruction. After watching it a few times and listening to the voiceover (if there is one), turn the sound off so you're not distracted. In particular, watch how the person is using both hands to position the work, the angles he or she is moving parts at, etc. Don't be discouraged by the individual's seeming lack of effort in spots that are proving tough for you. Remember, sometimes the demonstrator is working with a doctored boat; i.e., one with a particularly loose skin, "tuned" fittings, and the like.

For your first few assembly attempts, just make the frame. Without the resistance of the skin, which the frame is trying to stretch out and keep in tension, everything will go together easier. (This is why, generally speaking, it's easier to assemble those folding kayaks that allow you to make the entire frame, or most of it, first and then insert it into the skin.) You also have more room to see what is going on without having to deal with deck overhang obscuring the process. This will also convince you, for example, that those sliders *do* slide over those rod ends in the middle of the boat; the manufacturer has *not* made a mistake and shipped you mismatched parts! That confidence will help you when you are struggling to work with the frame inside the skin.

Mark every part with color-coded tape. Manufacturers are getting better at making it easier to identify what goes where, but you can always improve on even the best factory-provided identifiers. Keep it simple and easy to see, so an onlooker can immediately discern the pattern of your color-coding. You may even want to indicate starboard and port sides on gunwales such as Kleppers. While gunwales can go on either side, the wood does take a set eventually. Why not have the advantages of that proper curve when assembling the boat?

Lubricate everything that can be lubricated. Aluminum-framed boats benefit the most from this procedure, but so too do their wooden-frame brethren. Feathercraft generally provides a small bottle of Boeshield T-9 with its boats. Use it at every male and female joint and for any parts that slide, such as the sliders on the K-Light and any rods that are stretched out by the levering process used in some models. You only have to do it every couple of months. On Kleppers and Nautiraids, put a little grease or wax on the fittings so they will close or snap together more smoothly. On both these makes, you should wax the perimeter bead that is used to attach the deck to the coaming.

for assembling Kleppers, but you can adapt them to your own boat.

The military designates one person as team member A, the other as team member B. Team member A is responsible for the long bag with the keelboards, gunwales, etc. Member B is responsible for the hull bag and ribs. See what the duties below look like; they may help determine who will be A and who B. For example, whoever is handier with the several steps of rudder assembly should take the B role.

Here goes:

1. A empties the long bag, while B empties the hull and rib bags.
2. A sorts the long pieces into front and rear piles. B spreads out the skin and sets out the ribs in sequence alongside it.
3. A assembles the front half of the frame. B assembles the rear half. Both insert their halves into the skin. Together they join the frame halves and

put in any remaining long stringers. A puts in rib #3 and grabs the coaming, and B places ribs #4 and 5.

4. A puts in the masthead end of the coaming. Both connect snap locks of ribs and tuck the black edge piping into the coaming groove. Whoever gets to the rear first puts in the boomerang piece.

5. Each puts in his or her respective seat and seat back.

6. Each inflates either a port or starboard air sponson two-thirds full.

7. A inserts the foot-pedal assembly. B places the rudder, yoke, pins, and cables on the boat.

8. A attaches the front of the tuck-under spraydeck, and B attaches the rear. Each tucks under one side. A and B then finish inflating the sponsons.

DEALING WITH ASSEMBLY AND DISASSEMBLY PROBLEMS

Frame Twist During Assembly

Have you ever had any of the following happen to you when putting together your folding kayak? You assemble a frame half and then go to push it into the skin only to find it going in crooked. Or you succeed in getting the frame halves in straight, but when you try to connect the frame halves and stretch them inside the skin, the full frame winds up going off center.

Manufacturers' written instructions don't always tackle such vexing problems. You can sometimes find a solution through experimenting, or by mentioning your problem to a savvy dealer.

Frame half goes awry. **Make certain to stretch out the skin fully.** That means *fully*; not just having it laid out fully end to end but also opened up wide, side to side. Most people take care of the first—the end to end—and ignore the second.

It is easy to overlook this step when you're in a hurry, but it will save you a lot of time. This problem often crops up during the first assembly of a new season, when the boat's been stored for a while in the off-season. The skin gets wrinkled while in its folded or rolled-up storage condition, and when you lay it out the wrinkles are still there, or the sponson sleeves may have gotten twisted. The result is that you don't have a clear opening for the frame.

Give the skin a good shaking. Grab an end and shake it up and down. Go to the other end and repeat. This helps move the sponsons out of the way. Then go to the cockpit area and grab the skin at the front end and shake the skin up and down again. Do the same at the back of the cockpit. If you have a single folding kayak with a small cockpit opening, you can do this shaking in one motion by grabbing both ends of the cockpit opening.

As you insert the frame half in, pay attention to alignment. When the first quarter or third of the frame half is in under the deck, start straightening the frame half's position in the skin; don't wait until the frame half is well into the skin.

In some folding kayaks with large sponsons and openings such as a single Klepper, you have a little more leeway than you do in a Feathercraft single, and certainly more than you do in the Nautiraid singles.

Use a sawing motion. Instead of shoving the frame half in all at once, use a a back-and-forth or in-and-out motion, like using a handsaw. Ease the frame in a foot or so at a time. With this motion you gently push aside any folds in the skin that may be throwing the frame half off-kilter or that are stopping it from going in smoothly.

Many Nautiraid owners use this trick since Nautiraid openings tends to be tighter because the boats have external sponsons. If you try to put a Nautiraid frame half in all at once, you're almost certain to wind up getting it jammed in out of alignment.

Frame twist when extended. This can happen with some models such as Feathercraft and Nautiraid singles. Their frame-to-skin tolerances tend to be tight by design. But even models of other makes can experience this.

First, make certain the frame halves are all the way into the ends of the skin. If they aren't, when you extend the frame halves something will have to give, which usually is alignment of long frame pieces such as the keelbar. There are several tricks to try depending on the model.

If you've had problems with the full frame twisting off center in previous assembly efforts, get inside the cockpit and push against the cross-rib with your feet. This ensures that the frame halves are as far in as they can go.

With the K-Light, and now the Kahuna, you can't really push with your feet because of the placement of the crossribs. But you can still get the frame halves to seat better into the ends of the skin via a two-step process. First, place the telescoping center keelbar in place and start extending it out with just hand pressure. Next, as you start the extension process of the keelbar with the levering rods, do so just a bit without getting to the point where the snap button pops through its intended hole. At this point, pause and straighten out the frame. Then go back to extending the keelbar all the way until the snap button pops through the hole.

Vigorously shake the boat up and down. If the full frame has twisted out of alignment after extending the frame halves, try grabbing the cockpit opening (without the coaming in place) with both hands and shake the boat vigorously. You may have to play a bit with manipulating the frame by kneading it from the outside through the skin.

Sequence the inflating of the sponsons. This trick often gets the frame straightened out. You should never fully inflate one sponson before moving on to the next one. If you do, you are pulling the skin tightly on one side, and the frame will most definitely go off center inside the skin. Instead, inflate the first sponson just about a third or so. Then almost fully inflate the next one before you finish inflating the first. Be careful about which sponson you inflate first: you should start with the one on the side where the frame is off center. As you inflate the first sponson you will see the frame slowly move to a centered position. If the frame was quite off center when you started, then inflate that side about half to two-thirds of the way toward full inflation. That will ensure that the frame won't get crooked again when you inflate the second sponson.

Try changing the assembly sequence described in the manufacturer's instructions. The suggested sequence generally works as the best ordering of steps, but sometimes, if you switch the order, you'll find that assembly turns out to work better. This is probably because frames and skins are fundamentally made by hand, and variations in manufacturing can change dimensions enough that what works for the majority of boats in a model may not work for yours.

Try something unorthodox. When the frame halves are in the boat but you haven't started the extension process yet, partly inflate the sponsons. This sounds crazy since you would ordinarily not inflate the sponsons until after the boat is fully assembled, but if the frame is twisting, partly inflated sponsons may help hold the frame from twisting as the frame halves are extended. Don't put too much air into the sponsons—use just enough so they start stiffening a bit.

Remember that everyone's anatomy is different, and people favor different sides of their bodies. Usually this doesn't matter, but particularly strong individuals may be applying too much thrust as they insert the frame half, and it may go in crookedly. If this happens to you, try using your weaker side.

TIPS FOR DISASSEMBLY

Disassembly is generally pretty straightforward, but snags can occur. Steps that should go smoothly can often pin you down longer than the process should take. Below are tips to ease disassembly.

Loosen any deck bungees. On some boats, deck bungees may tend to hold the frame halves in. They also may apply enough tension to the skin to make it difficult to release the deck hem bead that fits into the groove of the cockpit coaming.

Take out rudder assemblies, footboards, etc., especially if these were added as a modification. These can get in the way of separating frame halves and removing them from the skin.

Be aware of any other item that may be holding the frame in position. It could be an air bag or some gear still left inside.

In general, make a habit of removing the cockpit coaming as soon as you can. Kleppers and Folbots seem to have a linear logic to them, and the coaming practically screams at you when it is time for it to be removed. But with Feathercrafts, you can remove the coaming at just about any time. Some people leave the coaming on, and it can get in the way of other disassembly steps. This may happen because the instructions tell you to put on the coaming fairly early, so people follow that process in reverse. But you should take it off right away to give yourself more room.

A preventive step. When assembling the kayak, remember to leave those little tabs in the cockpit hem out of the cockpit groove. This applies to Feathercrafts and to a degree to Kleppers and Nautiraids. If the tabs have accidentally been buried under the coaming or inserted into the groove, it may be difficult to get enough of a grip on the beaded material to take it out of the groove.

When you're about to remove the frame halves, stop and give the entire boat a shake. Grab the boat by the cockpit area of the skin and shake it. Also go to the front and back of the skin and bang slightly on the sides of the hull. This helps loosen the skin, especially when it's still wet as the coated material tends to cling to the frame.

If the boat has been left assembled for a while, the frame halves may be stuck inside. A preventive measure would be to use the plastic-bags solution. If you're planning to store the boat assembled for a long period, before putting in each frame half (or the front of the boat, in which you make the entire frame outside the skin), place a plastic grocery bag over the bow and stern ends, and then slide the halves in. The plastic bags provide a sliding surface for when the frame half is taken out and reduce adhesion of the skin to the frame.

Release the keel rod or keelboard just before you release the frame halves at the gunwales and other long pieces. Some people get sloppy or are in a hurry, but if the keel is released too early, the other long pieces may not come apart easily.

LEAVING A KAYAK ASSEMBLED

Just how long can you leave a folding kayak assembled? The answer varies by manufacturer and even among models. Here is a rundown of the major makes.

Feathercrafts

Feathercraft frames fit together with close tolerances, which makes them very strong and able to withstand punishment. However, this can lead to trouble with storage and long-term assembly. Frames have numerous places where connections are male and female; i.e., the ends of aluminum tubes fit into each other. Sliders in one model connect abutting aluminum tubes. In several models, the frame halves extend inside the skin through the movement of tubes that are nestled one on the other and locked in place with snap buttons.

It's OK to keep a Feathercraft assembled for a while, but don't do it for too long, generally no more than three months or so. That period would take up a good part of the paddling season in temperate climates.

What happens if you leave a Feathercraft assembled too long? It may seize up on you if frame parts get gummed up with dirt and salt. This has also happened to shops that have kept a demo model assembled for too long.

Lubricate with either Super Lube or Boeshield T-9. A tube of Super Lube comes with the boat. Use the liquid or paste form of these lubricants, which adhere better, not the aerosol version. After wiping off any grit, lubricate all male and female connections. Also, lubricate all sliding tubes at the chines and gunwales. The extension bars that form the keel should also get a good dose of lubricant. Lubrication not only assures that parts will slide better; it also helps prevent corrosion and keeps the surfaces clean.

Let air out of the sponsons. This has nothing to do with reducing stress on the hull stitching as some people surmise. Partly deflating the sponsons reduces the amount of contortion on the sliders on the K-Light and the extension bars of the other models. This sideways pressure is often why parts get stuck together.

Regularly check the telescoping tubes that extend the frame halves. To do so, let air out of the sponsons, and then check to see if the sliders will rotate freely. Also, without actually taking the frame apart, push in the snap button on the keelbar to see if it depresses and that the two nestling keel parts slide freely. Don't forget to extend the frame again.

If you can, store the boat upside down. This allows dirt to fall to the underside of the deck and away from the keelbar. Stored this way, the inside gets better and warmer air circulation, and the keelbar is under less tension, so it's less likely to seize up. This also partly relieves pressure on the chine and gunwale bar extensions. If in the process your deck bars stick, you have less of a problem than if the keelbar or chine bars seize. It is much harder to deal with a stuck keelbar than a deck bar. You can at least get frame halves separated and out of the hull, and then you can work on the stuck deck bar outside the skin.

Use a sea sock when you paddle. This reduces the amount of grit that can gum up aluminum connections. Rinse out the inside of a Feathercraft that is being left assembled any chance you get. You don't have to do it every time you are near the boat—just every so often.

Folbots

Folbot, like Feathercraft, uses aluminum frame parts for all its long pieces. However, the tolerances are more generous. Moreover, the method of extending frame halves within the skin relies on a mechanism that is virtually seize-free. So you can be somewhat less cautious in keeping a Folbot assembled for longer periods than a Feathercraft. You would be pretty safe in leaving a Folbot assembled over a winter, for example, but there are some areas you should watch and take precautions with.

The way a Folbot's frame halves are extended inside the hull is via a horseshoe and block mechanism. One frame half of the Folbot has a horseshoe-shaped part at the keel and gunwales. To extend the frame, these horseshoes on one half frame are engaged with block-type structures of the other frame half and pressed down or to the sides. This form of open connection is highly unlikely to ever get stuck no matter how long the boat is left assembled. It is seldom affected by corrosion or gum-up.

Folbot does use sliders at the chine tubes, but the sliders have a looser fit. Conceivably a Folbot slider can seize, or the snap button that pops through a hole could stick, but they are easy enough to free up if banged with a mallet or given a shot of WD-40 or a similar product.

If you want to leave a Folbot assembled for an extended period, here is what you should do (in addition to letting some air out of the sponsons).

Lubricate all the male and female connections. While the tolerances are fairly loose, lubing these parts with the lubricants suggested above will prolong the period you can safely leave a Folbot assembled. If these tubes do stick, it would be within the frame halves and wouldn't prevent taking the boat apart in the middle and getting the frame half out. With the frame halves separated and outside the skin, you would be able to deal with any stuck male or female connection.

Pay special attention to the chine sliders. Heavily lube the connection and the snap buttons. While the boat is assembled and in storage, tap on the sliders every so often with a mallet and see if they can turn a bit.

As with Feathercrafts, wash the inside with fresh water every so often. You may also want to store the boat upside down to make certain grit doesn't get into the chine sliders.

Kleppers

The assembly of Kleppers uses virtually no metal parts that could get stuck together. The only place you will see male and female connections is in the chine rods. These rods are made of wood and connect to each other with metal ends. The tolerances are loose, however, and are at the end of solid pieces of wood through which no water and dirt can flow to foul up the male and female connections. Metal sliders are used in the chine rods in the center of the boat, but there are no snap buttons, and the sliders are under minimal tension. If

a Klepper is left assembled for several years, the slider may get a bit stuck, but it will most definitely respond to banging and WD-40. And, in a worst-case scenario, you could cut the wood at the joining part with a wood chisel, which is much easier than cutting through aluminum.

Kleppers do have aluminum fittings that connect long pieces to the crossribs. These can corrode or clog up a bit, but never enough to keep the fitting from opening and prevent taking the boat apart. Kleppers have been left together for years and then successfully taken apart without a problem with these fittings. Kleppers also use horseshoe and block mechanisms to extend the frame halves, similar to what you see in Folbots. Such means of stretching the frame halves inside the skin cannot ever freeze up.

While you can safely leave Kleppers assembled for years with only a rare chance of anything getting mildly stuck, there are precautions you should take in storing a Klepper assembled.

Keep the boat as dry as possible. If the deck constantly gets wet, it will tend to shrink, and you may have problems later when assembling the boat again.

Keep water out of the boat. The wooden parts may deteriorate if they are left sitting in bilge water while in storage. The wood may blacken in spots, and screws may come loose where wood rots around them. Also, bilge water may warp the bow and stern end pieces. This will not happen in ordinary use, but it will if the parts are resting in bilge water for long periods of time while in storage.

Let air out of the sponsons. This will allow air to get in under them and prevent the canvas from holding water and remaining damp. Partly deflated sponsons will also reduce any tendency of wet wooden parts to warp.

You need not store it upside down. Unlike other makes of folding kayaks, Klepper and Nautiraids (see below) are not affected by any grit at the keel and chines.

Nautiraids

Nautiraids are blessed with all open fittings, and the company proudly advertises this in its literature. There is no spot in any Nautiraid where any part is fully enclosed or locked within another. Where parts do meet the fitting or connection is an open one, so it cannot get stuck together.

Still, you can have some problems with a stored Nautiraid. While you can leave one assembled for years, as you can a Klepper, there are places to exercise a bit of caution.

Beef up some of the connections. Unlike in the case of Kleppers and Feathercrafts, the long pieces of a Nautiraid do not snap snugly into place on the crossribs. Instead, they sit in notches. For an ordinary day trip or even weekend camping trips, this arrangement is OK as it can't cause any problems. However, if you leave the boat assembled for long periods and continue to use it, it's possible that one or more of the wooden long rod pieces will slip out of the open notches of the crossribs; if left that way, the wooden rods can warp out of shape. So, if you plan to leave a Nautiraid assembled for a season or longer, use plastic wire ties at these connection points in order to make certain nothing slips out of place.

Watch for swelling of the ends of long pieces where they lie in the open channel hinges. The subassemblies have several places where wooden ends nestle into open metal channels at the chines, gunwales, and even the keelbar and top bars. If the wood swells, it may take a bit of effort to release the wood from the channel. If you decide to varnish in these areas, be extra careful—you don't want to build up too much of a varnish layer that would stick in the open channel.

Chapter Seventeen

Repair and Maintenance

If you're like most paddlers, chances are you'll never need to make any repair on your folding kayak, even patching. Turn over a dozen foldables that have been used regularly for five years, and only one or two are likely to show even one patch. The rest will have clean bottoms.

And if you're like most folding-kayak owners, you won't do much maintenance beyond washing the skin-and-frame members occasionally to remove mud and saltwater residue. Your boat won't look any more worn than that of the paddler who polishes and varnishes every surface in sight.

Nevertheless, you should know how to patch and repair your boat just in case something happens when you're far from home. It's a jungle out there: you'll encounter hidden wrecks, sunken tree trunks, barnacle-crusted rocks, and broken-bottle beaches. And the power of the sea is enough to trash even large ships when it's riled up. Surf landings are rough on any vessel.

If you want to get the longest service out of your folding kayak and enjoy hassle-free assembly and disassembly, a regular maintenance schedule may very well help it last a century, at least the frame anyway. This need not be a boot-camp regimen; fairly simple attention will work wonders. It will also help you spot and fix any potential problems before they become a real problem when you're out on a trip somewhere.

REPAIR

Repairs can be organized into two categories: emergency repairs done in the field, and repairs that can be completed at your own pace at home or during a break in a multiweek trek. Surprisingly few things can go wrong with a folding kayak that demand your immediate attention while you're out paddling. Even then, you can make a quick fix that will hold until you can correct the problem more permanently.

Field repairs are not very elaborate, and they don't need to be pretty. You just need to do something fast that will allow you to keep going. Some permanent repairs can take time, but with a foldable, you may be able to replace, not repair, an errant item, which takes very little time.

Field Repairs on the Run

You probably received a repair kit with your foldable, and it most likely contains some or all of the following: large pieces of deck material to patch a torn deck; a large piece of hull material, possibly including some keelstrips; cement to attach the hull-repair patch to a tear; sandpaper for roughing up the hull surface to accept the patch; clear vinyl solvent that will seal pinholes in the air sponsons; duct tape; and a spare part or two.

Take that kit and put it away at home someplace where you can find it if it's ever needed. You won't need all those items on most trips. Many paddlers dutifully carry the kit with them without ever asking themselves some very useful questions: "How likely am I to sew on a patch during a day trip or weekend camping outing?" "How willing am I to go through the ritual of roughing up hull surfaces and cementing and recementing patches with fifteen- to twenty-minute waiting periods between coatings while sand is blowing over everything and the mosquitoes are biting?"

Klepper repair items. *(Walther/Klepper)*

You need very few items from that kit for emergency field repairs. The duct tape is one, and it's probably all you'll need for most emergency repair situations. In fact, you should purchase extra duct tape so you'll have enough for some emergencies you may run into. Be careful about duct tape, however. The shiny aluminum-faced kind isn't up to marine-environment repairs. It certainly will not hold tenaciously to parts and boat skins. Get the good stuff from your boat dealer or in the aftermarket. A good version is sold in photography shops, where it's known as gaffer's tape. The best duct tape comes from folding-boat manufacturers.

You'll want to retrieve any specialized item from the factory-supplied repair kit and take it with you when paddling. For example, if the kit has a spare air stopper for the sponsons, that's a good item to have in case you lose one.

If you have a foldable with an aluminum frame, your repair kit probably contains a repair sleeve of aluminum tubing sized slightly larger than the thickest long aluminum frame member. Bring that along. It takes a lot to bend or crimp an aluminum long piece tube, but if it happens, the quickest repair is to slip that emergency sleeve over the broken or bent part and secure the sleeve in place. You could also bring a short length of

PVC pipe that is slightly larger in diameter than the aluminum rods of your kayak; it would make a good splint if a bar gets bent or broken.

Look at the sidebar on pages 74–75 for other items to bring with you. Chief among these is a multitool like the Leatherman tool. You'll also want to carry some spares for parts that can break down and would be easier to replace than to try to jury-rig. The most likely weak points are the rudder pin and yoke. The pin can get lost, and the yoke can snap or bend.

Here are some emergency repair principles.

Duct tape is the solution to nearly any problem on a foldable. Duct tape will adhere to the smooth surface of your hull for months, and it will hold on to the canvas for weeks. It will keep cracked ribs and long pieces together for years.

Much depends on how you apply it. It will stick on the hull only if the surface is truly dry, so take the time to dry the surface thoroughly and then apply duct tape to the damaged hull with an inch or so of overlap. Place duct tape on both the outside and inside surfaces, if you can reach the inside easily. Round off the ends of the tape so you leave no right-angle corners that could catch and lift the patch. Press down on the tape and out from the center to expel air.

The tape should be applied to the deck in a similar way. Since most deck surfaces have a grainy texture, not smooth like the hull, it's important to apply pressure until you can see the grain bumps through the tape surface. Apply duct tape more generously with more overlap than on the hull. You may want to apply several layers.

Duct tape needs help when applied to frame members. If you have a broken or splintered long piece, you should apply not only duct tape but also some form of splint to bridge the break. You can achieve quite a long-lasting repair of a broken long piece if you do the following. Put some duct tape at the break, enough to smooth out burrs and jagged edges. Then find a piece of wood, maybe part of a tree branch or a stick of driftwood, and attach this as a splint by first wrapping it in place with light cord or dental floss. If you don't have cord or floss, long strands of cloth from a T-shirt or bandanna will do. Then wrap the repair with plenty of duct tape in overlapping layers.

Don't fret over broken or loose fittings. Folding kayaks have built-in redundancy. No one, two, or three broken fittings are going to affect the boat's ability to keep going. Other fittings will take the load. Also, the tension of the skin over the frame will help keep the frame snug and solid. You can wait until you get home to fix fittings. If it does bother you, use some cord to tie the long piece and rib together temporarily at the point of the errant fitting.

Klepper owners in particular seem to fret about fittings. If a fitting won't stay locked, they worry about the boat holding together. They fail to see that each rib is connected to the long parts in as many as seven places, more than in any of the other foldables. Even if three fittings aren't holding on a rib, the rest are enough to do the job.

Keep your mind open to indirect solutions. Don't get caught up in linear thinking. You can repair a broken aluminum part with a wood splint. You can use a metal splint such as a tent peg to span a broken wooden part.

Speaking of tent pegs, not only are they good splints, they also come in handy for other repairs. The metal pegs that come with most tents, for example, can be used to temporarily replace a lost rudder pin on a Klepper.

The tent-peg idea should alert you to see if you can use any other items in ways they weren't intended. If you don't have what you need, rummage around in your things. As mentioned above, a torn-up T-shirt makes a good wrap for a repair. So will a belt. A quick walk along almost any beach or shoreline is bound to turn up some flotsam that could be put to use.

Permanent Repairs

You usually will want to wait until you get home to make a permanent repair, but if you have enough time, you can do almost any permanent repair on a folding kayak in the field under all conditions, including extreme cold. Foldables are the only sea kayaks that can make this claim, and it's one reason they're the first choice for long-range expeditions, especially in northern climates. You cannot permanently repair the holed or cracked hull of a rigid plastic or fiberglass sea kayak in such locales because their repair materials will not work reliably in temperatures lower than about 45°F. Hypalon hulls, on the other hand, will accept a permanent patch at temperatures below freezing.

Here are some guidelines for permanent repairs.

You may want to exercise your replace-not-repair option. With a folding kayak, you have that unique choice, at least when you get back home. With a rigid boat, you don't. Say your loaded double foldable gets bashed against huge boulders by mean surf and you break the coaming. You can make an emergency repair and continue your trip. When you're back home, you may want to buy a new coaming or a part of one since you can get just one side.

Consider the cost of that item versus messing with repair materials and their costs. Much depends on the nature of the part. If it's truly a minor component in the boat's structure, say a stringer, you can just leave it taped and never permanently repair it or bother with a replacement. Some major pieces, such as the main connectors holding the two frame halves together, would merit replacement, certainly at least a permanent repair.

Always opt to use the materials furnished by the manufacturer. Be wary of substitutes from the outside world. Not all Hypalon-type materials are the same. A Hypalon strip purchased from a rubber-raft catalog may not have the same composition, adhesives, and core material as the original manufactured equipment. Some materials may only seem to work better than what the manufacturer provides. For example, Barge cement adheres permanently when the contact cement from Klepper won't. You may regret permanence, however, if in the future you need to lift that Barge-cemented patch to put on keelstrips.

Get the latest advice from the manufacturer and follow it. Your boat may be a dozen years old and finally bend an aluminum rod. Call the company. The written instructions you received with your boat may be out of date. The company may have found better or easier solutions. It's even possible that the company may be willing to replace a piece that broke, if it suspects that the piece may have been part of a bad batch.

Be thorough when making a hull repair. Generally you repair Hypalon the way that was described for attaching D-rings to the hull (see page 207). Take your time and have all the materials at hand before you start the job. It's critical that you really work on preparing the surface, the secret behind a lasting repair.

Use sandpaper to roughen the surface really well. If you don't get the surface sufficiently scratched up, the contact cement and the patch will not hold well. On the other hand, you don't want to sand through the surface down to the core material underneath. That's why it's important to take your time; scratch the surface some, blow away the dust, and scratch some more.

Apply the contact cement in several stages as instructed earlier. Be patient. Wait for the surface to get just a bit tacky. If you're going to err, it is better to wait longer than rush the job. Five minutes too soon is bad; five minutes too long is OK.

Remember to round off the edges, as you would with any patch. If you leave the right-angle corners, your patch will most certainly lift off over time.

Other hull materials, such as vinyl or urethane-coated nylon, have their own set of repair instructions. You should follow the company's directions.

Aquaseal can work wonders. This product, which had its origin as a repair glue for neoprene wet suits, has wide application for permanently repairing folding kayaks. Aquaseal can be used in a number of ways, but always use the accelerator material known as Cotol-240 that you buy separately.

You can use Aquaseal to attach a patch to the deck instead of sewing it on. Here's how. Get the deck material out of your repair kit. Cut it to a size that gives you at least a 1½-inch overlap beyond the damaged section. Round off the corners. Apply Aquaseal to both the patch and deck. Press the patch down hard, and then apply a bead of Aquaseal around the perimeter of the patch.

Aquaseal can be used directly on nicks in the hull that are too minor or small to warrant a patch. It will also repair ripped spray skirts and clothing.

Frame members will respond to a number of commercially available repair materials. Many repair materials will work with aluminum, polycarbonate, polyethylene, and wood frame members. Again, see what the manufacturer recommends. If you're unsure, go to a marine supply shop and look through the repair section. Powerboats and sailboats use much the same materials that go into the frame of your foldable. By buying your repair products from a marine shop, you assure yourself of getting something that will be waterproof and hold up in a saltwater environment. A very useful product is rigging tape. Its marine application is to prevent metal devices such as turnbuckles from chafing sails or line, but it is also ex-

cellent for wrapping broken parts together. It stretches to three times its length and thus sticks tightly through tension, not adhesives. Applied this way, the tape is air- and watertight. It comes in black or white.

One product you may want to look into is 3M's Urethane Adhesive 3532, which has a high viscosity, is puttylike in consistency, and can be used either for bonding broken pieces together or in conjunction with cloth as you'd use resins. It takes about ten minutes to harden, but you should wait twenty-four hours before putting full stress on the repair. The adhesive is expensive, about $25 for a 4-ounce kit.

You may also want to take a look at cold epoxy, which is sold under a variety of brand names. It generally will work for marine applications.

MAINTENANCE

You don't have to go overboard on maintenance. As stated earlier, many paddlers never varnish the wooden frames of their Kleppers, Nautiraids, and older Folbots, yet they get away with it. For example, the German-language copy of maintenance instructions for Kleppers tells you to varnish yearly, but that advice is absent from the English instructions. Yet there is no evidence that Kleppers last longer in German-speaking countries than in English-speaking ones.

Your most important maintenance material is not varnish, lubrication, wax, or anything exotic—it's water. Fresh water. Wash your boat regularly. If you can, wash it after each use. If you can't, then plan to wash it at least once or twice during the paddling season and before you put the boat away, assuming you're not a year-round boater.

Wash everything: the hull, inside and outside; the deck, topside and underside; and the frame members. Use a mild soap on the deck to wash away salt crystals and the oiliness that salt water tends to have. Aluminum frame pieces need special attention. Wash the tubes inside and out. Dropping the pieces into a bathtub is an easy way to remove grit from the inside. If you don't, that grit will wear away at shock cord and gum up the male and female connection points.

You can get by without washing your boat. Some city apartment dwellers never get a chance to do anything with the hull. Your foldable will be happier, however, if it does get washed every so often.

Here are two other maintenance steps to take with your boat during the season. One, wax the hull with whatever the manufacturer sells or recommends. A well-waxed hull is better protected against damage from sun and salt, and wax will keep Hypalon and other hull materials from drying out prematurely. A waxed hull slides off sharp rocks and other abrasive surfaces better than an unwaxed one.

Two, if you have an aluminum frame boat, lubricate the joining ends regularly. A good preventive schedule calls for lubrication every two months, especially if the boat is left assembled and gets wet on the inside all the time, particularly in salt water. Of course, wash the frame just about as often, too.

Getting Ready for the Season

The "boating season" may not open in your local waters until last winter's ice disappears. In the western-rivers region, the paddling season has more to do with rainfall amounts than temperatures. If you live where water sports are possible year-round, your local boating season may revolve around an annual profusion of flowers, migrations of wildlife, or around your family's vacation schedule. If you prefer to travel elsewhere to do your boating, your season could begin and end at any time. But no matter where you live or what

your lifestyle, you can think of the boating season as whenever you most frequently get to enjoy adventuring on the water.

Every boater, from rafter to yachtie, knows that you have to get your craft ready for the season. Problems may have developed unnoticed while the boat was in storage. Annual maintenance duties may never get done later when you're just too busy having fun with your boat, so you'd better see to them now. Although folding kayaks are no more delicate than other boats, they do need some specialized attention. Here is a checklist of things to do before the upcoming season and tips to making it a happy one.

All Folding Kayaks

Check to see if the airbags you are using in the bow and stern sections of your folding kayak are holding air. What, you don't use extra flotation bags? Get some!

The easiest way to check your airbags is simply to inflate them to full capacity and then come back an hour later. If the flotation bag is not holding air, take it over to a filled bathtub and look for telltale bubbles coming from any holes. Repair with whatever product is appropriate for the bag's material, either a patch or just a sealant for pinprick holes.

Go around the deck and tug at all D-rings, handles, paddle pockets, etc. This means all fittings that are sewn or glued on to the deck. Now is the time to see if any of these components may fail later when you may need to depend on them. Also, this cautionary checking will avoid later leakage in the deck if some stitch pulls loose.

Go around the entire seam line that connects the deck to the hull. See if any stitch is lifting or fraying. This happens rarely, but it is good to check anyway.

With this seam line, as well as D-rings and the other items mentioned in above, you will have to repair any spots that are failing. You have several choices. One is simply to apply some glue or sealant, such as Aquaseal, Shoe Goo, or Marine Goop. This will work for most small spots. It is good to do this early, a week or more before you intend to start paddling so you will see if your repair holds.

With older skins, fifteen years or more, you may see some deterioration of the seam line, depending on how the boat was used or stored. The only remedy that will work is to have it repaired professionally. A good place to go would be the Long Haul Folding Kayaks Sales and Service Center (see appendix), which is ready to handle just about any make of folding kayak and do a repair to make the boat look like new.

Inflate the built-in air sponsons to see if they hold air. Let them stand for an hour or so. If air is slowly leaking out, first ascertain if it may just be the inflation tube. This will avoid taking out the entire sponson, checking it, and reinserting it into the skin, which is a time-consuming chore on all folding kayaks, and some are harder than others. In most instances, the leakage is in the tube, either its stopper or where it enters the sponson proper. To check the air stopper, insert it into a clear cup of water to look for any bubbles. The point of connection for the inflation tube to the sponson can be checked by spraying on a soapy solution, which will reveal bubbles.

If a lot of air is leaking, the problem is certain to be the sponson itself since you would probably have seen any large hole in the inflation-tube area. Take your time. Read the instructions on how to remove and repair or replace a sponson. If you're uncertain or want to double-check, call the manufacturer. There may be an easier way than what was suggested in the original instructions.

Check any reinforced parts of the hull, such as end-protective pieces and keelstrips. Sometimes these can loosen at their edges and, over a season, start to peel away further or fill with grit. Take care of them now with cement or sealant used to attach repair pieces to the particular hull of your boat. If in doubt, contact your boat's manufacturer.

Wax the hull. This serves several purposes. First, it nourishes the hull material and keeps it from drying out over time. Second, it makes the surface slicker so it's more apt to slide over obstacles rather than snag or abrade on them.

You can use any one of several products. Klepper sells a rubber polish that works on all hulls. You can also use 303 Aerospace Protectant.

Of course, before waxing the hull, see if you can spot any damage or holes. Also check to see if the skin is getting flaky or stiff with hairline cracks, a sign of aging that comes after twenty or twenty-five years.

Folding Kayaks with Cotton Decks

This applies mainly to Kleppers and Pouchs but may also be seen in some early Nautiraids. Poke along the entire length of the deck with your finger. You are looking for potential dry rot that may not be visible. Cotton decks start becoming susceptible to this after about twenty years, but it could happen sooner than that if the boat has been stored out in the weather uncovered when not in use.

The seam lines of such decks are also more susceptible to fraying than synthetic decks. This comes with age. If you have dry rot, then no amount of patching will work for long. Get a new skin or have a new deck sewn on (again, by the Long Haul Service Center), but only if the deck damage has occurred sooner than expected and the hull is still quite supple and full of useful life.

Folding Kayaks with Synthetic Decks

While synthetic decks are generally impervious to dry rot, you are not necessarily exempt from checking this during your preseason inspection. While cotton canvas decks keep water out through the swelling of the surface threads, synthetic decks depend on coatings that can wear away over time, even though they are quite strong and tend to last a long time.

With older Feathercrafts and all Folbots, the coatings are on the underside. To check them, it's best to turn the skin inside out. If you see worn spots, recoat with whatever the manufacturer suggests or some general tent-recoating material. You may also want to replenish the water repellent on the outer side. Many outdoor products are available that would suit this purpose, but it is good to check with the folding-kayak company first.

Older Nautiraids are unique in that they have the waterproof coatings on the outside, so you can make a quick visual check for any places where the coating may have worn thin through constant rubbing. Recoat any bare spots.

Folding Kayaks with Wooden Frames

This applies to Kleppers, Nautiraids, Pouchs, and older Folbots. Check the frame for any major bare spots where varnish has vanished. You are looking to revarnish large areas really, but if you want to be fussy about it, you can even varnish tiny spots.

Be advised that few owners revarnish the entire frame, or even parts of it. If you do decide to revarnish, then do so sparingly. Overvarnishing can get in the way of parts that are meant to fit together.

Look at all the fittings that connect wooden parts, particularly rivets, screws, and bolts that may be coming loose. On Kleppers, which use special fittings, look at the rivets holding them in place as well as the tiny springs in the latch fittings. If they have lost their springiness, they can be a nuisance. You should also check to see if the horseshoe and block that connect the frame halves at the gunwales and keel remain securely in place.

In Nautiraids, which have numerous pre-assemblies that hold parts semi-permanently together, see if any of these are starting to fail. For example, wiggle the bolts holding stringers to the bow and stern end pieces.

Folding Kayaks with Aluminum Frames

A good place to start when you're getting such frames ready for the season is to soak the aluminum tubes and lubricate the tube ends. But there are other steps to take as well.

Check any preassemblies. For example, Feathercrafts have their longerons preconnected to the bow and stern end pieces. See if the bolts holding them have come loose. Remember that on Feathercrafts there should be some play in them; i.e., they should not be held rigidly.

On Folbots, see if any of the flanges located in front of the keyholes that hold the crossrib pieces in place have broken off or been weakened.

Examine tube ends. You are looking for any burrs that may have resulted from nicks that may tear at dry bags or clothing.

Odds and Ends

Folding kayaks vary widely in their design, so troubleshooting for them varies as well. Here are two common trouble spots to watch out for. You have probably run across more over time in dealing with your boat.

The sponson sleeves on Kleppers. Unlike other manufacturers, Klepper sponsons rest in light fabric sleeves that are sewn to the skin only along the top edge. These hanging sleeves have several slits in them meant for easy replacement of a sponson. However, during the insertion of the frame halves, sometimes the frame catches on these slits and starts to tear the sleeve loose. This should be repaired. Also, with the sponsons set up in such hanging sleeves, Klepper sponsons are more prone to migrate away from the ends of the kayak than those on other boats. You may have to realign the sponson in its sleeve.

The zipper and zipper pulls on Folbots. Folbot is noted for its zippered decks and the ease of assembly and access to gear they provide. (Nautiraid and even Klepper have started using zippers, too.) These zippers are heavy-duty but should be checked as they could be damaged if overstressed (something that can happen if you have air sponsons fully inflated when working the zippers open or shut). Also see if the Velcro strips that keep down the overflap are holding well and not pulling out.

WHAT TO DO WITH AN OLD HULL

What do you do with a tired old hull that has already seen twenty-five years of service? The issue comes up, for instance, when someone has found an uncle's old Folbot Super in the attic. Or it could be a hard decision you're facing with a thirty-year-old Klepper for which a replacement hull costs considerably more than what you originally paid for your double when it was new, including sail rig, rudder, spraydeck, et al.

Here are your options.

The Economies of a New Hull

When you think about it, a new hull is a bargain. No other kind of vessel can be brought back to like-new condition so simply, although it does take a stroke of your pen to a check or credit card form. Rigid kayaks don't offer that option. When their hulls go at around ten to fifteen years, depending on their hull material and your usage, you chuck them.

A foldable can have any part replaced, including the hull. So, if you've had a kayak for twenty-five to thirty years, you can replace the skin, place it on your existing frame—good for probably

half a century or more—and be on your way for another twenty-five or thirty years of fun.

The cost and availability of a new hull depend on the manufacturer. They run from fairly inexpensive to costly. Folbot can replace the hulls on most of its models. The exception is the models with wooden longerons, for which the company no longer has the patterns.

A Klepper hull is costly, but it's certainly worth the price. A gray-bottomed Classic or Magic hull replacement for a Klepper double costs $1,700. You'll get a good twenty-five to thirty years out of it, and it will have the latest fittings and improved deck webbing. The Expedition hull is more expensive at $2,400. It's a lot of money, but your boat will be able to take unbelievable punishment on the roughest of surfaces, and you'll have paddle pockets and some other nice deck goodies.

Traditional Revitalizing Methods

Follow Occam's razor: Don't go for a complex theory or solution when a simple one will do. Your problem may respond to some liberal use of keel-strips without going to the complexity of cold cash. These strips can buy years and years of happy paddling. The cost is much less than a new hull.

If you're tempted to slap on plain old paint or some other such covering liquid, think twice. Unless it's a specialized product like Gacoflex (described below), it may not work well. Ordinary paint-type products won't hold onto a surface intended to be folded and flexed or take the abuse of sun and salt water.

Gacoflex

Gacoflex H-22 is a specialized Hypalon coating meant for all sorts of applications, from roofing and decks to coating rubber rafts and folding kayaks. It will work on Hypalon, neoprene, and polyurethane but not vinyl. It coats the hull completely, filling in scaling areas and pinholes.

Putting on a keelstrip.

To use it correctly, you must first scrape off any loose hull material. Then wipe the hull with a special thinner called N-450-1. Brush on the Gacoflex, applying several coats. The first coat should be well brushed on to the hull's surface. Additional coats should be applied one right after the other to assure good adhesion between layers.

The hull should be on the boat frame when you apply the coating, and you should plan to leave the folding kayak assembled for a week or so. If you take it apart too soon, you risk having the hull stick to itself. This product is toxic to breathe, so plan to have adequate ventilation. Gacoflex H-22 costs about $40 a gallon.

It's tricky stuff to work with. Some paddlers have had problems applying Gacoflex. The product remained tacky for them and tended, at times, to stick to itself in the bag. Others find it simple to apply and are happy with the results.

Attach a New Surface

You may be able to cover the existing skin with a new covering layer. The benefit of attaching a new surface is that you don't have to be all that precise since you're covering an already formed material with another. This idea comes from *Folding Kayaker* reader Robert Grant of Indiana.

EPDM is a rubberized fabric used by building contractors for roofing and other jobs. Feathercraft uses EPDM in small sections to protect the nose and stern of its kayaks. The EPDM fabric is 0.045 inch thick and costs 32 cents a square foot. It comes in 20-foot-wide sheets in long rolls. You get it cut to the overall size you need. A 4-by-20-foot sheet costs around $30. The adhesive needed for EPDM also costs around $30 a gallon. A gallon is more than you'll need, so try to buy it in a smaller can. You'll also need a special cleaner that helps prepare the surface. Be warned: EPDM is heavy and will add to the weight of your kayak. That's why Feathercraft doesn't use it for its full keelstrips.

Before going through all the expense and work, first see if EPDM will hold on your boat and bond to it properly. Try it first on a piece of hull material from your repair kit. Then, to be doubly certain that your actual hull is not too chalky to bond with the EPDM, place a small patch of the fabric on some spot. If EPDM passes both tests, then proceed as follows.

Clean the existing hull with the special cleaner for EPDM. Then cut the material into three long strips. Make chalk marks on the hull for lining up the EPDM strips. Work from the center of the boat to one end and then to the other. To make the material easier to handle, you can double it over itself while working on it.

When you're sure of the position of the EPDM in relation to the hull, apply the EPDM adhesive cement to one strip of the EPDM fabric at a time and to the area of the hull where it will be placed. Wait for the adhesive to dry to a slightly tacky state. The contact-adhesive surface sticks only to another adhesive surface; therefore, you can place layers of newspaper in between to allow you to get the strip into position without sticking it prematurely to unintended areas of the hull. Then, pulling out the newspaper, press the EPDM fabric into contact with the hull. To finish the job, apply EPDM caulking to the area around the ends. This caulking comes in a tube.

Appendix 1: Resources

SUGGESTED READING

Other than the book you're holding and the newsletter *Folding Kayaker* (see Periodicals, page 238), few direct sources of information concentrate on hands-on advice about folding kayaks. That's one of the reasons this book was written.

Still, there are a number of books and periodicals that you will find worthwhile reading. Some are inspirational, with a strong folding-kayak theme, while others offer specific information vital to any sea kayaker.

Books

The following reading list is eclectic rather than a broad survey of what's available. For example, it lists just one book on navigation, *Fundamentals of Kayak Navigation*, which is the best and probably only such book you'll ever need.

The listing is divided into three sections: books in English, books in German, and guidebooks to paddling in several choice areas.

IN ENGLISH

Alone at Sea by Dr. Hannes Lindemann. (Oberschliebheim Germany: Pollner Verlag, 1993.) This is a "must-read" for any folding kayaker, for any sea kayaker for that matter. Dr. Lindemann's account of his transatlantic journey in a stock Klepper folding kayak will inspire you and should convince anyone of the underlying toughness of these boats. This new edition contains an important chapter that was missing in the previous English version.

Arctic Crossing: A Journey Through the Northwest Passage and Inuit Culture by Jonathan Waterman. (New York: Knopf, 2001.) This tale of an adventure across the top of the world exemplifies what a folding kayak can handle and its enormous versatility. The author put several models of foldables through their paces, and they came through with flying colors.

Baidarka by George Dyson. (Edmonds WA: Alaska Northwest Pub. Co., 1986.) An unbelievably beautiful book to read and look at, it traces the origins of skin-and-frame boats, which folding kayakers can closely identify with. Dyson details the vivid history of European encounters with the Northern cultures along the West Coast of North America, and he runs through how to make your own skin-and-frame kayak. If you're contemplating making your own foldable kayak, this is a good place to start.

A Boat in Our Baggage: Around the World with a Kayak by Maria Coffey. (Camden ME: Ragged Mountain Press, 1995.) The author and her husband take a double folding kayak to a number of places, from the Ganges River to the coast of Ireland. Well written and inspiring.

Cockleshell Heroes by C. E. Lucas Phillips. (London UK: Pan Book, 1977.) It's out of print, but you can find it in many libraries. This is a true account of the 1942 British commando raid on Axis shipping in the French port of Bordeaux, 62 miles up the Gironde estuary from the sea. They got there by folding kayak. Also look for the movie of the same name that stars José Ferrer and appears on TV every once in a while.

The Complete Sea Kayaker's Handbook by Shelley Johnson. (Camden ME: Ragged Mountain Press, 2002.) This is one of the most thorough instruction books around. Plus it contains useful information on such subjects as camping, maintenance, and expedition planning.

The Essential Sea Kayaker, 2nd ed., by David Seidman. (Camden ME: Ragged Mountain Press, 2001.) Though directed to hardshell kayakers, this comprehensive guide offers much to both beginning and experienced sea kayakers. Its approach is that of teacher and pupil, and it works.

Folbot Holidays, 3rd ed., edited by J. Kissner. (Raleigh NC: Graphic Press, 1966.) This quaint book was compiled and partly written by Kissner, the founder of Folbot. Whimsically organized, it consists mainly of first-person accounts from early Folbot users, with some ad hype thrown in. You won't find it in bookstores, but Folbot has boxes and boxes of the book for the asking.

Fundamentals of Kayak Navigation, 3rd. ed., by David Burch. (Guilford CT: Globe Pequot Press, 1999.) This has been a classic since the day it went to press. You will find yourself returning over and over again to read sections as you encounter new problems of moving about on open water. It may be the only navigation guide you'll ever need.

Gathering Paradise: Alaska Wilderness Journeys by Larry Rice. (Golden CO: Fulcrum Publishing, 1990.) Rice takes you on a number of kayaking journeys that you will find both memorable and instructive.

The Happy Isles of Oceania: Paddling the Pacific by Paul Theroux. (New York: G. P. Putnam's Sons, 1992.) Theroux's travels by folding kayak allow him to get a different, up-close perspective on this corner of the ocean sea. It's excellent reading, as are all of this author's books on offbeat conveyances to reach unusual destinations.

The Hidden Coast: Coastal Adventures from Alaska to Mexico, 2nd ed., by Joel W. Rogers. (Portland OR: West-Winds Press, 2000.) Rogers writes about more than a dozen trips of personal discovery along the Pacific Coast from Alaska to Baja. Beautifully photographed, it'll make you want to drop everything and go paddling.

Keep Australia on Your Left: A True Story of an Attempt to Circumnavigate Australia by Kayak by Eric Stiller. (New York: Forge, 2000.) This is a fascinating, well-told adventure story. There's also frequent discussion of the folding kayak used, from assembly and placement of gear to technique and maintenance, and succinct insights on sea kayaking the open coast. If one were just to piece these pages together, you would have a darn good sea-kayaking primer.

Movin' Out: Equipment and Techniques for Hikers, rev. ed., by Harry Roberts. (Boston: Stone Wall Press, 1979.) This book and a companion piece on winter camping, *Movin' On*, offer some of the best and most practical advice ever written about camping. It was written in a very personal style by Roberts, a well-known canoeist who edited a number of leading paddling publications.

Qayaq: Kayaks of Alaska and Siberia by David W. Zimmerly. (Fairbanks AK: University of Alaska Press, 2000.) This is another skin-and-frame book, but from a scholarly perspective. It makes fascinating reading for folding kayakers. As you look at the many drawings of the different types of kayaks, you'll appreciate more and more the lineage of foldables.

A Scientist at the Seashore by James Trefil. (New York: Collier Books, 1987.) This is a scientific look at the ocean and beach and the transitional zone between them. You'll learn why salt water is salty and how sandy beaches are formed, and you'll gain a deeper understanding of tides. The discussions are sometimes quite complex, but if you stay the course, you'll be a savvier paddler because of the knowledge you'll gain.

Sea Kayaking: A Manual for Long-Distance Touring, rev. ed., by John Dowd. (Seattle WA: University of Washington Press, 1997.) This is the seminal sea-kayaking manual. It is written with a respect for folding kayaks that befits a man who has done some epic voyages in one. A good all-around book.

Seekers of the Horizon: Sea Kayaking Voyages from Around the World edited by Will Nordby. (Chester CT: Globe Pequot Press, 1989.) This anthology of sea-kayaking adventures includes an abridged account of Dr. Lindemann's classic voyage and other pieces by folding kayakers such as Larry Rice and Dr. Paul Kaufmann.

The Starship and the Canoe by Kenneth Brower. (New York: HarperCollins, 1983.) The narrative parallels two men of vision: Freeman Dyson, noted physicist, and his son, George Dyson. One seeks to build a spaceship and the other a kayak. This is a thought-provoking book that you will find hard to put down.

Waves and Beaches, 3rd ed., by Willard Bascom, edited by Andy Nordhoff. (Flagstaff AZ: Best Pub. Co.,

2000.) This book will help you fathom the dynamic environment on which our vulnerable-looking craft venture forth. It's lots of reading but will pay off in practical understanding of beaches and waves.

In German

As in physics and some other sciences, a good deal of the written work on folding kayaks is in German. Here are some key titles you may want to pick up even if your command of German is limited. One in particular should be on the bookcase shelves of every folding kayak owner, *Der Hadernkahn*.

Alleingang im Kajak by Dieter Kreutzkemp. (Pietsch-Verlag, 1990.) This is the narrative of a 3,000-kilometer trip down the Yukon River in a Pouch single-seater.

Das Baldverlorene Paradies by Herbert Rittlinger. (Pollner Verlag, 1993.) This is a new edition of Rittlinger's classic account of traveling through Europe by folding kayak, which was originally written in the 1930s. Rittlinger did a lot to popularize the sport of kayak wandering.

Das Faltboot by Klaus Bovers. (H. S. Walther, 1984.) This was published by Klepper, but it is more than a promotion piece for the company's products. It's nicely done, with concise discussions of history, some of what goes into making a folding kayak, and broad information on using one.

Der Hadernkahn by Ursula and Christian Altenhofer. (Pollner Verlag, 1989.) Get this book even if you don't understand a word of German. It traces the history of folding kayaks from before Heurich and Klepper to just after World War II. The photos and illustrations are priceless. English-German cognates will help any open-minded reader comprehend the valuable information the book provides.

Ganz Allein zum Amazonas by Herbert Rittlinger. (Brockhaus, 1977.) This book chronicles the extensive travel through South America in a Klepper by the folding-kayak wanderer Rittlinger, who was the first person to paddle the entire length of the Amazon River.

Im Banne der Arktis by Konrad Gallei and Gaby Hermsdorf. (Pietsch-Verlag, 1981.) This book covers kayaking the west coast of Spitzbergen.

Im Faltboot um Kap Hoorn by Arved Fuchs. (Delius Klasing Verlag, 2001.) This is an account of the first successful winter circumnavigation of Cape Horn that was done in a single Klepper. A true adventure story.

Nil und Niger by Achill Moser. (Pietsch-Verlag, 1989.) This is a book of adventurous river journeys through Africa in a Pouch two-seater. It includes a section on adventure-travel tips.

Ost-Grönland by Konrad Gallei and Axel Thorer. (Badenia, 1987.) This book is about a kayak adventure in East Greenland in a Klepper.

Guidebooks

Any number of informational sources can tell you about places you may want to paddle, and cruising and sailing guides are good ones. The sailing industry has given birth to a number of such books. Even though they're aimed at boats larger than yours, you'll find them useful.

Guidebooks devoted to canoeing and kayaking are another good source. The bookshelves of local paddling shops usually have a number of titles covering nearby areas. If you plan to kayak in a particular spot, find a local shop, and then call to ask if some books can be mailed to you.

As a starter kit, a few such books are listed below. Some of the publishers have other titles you may want to get.

The Alaska River Guide: Canoeing, Kayaking, and Rafting in the Last Frontier, 2nd ed., by Karen Jettmar. (Anchorage AK: Alaska Northwest Books, 1998.) Many of the rivers covered in this book are doable in folding kayaks. Jettmar gives some good advice on camping and paddling in this last frontier.

The Coastal Kayaker: Kayak Camping on the Alaska and B.C. Coast by Randel Washburne. (Seattle WA: Pacific Search Press, 1983.) Washburne's book is a practical guide to extended trips in these areas and contains some good general information as well. Washburne also authored another guide you might want to check out: *Kayaking in Puget Sound, the San Juans and Gulf Islands: Fifty Trips on the Northwest's Inland Waters,* 2nd ed., edited by R. Carey Gersten. (Seattle WA: Mountaineers, 1999.)

Sea Kayaking Along the Mid-Atlantic Coast: Coastal Paddling Adventures from New York to Chesapeake Bay by Tamsin Venn. (Boston: Appalachian Mountain Club Books, 1994.) This terrific book guides you to great paddling that is just a few hours' drive away for many people. The descriptions of each spot are quite complete and include historical and practical information to help you understand what you're looking at and keep out of danger.

Sea Kayaking Along the New England Coast by Tamsin Venn. (Boston: Appalachian Mountain Club Books, 1991.) Like the author's other book, above, this includes complete descriptions and is a terrific guide to the New England area.

Sea Kayaking Canada's West Coast by John Ince and Hedi Kottner. (Seattle WA: Mountaineers Books, 1992.) This excellent guide was written by two folding-kayak paddlers, who provide good explanations on how to get to put-ins and what you will find along the way as you paddle.

Periodicals

Even though general paddling magazines only occasionally offer direct information on folding kayaks, they are worth receiving on a regular basis. They provide features on gear and techniques as well as safety advice that applies to all sea kayakers. Many of the adventures covered have been done in folding kayaks, although little mention is made of this, nor are any specific tips offered on how these boats were used.

For direct information on folding kayaks, you may want to get my newsletter, *Folding Kayaker*, which has been published since 1991. It is devoted entirely to folding kayaks, with boat reviews, advice on gear, techniques specific to folding kayaks, tips on modifications, and just about anything you'd ever want to know about foldables. It also includes a classifieds section for used folding kayaks. Part of this book is based on articles that first appeared there. For information,

write to *Folding Kayaker*, P.O. Box 0754, New York, NY 10024 or call 212-724-5069. You can e-mail me at rdiaz@ix.netcom.com.

Below are some general paddling publications that you'll find useful.

ANorAK (Association of North Atlantic Kayakers), 538 Rt. 679, Chatsworth Rd., Egg Harbor City, NJ 08215; 609-296-9510; http://members.aol.com/gokayak/anorak. This newsletter is entirely written by readers. Between the quirky contributions, you will find some good information.

Atlantic Coastal Kayaker, P.O. Box 520, Ipswich, MA 01938; 978-356-6112; www.ackayak.com. This excellent publication has insightful articles on a wide range of sea-kayaking subjects. The publisher is Tamsin Venn, who has written two guidebooks mentioned above.

Canoe & Kayak, P.O. Box 3146, Kirkland, WA 98083; 800-MYCANOE (800-692-2663); www.canoekayak.com. The oldest and most widely circulated of the paddling magazines, this has good information in each issue on gear and techniques. The December issue offers an excellent Buyer's Guide, and there's also an annual issue about kayak touring.

Paddler, P.O. Box 775450, Steamboat Springs, CO 80477; 970-879-1450; www.paddler-magazine.com. This is another good general magazine, with articles on travel, gear, and techniques.

Sea Kayaker, P.O. Box 17029, Seattle, WA 98107; 206-789-1326; www.seakayakermag.com. Entirely devoted to sea kayaking, this magazine has little coverage of foldables, except for the many trips that are taken in them. There are excellent general articles on technique and gear that you'll find useful.

WEB SITES AND THE INTERNET
Folding Kayak Manufacturers

All the manufacturers have Web sites where you can see their products and glean more information about their construction. Some even have assembly instructions in PDF format in case you lost yours or are buying a used boat.

Feathercraft Folding Kayaks: www.feathercraft.com

FirstLight Folding Kayaks:
www.firstlightkayaks.com

Folbot: www.folbot.com

Fujita (FoldingCraft): www.foldingcraft.com

Klepper: www.klepper-usa.com; www.klepper.com

Long Haul Folding Kayaks:
www.longhaulfoldingkayaks.com

Nautiraid/SEDA Products Inc.: www.nautiraid.com;
www.sedakayak.com

Pakboats: www.pakboats.com

PouchBoats: www.pouchboats.com

Weather, Currents, and Tidal Information

You can also find critical information that will help you be more savvy before making any kind of trip, whether for just an afternoon or a multiday camping excursion.

For example, you will want to know what to expect in terms of weather. You can use your marine radio or special weather radio or you can find the information on most weather related sites. A good one to check is www.weatherunderground.com/MAR/, which leads you to your local marine weather forecast.

Another way of getting similar information but with details about water temperatures and other useful things is to find out what's happening at weather buoys en route or nearby. To find this go to www.ndbc.noaa.gov, where you'll find a map you can use to zero in on the location you want. It also links to the local marine forecast, often in greater detail than you will find at a general weather Web site.

You also need to know the forecasts for tides and currents for the area you wish to paddle. Kayakers generally want to know about the currents more than the tides since the water is not likely to be too shallow for you to operate. A Web site to go to is http://tbone.biol.sc.edu/tide/sitesel.html. From there you select broad regions that lead to specific local tables for both currents and tides that you can print out for the dates you wish. Most of the tables are for tides but there enough on currents for you to get an idea of what to expect regarding changes between ebb and flood currents as well as the times of maximum flows.

Other Web Sites

Michael Edelman has an interesting Web site (www.foldingkayaks.org) entirely devoted to folding kayaks that is worth visiting. Mike keeps up on happenings in the field and includes this information on his Web site. There are also lots of good links to other sources of folding-kayak information. Edelman reads my newsletter and often cites articles from it, so that is a way to learn if there are any new reviews you may want to see.

If you read German, or even if you don't, take a look at several good Web sites in German. These may or may not have an English version by the time you read this. One is www.faltboot.de, maintained by Juergen Hoh and Marian Gunkel. It contains tips, trips, and a forum. Another one to look at, www.faltboot basteln.de, has photos and catalogs for some seventy folding kayaks. Of great value are the old catalogs, just in case you run across some 1930s or 1950s model from a now-defunct company. Lastly, there is www.faltbootkabinett.de, created by Dirk Bredow, curator of a folding-kayak museum.

Internet Forums

Bagboater is a specific forum devoted to all things folding and offers lively discussions. Often manufacturers will pop in to answer questions, and I frequent it as well. To subscribe, go to http://groups.yahoo.com/group/Bagboater.

Of the manufacturers, only Folbot has a truly active forum (www.folbot.com/yak.htm) for Folbot enthusiasts and owners. It is a good place to post a specific question about your Folbot, and it's also a good place for a prospective buyer to monitor or ask questions.

There are also some sea-kayaking listserve groups that you may want to join. The one with the greatest breadth and flow of informed ideas and comments is Paddlewise. Subjects discussed include every aspect of sea kayaking, gear, destinations, technique, etc. Paddlewise is truly international in scope. You can feel free to ask what you may think is a pretty basic question and not be embarrassed. I also frequent this listserve. Visit www.paddlewise.net for information on signing on and also to look at its archive of past posts and other highly useful information.

You should also check local listserves in your area or in ones where you'll be paddling. Check a local kayak dealer or touring and instruction service for a popular one in your area. For example, New York has NYCkayaker (join by visiting www.hrwa.org, the home of Hudson River Watertrail, which maintains this listserve), and the Washington, D.C., area has CPAkayaker (go to www.cpakayaker.com to join). Local clubs have them, too, such as Bay Area Seakayakers (www.bask.org); its listserve is BUZZ and you have to be a member of the club to get on it.

VIDEOS

Several of the manufacturers offer videotapes, either free or for a nominal charge. They generally are aimed at giving assembly instructions or promoting their products, but they do a lot more. One way of deciding whether you want to purchase a particular model is to review its assembly video.

Jonathan Waterman, whose book appears in the above list, has two videos that document his Northwest Passage odyssey. It will make you appreciate what a folding kayak can do and its reliability under extreme circumstances. To purchase the video, go to www.adventurevideos.com.

William Longyard has a great video about traveling in Europe with a folding kayak. It is both a picturesque travelogue and a hands-on guide for the folding-kayak traveler. There are lots of practical trips, as well as suggested places to paddle with accompanying directions via public transportation. Go to longyard@ix.netcom.com to buy the video.

Trailside offers at least three videos that feature folding kayaks: *Kayak Sailing the Exumas*, *Kayaking New York City*, and *Glacier Kayaking*. For more information, go to www.trailside.com or call 800-TRAILSIDE (800-872-4574).

KAYAKS AND ACCESSORIES

Following is a list of the folding-kayak manufacturers and/or importers for the kayaks mentioned in this book.

Folding Kayaks

Feathercraft Folding Kayaks Ltd., 1244 Cartwright St., Ste. 4, Granville Island, Vancouver, BC, Canada V6H 3R8; 604-681-8437; www.feathercraft.com. Besides kayaks, the company offers accessories including paddle floats, pogies, etc. The company will make some accessories to order, such as spray skirts with hand warmers and pouch pockets. You can buy direct from Feathercraft or from dealers spread throughout Canada, the United States, and Europe. There is no discount for buying at the factory.

Folbot, P.O. Box 70877, Charleston, SC 29405; 800-533-5099, 843-744-3483; www.folbot.com. It sells several models of boats, plus some accessories such as boat carts, sails, etc. These are mainly sold direct, although there are some dealers around.

Klepper products are distributed in the United States by Klepper USA, 18011 Sky Park Circle, Ste. F, Irvine, CA 92614; 800-500-2404; www.klepper-usa.com. Klepper sells boats and accessories such as sails and boat carts.

Long Haul Folding Kayaks/Sales and Service Center, 1685-2075 Drive, Cedaredge, CO, 81413; 970-856-3663; www.longhaulfoldingkayaks.com. This company sells its own brand of kayaks and is also a reputable service center for all makes. It can make replacement hulls or repair old ones. Long Haul also sells accessories usable for many makes as well.

Nautiraid kayaks are distributed in the North American market by SEDA Products Inc., P.O. Box 997, Chula Vista, CA 91912; 800-322-SEDA (800-322-7332); www.sedakayak.com.

Pouch boats are imported into the United States by Ralph Hoehn Associates, 203-324-0901 (voice mail); www.pouchboats.com.

Accessories/Major Dealers

Baidarka Boats, P.O. Box 6001, Sitka, AK 99835; 907-747-8996; www.kayaksite.com. Baidarka sells several makes of folding kayaks. It stocks good repair materials such as marine-grade plywood, as well as special folding-kayak accessories including Kaipaks, side bags that strap onto nearby cross pieces in a folding kayak.

Balogh Sail Designs, 2188 Laconia Rd., Red Oak, VA 23964; 434-735-8292; www.baloghsail designs.com. BSD is the maker of several sailing rigs that will fit most folding kayaks. Its line of products include the Batwing, BOSS outrigger system, and Twins sail.

New York Kayak Company, Pier 40 South Side, West Houston and West Sts., New York, NY 10014; 800-KAYAK-99 (800-529-2599); www.nykayak.com.

Located in the heart of Manhattan, this company sells a number of brands of folding kayaks and accessories.

Western Folding Kayak Center, 6155 Mt. Aukum Rd., Somerset, CA 95684-0130; 530-626-8647, 888-692-8092; www.klepperwest.com. This company sells more brands of folding kayaks than any other outlet and has a good selection of books, including the new edition of *Alone at Sea* by Lindemann and *Der Hadernkahn*.

Appendix 2: Metric Conversions

1 inch = 2.54 centimeters
1 inch = 25.4 millimeters
1 foot = 0.3 meters
1 ounce = 28.35 grams
1 pound = 453.6 grams = 0.45 kilograms
2.2 pounds = 1 kilogram
1 quart = 0.946 liters
1 mile/hour = 1.609 kilometers/hour
$(°F − 32) \times 0.555 = °C$
$(°C \times 1.8) + 32 = °F$

Index

(continued)